CHRISTIAN WORSHIP WORLDWIDE

The CALVIN INSTITUTE OF CHRISTIAN WORSHIP LITURGICAL STUDIES Series, edited by John D. Witvliet, is designed to promote reflection on the history, theology, and practice of Christian worship and to stimulate worship renewal in Christian congregations. Contributions include writings by pastoral worship leaders from a wide range of communities and scholars from a wide range of disciplines. The ultimate goal of these contributions is to nurture worship practices that are spiritually vital and theologically rooted.

Published

CHRISTIAN WORSHIP WORLDWIDE

Expanding Horizons, Deepening Practices

Edited by

Charles E. Farhadian

William B. Eerdmans Publishing Company
Grand Rapids, Michigan / Cambridge, U.K.

Published 2007 by
Wm. B. Eerdmans Publishing Co.
2140 Oak Industrial Drive N.E., Grand Rapids, Michigan 49505 /
P.O. Box 163, Cambridge CB3 9PU U.K.

Printed in the United States of America

12 11 10 09 08 07   7 6 5 4 3 2 1

Library of Congress Cataloging-in-Publication Data

Christian worship worldwide: expanding horizons, deepening practices /
edited by Charles E. Farhadian.
p.   cm. — (The Calvin Institute of Christian worship liturgical studies series)
Includes index.
ISBN 978-0-8028-2853-8 (pbk.: alk. paper)
1. Public worship.   I. Farhadian, Charles E.

BV15.C47   2007

264.009 — dc22

2007009966

www.eerdmans.com

Contents

Contents

Illustrations

Additional photographs and video clips to complement some of the chapters of this book can be found at www.calvin.edu/worship/Farhadian

Acknowledgments

Any edited volume of essays is a team effort, and this book is no different. The idea of publishing a book that focuses explicitly on non-Western Christian worship was concocted over an American-style breakfast shared between John Witvliet and me in Grand Rapids, Michigan, in the fall of 2001. Calvin College's Institute of Christian Worship had received a generous grant from the Lilly Endowment for supporting worship renewal, and it seemed timely to highlight the ways that non-Western worship practices may give insight into the relationship between Christianity, cultures, and worship worldwide, particularly in a period in which the worldwide Christian movement had shifted numerically from the Northern (i.e., Western) to Southern (i.e., non-Western) Hemispheres. Today the non-Western church is the majority church worldwide, with astounding resurgence and growth outside of the Euro-North American region. As we set out to shape the discussion that would become this book, the contributors to the volume all affirmed Michael Hawn's suggestion that the book not be read as a guide to "liturgical tourism" that introduces the reader to the "exotic" nature of non-Western worship. Rather, we desired that this volume would help its readers appreciate the immense variety of expressions of Christian worship in order to take seriously the social and cultural context that plays such a significant part in worship. Contributors affirmed the emphasis on culture as the potential, not the problem of worship, and stressed the importance of moving past a "worship war" mentality that loses sight of the ways in which worship is a social act, embedded in cultures and societies, rather than an individual act alone.

The chapters of this book emerged out of discussions among its contributors at two meetings, the first of which took place at Yale Divinity School in 2002, where we held a worship and cultures colloquium hosted by Lamin Sanneh. I want to thank Chun Chae Ok, Dean of the Graduate School of Theology, Ewha Womans University, Seoul, Korea, who joined our colloquium and introduced us to the ways in which some Korean churches today are trying to "Koreanize" their worship by introducing local Korean cultural elements, such as musical instruments, into Sunday worship services. Unfortunately, M. L. Daneel, who co-authored the chapter on worship in Zimbabwe with Dana Robert, was unable to join our meetings because of commitments in Zimbabwe. The conversation at Yale was improved significantly by keen insights brought by discussants Susan Felch, Arie Leder, and Nicholas Wolterstorff, who helped move the conversation forward without losing sight of our overall goal. A word of thanks also goes to Yale University Law School student Shirley Udekwu, who tirelessly recorded our conversation.

Our second meeting, organized as the Christianity, Cultures, and Worship Worldwide Conference, was held at Calvin College in 2003, and gave us the opportunity to present and discuss our research with worship leaders and scholars from a variety of church traditions. I want to thank Jim Ault, documentary filmmaker, who participated in the conference by showing selections from his film work of Christian worship in Zimbabwe and Ghana. Without traveling to Africa, we could see through Jim's presentation non-Western worship in the larger contexts of African cultures. Calvin College's Seminars in Christian Scholarship office, led by Susan Felch, Kara Vandrie, and Alysha Chadderdon, orchestrated the weekend event without a glitch. At the conference we enjoyed the wonderful sounds of Calvin College's African a Capella, a vocal group whose student-members come from various countries on the African continent. In addition, we were delighted to be led in worship throughout the conference by Michael Hawn, who introduced the conference attendees to a variety of Western and non-Western worship songs. Thank you, Michael.

I want to thank Lewis Rambo from San Francisco Theological Seminary and Calvin College students Daryl Holmlund, Joyce "Sam" Huizenga, Sara Ladenburger, and Jared Jonker for their helpful comments on the introductory chapter of the book. I am grateful particularly to John Witvliet, whose creative vision, intellectual acumen, and inexhaustible energy helped us dream about this project, and to Nathan Bierma for expert editorial advice and for shaping the introductions to each chapter. Naturally, I thank all the contributors for their fine essays that introduce us to worship worldwide. Finally, I want to thank my wife, Katherine, and two sons, Gabriel and Gideon, for permitting me to take time away from the family in order to complete this book.

CHARLES E. FARHADIAN
Santa Barbara, California

Series Preface

The topic of this volume is endlessly interesting, profoundly instructive, and unmanageably large. The scope is nothing short of the worship practices of the world's two billion Christians.

In that single sentence description, there are two boundlessly expansive terms. First, there is "worship." For our purposes, we will focus on one sense of this term, worship as a public ritual event, an assembly usually conceived as an occasion for a kind of divine-human gift exchange of sung and spoken prayers, scriptural preaching, and sacraments or other ceremonies.[1]

The topic of public worship includes a dizzying array of subjects. There are the various elements of worship that may be a part of the liturgy in a given congregation: scripture readings, prayers, preaching, baptisms, the Lord's Supper, exorcisms, healing, testimonies, blessings, offerings, and more. There are varied art forms through which each of these actions is expressed, including (at least) congregational singing, instrumental or vocal music, visual art, architecture, oral and written rhetoric, drama, dance, gesture, and posture. There are also varied occasions for worship and types of services: regular weekly services, occasional evangelistic services, festivals to celebrate or observe events in the ecclesiastical or cultural calendar, revivals, healing or memorial services, informal prayer gatherings, as well

---

1. Note that the term "worship" also has an important broader meaning (all of life is an act of devotion to God), and a narrower one (an act of praise or adoration, often expressed in music, by which we extol the virtues of God, either as one element in a public worship service or in private devotion). Several of the essays in this volume allude to these other meanings of the term. But the focus of this book is on the public assembly of the church.

as personal and family worship practices. Each of these elements, art forms, and types of services features complex patterns of leadership, community interaction, historical roots and precedents, embodied ritual, and sensibilities about time and space. Public worship is a complex interdisciplinary topic that eludes exhaustive analysis.

The second impossibly large reality to comprehend is the stunning fact that there are two billion people on the planet who worship in the name of Jesus. These Christians represent Orthodox, Roman Catholic, Protestant, and Pentecostal traditions and hail from over 200 countries and hundreds of cultural and ethnic groups, each of whom has unique patterns of dress, speech, aesthetic sensibilities, and interpersonal communication habits (to say nothing of their unique understandings of when exactly a worship service has gotten to be a bit long!).

Suppose we were to distinguish the world's 200 largest countries or regions, the largest twenty Christian traditions or denominations, and the five most prominent recent impulses or movements for change, as three ways of limiting the scope of a series of case studies, so that studies were produced, for example, on "The Charismatic Movement Among Methodists in Bali." This strategy would suggest over 20,000 combinations to discuss — each with a window into one of the myriad ways the world's two billion Christians offer worship. Focus more narrowly on just one of the elements of worship mentioned above, and our math suggests enough interesting and significant research topics to keep busy an army of researchers that could fill a dozen of the largest football stadiums on the planet.

Such a wide-angled vision places before us a dazzling variety of ritual practices: everything from elaborate Byzantine vigils to exuberant Methodist frontier camp meetings, from the Dionysian ecstasy of Pentecostal singing in Brazil to the Apollonian reserve of a Presbyterian sermon preached in the Kirk of Scotland, from the trancelike worship of Asian monks to the precise rhetorical patterns of *The Book of Common Prayer;* from the visual brilliance of Michelangelo's Sistine Chapel to homey folk art on burlap banners, from the serene beauty of a Palestrina motet to the rugged earthiness of an Appalachian gospel quartet, from the sophisticated majesty of York Minster to the folk art that adorns a thatched-roof sanctuary in New Guinea, from the enforced silence of Quaker corporate mysticism to the sustained exuberance of an African-American ring-shout sermon.

The topic is happily but stubbornly broad. And we must not narrow it too quickly. Narrowing the topic too quickly risks losing the opportunity to reconsider our understanding of the church as a whole and the very nature of Christian worship.

Whether we are journalists asked to cover Christianity, missionaries called to promote it, anthropologists mandated to study it, teachers called to explain it, or ordinary Christians invited to describe it in an over-the-backyard fence interfaith conversation, all of us need a fair and balanced understanding of the Christian faith as a whole. Though we can qualify our answers endlessly, we cannot avoid general descriptions, especially in a religiously pluralistic age. We must work to speak about the Christian church on the basis of attempts to understand as much of the church's life as possible and to avoid generalizations that are simply false. If we were to say, "No Christian believes in nature miracles anymore" or "Christians are, on average, quite wealthy," we would, as Philip Jenkins points out, be neglecting the existence of several hundred million Christians.[2] A worldwide purview serves to discipline and chasten us when we make assertions about "what Christians believe" or "how the church is changing." So there is great value in lingering inside a topic that is admittedly too large to fully comprehend.

One promising way to begin to handle such a broad topic is to begin inductively by analyzing illustrative examples of worship practices that will take us to places many of us have never been: Peru, Zimbabwe, India, Samoa, Indonesia, Korea, and lots of places in between. We will also attempt to be clear about the limitations of our work. We will not be able to come to anything that approximates exhaustive knowledge of worship practices worldwide. We aspire instead to paint a few strokes in this broad mosaic, to merely begin to better understand the large scope of the topic and to gain some sense of its complexity.[3]

2. Philip Jenkins, *The Next Christendom* (New York: Oxford University Press, 2002), 3. For efforts to expand international awareness and accuracy in teaching and writing about Christianity, see Wilbert Shenk, ed., *Enlarging the Story: Perspectives on Writing World Christian History* (Maryknoll, N.Y.: Orbis Books, 2002).

3. For other books that help paint this picture with international awareness, see Geoffrey Wainwright and Karen Westerfield Tucker, *The Oxford History of Christian Worship* (New York: Oxford University Press, 2006); Thomas Best and Dagmar Heller, eds., *Worship Today. Understanding, Practice, Ecumenical Implications* (Geneva: WCC Publications, 2004); Thomas Best and Dagmar Heller, eds., *So We Believe, So We Pray: Towards Koinonia in Worship* (Geneva: WCC Publications, 1995); Lukas Vischer, ed., *Christian Worship in Reformed*

Why Study Worship?

Still, one important question must be addressed. Given the significance of worldwide Christianity, why study *worship?* Indeed, many studies of Christianity worldwide seem to ignore worship altogether, focusing instead on how Christians participate in culture, what theological work they produce, or some other dimensions of Christian thought and practice.

The importance of worship is initially established by the obvious fact that "going to church" in many languages often means, "to go to worship," to go to a public event or ritual of some kind. The writer of Hebrews mandates that we "not neglect meeting together as is the habit of some" (Hebrews 13:15). And Christians ever since have maintained public events for prayer, proclamation, and sacramental participation as central dimensions of the Christian life. There may be scattered examples of Christian life in some cultures that has thrived without a public event of some kind, or without emphasizing it much, but that would be a rare exception. Worship is a central Christian practice, no matter what tradition or country we are in.

More deeply, as cultural anthropologists tell us, worship is an occasion when the instinctive beliefs, dispositions, and values of a given community are on full display. Anthropologists have helped us see that worship is actually much more than just ideas acted out. As a fully embodied activity, worship expresses through cultural forms both explicit truth claims and basic intuitions about God's presence and the meaning of humanity, salvation, virtue, and time. As Frank Senn argues, liturgy is "nothing less than a way of doing the world."[4] It is no surprise, then, that the human sciences — psychology, sociology, and anthropology among them — have much to teach us about the inner dynamics and the external patterns of liturgical action. It is also no surprise that in the past genera-

---

Churches Past and Present (Grand Rapids: Eerdmans, 2003); Philip Tovey, *Inculturation of Christian Worship: Exploring the Eucharist* (Burlington, Vt.: Ashgate, 2004); F. Kabasele Lumbala, *Celebrating Jesus Christ in Africa: Liturgy and Inculturation* (Maryknoll, N.Y.: Orbis Books, 1998); S. Anita Stauffer, ed., *Worship and Culture in Dialogue* (Geneva: Lutheran World Federation, 1994); Elochukwu E. Uzukwu, *Worship as Body Language: Introduction to Christian Worship: An African Orientation* (Collegeville, Minn.: The Liturgical Press, 1997); and Mark MacDonald, *The Chant of Life: Inculturation and the People of the Land* (New York: Church Publishing, 2003).

4. Frank C. Senn, *New Creation: A Liturgical Worldview* (Minneapolis: Augsburg Fortress, 2000), p. 8.

tion, students of Christian liturgy have embraced these disciplines and begun a variety of conversations with social scientists that share a great deal of promise for generating insight into the dynamics of Christian communities at worship.[5]

Theologically, worship is perceived by most Christian traditions as an essential arena of divine activity. For Roman Catholics, according to Vatican II's *Constitution on the Sacred Liturgy,* liturgy is the "source and summit" of the Christian faith. For confessional Protestants, the "means of grace" and the "marks of the church" — two of the key defining categories in historic Protestant confessions — each have to do with enacted liturgy (typically focusing on preaching and the sacraments). For traditions as disparate as the Orthodox and Pentecostals, the distinguishing feature of each tradition is the way that public worship is understood to be a primary vehicle of divine presence and action. Across the spectrum of Christian traditions, distinctive worship practices are crucial for revealing the basic impulses of faith. We simply cannot comprehend Puritans without looking at meetinghouses, Pentecostals without considering tongue-speaking, the Orthodox without icons, or Catholics without the Mass.

Despite its rather obvious importance, worship only recently has become a topic of widespread study. Until the 1960s, no one taught worship full-time at any seminary in North America — Protestant, Orthodox, or Catholic. And though this is changing, relative blindness to liturgical practice can still be seen across the theological disciplines. Far more attention has been given to what the sixteenth-century Reformers thought happened in the Lord's Supper than to how they actually celebrated it. With some notable exceptions, missiology has generally been concerned more with cross-cultural apologetics than with common prayer, more with a theology of the purpose of mission than with theological guidelines to inform how to celebrate the sacraments. Further, cultural anthropological studies of worship practices are relatively rare. As Nathan Mitchell, one of many Catholic scholars with great interest in ritual theory, has often quipped, we have better "thick descriptions" of cockfights in Bali than we do of any celebration of the Catholic Mass.

---

5. See Nathan Mitchell, *Liturgy and the Social Sciences* (Collegeville, Minn.: Liturgical Press, 1999); Martin D. Stringer, "Liturgy and Anthropology: The History of a Relationship," *Worship* 63, no. 6 (November 1989): 503-21; and John D. Witvliet, "For Our Own Purposes: The Appropriation of Social Sciences by Pastoral Liturgists," *Liturgy Digest* 2 (1995): 6-35.

That means that we have before us a lot of uncharted territory. We have a myriad of truly fascinating and instructive examples to learn from.

Worldwide Learning, Probing Questions, and the Practice of Faith

Of the many goals that we could advance with a study of this topic, one significant goal for this volume is to work toward connecting learning about Christianity worldwide with Christians in North America in ways that will energize and deepen faith and common worship.

While recent academic exploration about Christianity worldwide is (arguably) more sophisticated and balanced than ever, many ordinary North American Christians often remain indifferent to both world events in general and the worldwide family of Christ.[6] As many international guests in North America notice, the world news sections of our newspapers and television newscasts keep shrinking. The same may be true of church publications in their reporting on the church worldwide. And yet it is precisely the practice of Christianity in other times and places that offers so much that can deepen our faith, create opportunities for service, and teach us about the deepest meaning of the gospel.

To that end, we hope that this volume both reflects and generates many constructive questions. How can missiologists, anthropologists, pastors, theologians, musicians, and artists best learn from each other? What particular examples of Christian worship practices are especially challenging and enriching? What are the most instructive examples of worship worldwide for North American Christians (or any other group) to learn about? How will the study of Christian worship worldwide challenge the methods we use to study and learn from practices in our communities? How will this wide-angle vision change the way we pray?

Consider some of the kinds of questions we might ask ourselves:

6. Note significant works that explore the worldwide scope of Christianity. See, for example, Lamin Sanneh, *Whose Religion is Christianity?* (Grand Rapids: Eerdmans, 2003); Andrew Walls, *The Cross-Cultural Process in Christian History: Studies in the Transmission and Appropriation of Faith* (Maryknoll, N.Y.: Orbis Books, 2002), and *The Missionary Movement in Christian History: Studies in Transmission of Faith* (Maryknoll, N.Y.: Orbis Books, 1996); and Dana Robert, "Shifting Southward: Global Christianity Since 1945," *International Bulletin of Missionary Research* 24, no. 2 (2000): 50-54, 56-58.

1. What do we make of John Stott's first visit to West Africa where he "saw Gothic spires rising incongruously above the coconut palms," "African bishops sweating profusely in medieval European ecclesiastical robes," and African worshipers speaking Elizabethan English?[7] Likewise, what are we to make of the fact that Warner Sallman's famous painting "Head of Christ" has been regularly used in Korean Methodist churches?[8] Or that Western boom boxes can now be found in the middle of worshiping communities in most continents?

2. How might we rethink our implicit assumptions about so-called "high" and "low" (or "classical" and "popular") art given the absence of folk music in many standard histories of liturgy in the West, and the absence of so-called "classical" music in treatments of Christianity worldwide, despite interest in such in Japan, Kenya, Singapore, and the Philippines? What are we to make, for example, of the Reformed Church of Japan's disciplined attention in the past decade to translating all 150 Genevan Psalms into Japanese?

3. A remarkable number of the studies we have about worship worldwide over the past thirty years speak consistently of the influence of both the charismatic movement and the liturgical movement. Is this historical interpretation accurate? What do these broad themes — accurate as they may be — obscure?

4. As legend would have it, in 987, Prince Vladimir of Kiev sent a delegation to Hagia Sophia in Constantinople to examine the Greek faith. After encountering the celebration of the Byzantine rite, the delegation reported, "we knew not if we were in heaven or on earth." In 1854, Thomas Birch Freeman, noted British Methodist missionary to Ghana, reported to his Missionary Society: "If our Public worship in Cape Coast is not heaven come down to earth, it is pretty nearly that of England come to Africa."[9] How are those narratives of cross-cultural description alike? How are they different?

7. John Stott, *The Contemporary Christian: Applying God's Word to Today's World* (Downers Grove, Ill.: Intervarsity, 1992), pp. 196-97.

8. Edward W. Poitras (Pak Tae In), "Ten Thousand Tongues Sing: Worship Among Methodists in Korea," in Karen B. Westerfield Tucker, *The Sunday Service of the Methodists: Twentieth-Century Worship in Worldwide Methodism* (Nashville: Kingswood Books, 1996), p. 207.

9. For the Orthodox example, see Robert Taft, *The Byzantine Rite: A Short History* (Collegeville, Minn.: Liturgical Press, 1982), p. 1. For the African example, see Paul W.

5. How might statistical summaries challenge our way of thinking about our way of assessing the spectrum of Christian worship practices? The Christian Reformed Church in North America, of which this author is a member, is a denomination of roughly 300,000 members with a history of fairly low-church, simple, sermon-focused liturgy, but a recent interest in forms of worship that originated in charismatic congregations has led some CRCNA members to think (ironically) that the more traditional approach to worship was "high-church." For members in this tradition, how would it change our thinking about our place in the worldwide spectrum if we realized that half a billion people worship with more charismatic forms of worship than our own, but also that 1.3 billion Christians worship with a liturgy more formal than our own? What would similar reassessments look like for others?

6. What does it mean to identify the marks or traits of worship in a given tradition? Given an international rather than a local or even national perspective, what is "Methodist" worship or "Reformed" worship? Here I think of a recent collection of essays on Methodist worship that includes the comment of a Brazilian pastor — "I have not experienced any real Methodist worship since I have been in Germany" — and a fairly sanguine defense of set prayers used by Methodist worshipers in the Caribbean.[10] Both experiences need to be embraced in nuanced understanding of what the Methodist tradition has come to be.

7. If Eastern Orthodoxy's worship became more ceremonial because of the collusion of the church and the imperial government in ancient Byzantium, how might we assess the collusion of American evangelicalism with the ritual impulses and preferences of Hollywood and Nashville? Is there a similar grafting of new ceremonial moves (such as Dove Awards for Christian music and publicity campaigns for Christian artist-worship leaders) into the church from its local cultural habitat? How are these examples of enculturation similar and how are they different?

Chilcote, "A Singing and Dancing Church," in Karen Westerfield Tucker, *The Sunday Service of the Methodists*, p. 244.

10. Walter C. Klaiber, "Building Up the House of God: Sunday Worship in German Methodism," in Karen Westerfield Tucker, *The Sunday Service of the Methodists*, p. 283.

8. Is North American imperialism over? Could part of the call for indigenous music in some parts of the world by North America leaders
   be just as imperialistic today as the efforts to prevent that
   indigenization a century ago? Could the influence of the Christian
   music industry, exporting North American boom boxes and iPods to
   remote villages be even more imperialistic? And if we decide that it
   is, is there anything to be done about it?

Once the questions start, they are hard to stop. And they begin to
challenge us to rethink nearly every category that we (as both academic
students of worship and local practitioners of worship) have used to comprehend the dynamics of our participation in the embodied living of the
Christian faith. While the topic of this volume seems hopelessly large, we
offer it with the modest hope that it will help us to ask better questions
about the relationship of Christian faith and its cultural habitats.

But these questions are not ends in themselves. The point of them is
to prod us to ponder all that is coming as part of God's coming kingdom.
The point is to help us better understand what we mean when we pray
"your kingdom come" — and then to live accordingly.

If there are 20,000 case studies that could have been included in this
volume, suppose that in the new heavens and new earth we will have the
luxury to hear all of them. Suppose in the fully embodied life we anticipate in heaven, we were to sign up for a "worship apprentice program"
with opportunities to learn how to play gamelans and pipe organs,
djembes and maracas, polyrhythmic drumming patterns, Bach chorale
preludes, spirituals, work songs, and Anglican chant, to design cathedrals
and store-front churches, to write hymn texts and improvise sermons, to
craft processional crosses, and weave tapestries. Our first millennium
there is bound to fly by!

In a sense, this volume is an exercise in eschatological imagination
formation. Can we imagine ourselves at worship in heaven alongside the
people we will encounter? Can we realize that we are already united with
them in the Spirit-formed sinews of Christ's body? May God's Spirit grow
in each of us a deeper, more vivid awareness of the sheer breadth of the
church, the privilege of worship, and overwhelming scope of the gospel.

JOHN D. WITVLIET

Beyond Lambs and Logos:
Christianity, Cultures, and Worship Worldwide

CHARLES E. FARHADIAN

How Can We Map a New Geography of Global Worship?

Today, Christianity is a post-Western movement with robust resurgence in the non-Western world, where the vast majority of Christians now live. The Christian diaspora finds unity not in ethnic similarities or political ideologies, but in its common worship, diversified by its refraction through cultures that span the globe. Religion scholars, missiologists, historians, and anthropologists increasingly find the massive numerical shift southward to be of such social and religious significance that many anticipate we are entering a new era of Christianity, a revolution in the way we see Christianity.[1] From its beginnings in first-century Palestine, Christianity has traversed cultural and linguistic frontiers, emerging in both hinterland and urban areas throughout the world, revitalizing local cultures and transforming lives.

This book highlights Christian worship in a rapidly changing and increasingly diverse body of worldwide Christians, and teases out lessons and challenges for the church today. The case studies give us a glimpse of

---

1. For instance, see Harvey Cox, "Christianity," in *Global Religions*, ed. Mark Juergensmeyer (New York: Oxford University Press, 2003), pp. 17-27; Philip Jenkins, *The Next Christendom* (New York: Oxford University Press, 2002); Jenkins, "After the Next Christendom," *International Bulletin of Missionary Research* 28, no. 1 (2004): 20-22; Dana Robert, "Shifting Southward," *International Bulletin of Missionary Research* 24, no. 2 (2000): 50-58; Lamin Sanneh, *Whose Religion Is Christianity?* (Grand Rapids: Eerdmans, 2003); Andrew Walls, "Converts or Proselytes? The Crisis over Conversion in the Early Church," *International Bulletin of Missionary Research* 28, no. 1 (2004): 26.

the future of Christian worship, showing us the changes afoot in representative regions in this worldwide burgeoning of Christianity.

Ahead lies a sea change in the way Christianity itself will be understood as it is re-contextualized and reemerges from non-Western cultures. The largest Christian communities in the next few decades will no longer be in the Euro-North American region, but rather in Latin America, Asia, and Africa, with the highest numbers of Christians living in the United States, Brazil, Mexico, the Philippines, Nigeria, Zaire (Democratic Republic of Congo), and Ethiopia.[2] We must recognize this new global imprint of non-Western Christianity. The West no longer occupies the center of gravity around which the non-Western Christian churches orbit. In the past, non-Western Christian worship practices were often legitimated by their Western characteristics — even though non-Western communities were historically and culturally closer to the birthplace of Christianity. No longer. The worldwide expansion of Christianity has left in its wake neither theological centers nor a particular cultural agenda. Instead, worshiping communities of all sorts gather in a spectacular array of cultural settings that glorify God in different ways.[3]

The gospel transforms personal and corporate lives, and worship is the proper response to God's grace. Whatever the immense cultural and social diversity found within worldwide Christianity, one thing holds true: Christians worship. Whether they gather on plains or mountaintops, in urban office buildings or high-school auditoriums, in magnificent cathedrals or basement apartments, followers of Christ assemble to glorify God, encourage one another, and remember the acts and promises of God. In the early church, healing, prophetic utterance, visionary experience, exorcism, speaking in tongues, body movement, and lengthy worship services defined the religious experience, and these practices have been present throughout church history. These same practices now have new resonance in the worship practices of non-Western Christians. This book highlights Christian worship practices in the non-Western world, to bring to light the winds of change blowing through the non-Western church.

To explore Christianity's worldwide shift southward, this introduc-

---

2. See Jenkins, *The Next Christendom,* p. 90. Jenkins's numbers are borrowed from the *Annual Report on International Religious Freedom* and the *CIA World Fact Book.*

3. The importance of the congregation as a center of worship in American churches is highlighted in Mark Chaves, *Congregations in America* (Cambridge, Mass.: Harvard University Press, 2004).

tion seeks to accomplish three goals. First, I suggest that a mark of Christian worship is its *openness*. Rather than being closed to innovation and transformation, Christian worship is organic, living, and celebrative. It is rooted in the remembrance of God's past actions, in God's abiding presence, and in the anticipation of God's fulfilled promises. Worship is a means to an end, rather than an end in itself. Worship is derivative of and responsive to God's activities and promises. Second, understanding Christian worship in a worldwide context requires that we acknowledge that our worship is deeply shaped both by our local culture and by larger, globalizing tendencies introduced from distant places. I further argue, following Lamin Sanneh and Andrew Walls, that there is a difference between "globalization" and the expansion of Christianity worldwide. Because Christian worship exhibits local flavorings and traditions that can make Christian worship most meaningful, it seems appropriate to separate the movement of worldwide Christianity from the "globalization" movement. Third, this chapter seeks to shed light on the answer to three questions: What actually happens in worship? What seems unique about Christian worship? And what is the relationship between local and worldwide Christian worship practices?

How Do Christians Worship Worldwide "in the Meantime," in Mystery and Anticipation?

Christian worship is always partly open to surprises; it is never complete. In worship, Christians take baby steps toward something eternal, full of substance and permanency. Perhaps this is what Michael Polanyi means when he writes that Christian worship "sustains, as it were, an eternal, never to be consummated hunch: a heuristic vision which is accepted for the sake of its unresolvable tension."[4] Worship necessarily entails a quality of mystery and knowability. The sacraments serve, in St. Augustine's apt phrase, as an "outward and visible sign of an inward and spiritual grace." Failure to recognize this element of mystery can easily lull the assembly into self-worship, where a community's own culture and lifeways become the focus and end of worship. On the other hand, worship must be mean-

---

4. Michael Polanyi, *Personal Knowledge* (Chicago: The University of Chicago Press, 1962), 199.

ingful to worshipers, or it inevitably becomes directed toward something other than its intended focus — God.

We know something of the "end" *(telos)* of worship, for it is hinted at in Revelation 7:9-17, which presents a colorful picture of "a great multitude which no man could number, from every nation, from all tribes and tongues, standing before the Lamb, clothed in white robes, with palm branches in their hands, and crying out with a loud voice, 'Salvation belongs to our God who sits upon the throne, and to the Lord!'" We do not live in that day. Nor are we today gathered from all tribes and tongues; for now, we are limited by our finitude and cultural particularity.

Christians worship today, as it were, "in the meantime," between the act of creation and its final consummation. The phrase "in the meantime" should be understood in two ways. On the one hand, it implies a quality of "between-ness," the middle time, as well as things fraught with potential, a domain of liminality, activity, growth, innovation, and the quality of intermediacy. We are, in the words of Lesslie Newbigin, "still in the middle of the story."[5] On the other hand, "in the meantime" denotes difficult times, times of burden and challenge. The "mean-ness" of time we know all too well; it ranges from the burden of ontological disquiet to physical intimidation or worse.

As such, Christian worship is inherently political, since it entails people giving glory to God and not earthly powers. Many of the earliest Christians were tortured, harassed, and put to death because of their insistence that the living God was to be worshiped above Caesar. The same is true today in many non-Western regions. Being witnesses (Greek, *martyria*) continues to be a central theme in the worldwide Christian movement.[6] Christian worship invigorates life "in the meantime," as glimpses of redemption and reconciliation of all creation inspire reconciliation with God and other human communities (see Romans 8:18-25). Christian worship is inseparable from its wider social impact.

---

5. Lesslie Newbigin, *The Finality of Christ* (Richmond, Va.: John Knox Press, 1969), p. 71.

6. It is interesting to note that the Greek New Testament term *martyria* (witness, martyr) meant sealing one's witness through suffering. All of Christ's disciples did just that.

How Does Worship Remain Contextual
amid a Globalized Culture?

How should we understand the relationship between Christianity and culture? What about the relationship among Christianity, culture, and globalization? Are all cultural perspectives of equal value? These questions are important because worship leaders have to decide what is "good" or "bad" worship, and what should be included in worship. Using electronic keyboards or organs, wine or grape juice, plain or ornate architecture — these are just some of the challenging decisions worship leaders face. Church and theological traditions have to set some parameters of worship. Are some cultural elements more sacred than others? How does one decide? What are the measures and criteria of "good" Christian worship? When we reflect on Christian worship, how important is it to consider our own cultural resources or "foreign" ones?

The globalization of culture necessarily involves a complex tension between globalism and localism, of embracing and resisting. The emergence of a global information technology, patterns of consumption and consumerism, political and military systems, extension of the concept of human rights, and the complex interchange between world religions would make it appear that local lifeways are being swept toward a single massive ocean of global culture. As social anthropologist Ulf Hannerz writes, "it has often been assumed that sooner or later other cultures will become more like those of the West, and American culture especially has been taken to be a bellwether culture for others."[7] The conditions of globalization are marked by a high degree of "extensionality," allowing for the diffusion of particular cultural forms into distant regions.[8]

The relationship between Christianity and culture is such an important one that assemblies worldwide are compelled to grapple with how their worship challenges, adopts, and adapts both local and distant cultural elements. Are worldwide worship practices necessarily impeded by the extension of Euro–North American cultural elements into non-Western churches? Should we assume, as we do with other forms of global

7. Ulf Hannerz, *Cultural Complexity* (New York: Columbia University Press, 1992), p. 5.

8. According to Anthony Giddens in *The Consequences of Modernity*, globalization can be defined as "the intensification of worldwide social relations which link distant localities in such a way that local happenings are shaped by events occurring many miles away and vice versa" (Stanford: Stanford University Press, 1990, p. 64).

culture, that worldwide worship will be reimagined in Western terms, and converge toward the same final cultural destination? Philip Jenkins asks, "If in fact every corner of the world is being subjected to a common barrage of media influences that are overwhelmingly from the West, why are we not seeing a kind of cultural homogenization? Why is the global South not absorbing Western moral and religious liberalism?"[9] The relationship between processes of globalization and worship practices has become complicated by the increased pervasiveness of ethnic plurality throughout the world, where it is difficult to make facile distinctions between local and non-local forms. Learning about the worship practices of non-Western Christians sheds light on a different reality — one in which local cultural forms, whether dance, architecture, or music, are employed in meaningful ways (see the case studies by Kane, Robert and Daneel, and Escobar and Palomino).

One flaw in the "global homogenization scenario" is the failure to recognize the persistence of cultural particularity even in the face of the apparent juggernaut of globalization.[10] In the words of Claude Lévi-Strauss,

> We can easily now conceive of a time when there will be only one culture and one civilization on the entire surface of the earth. I don't believe this will happen, because there are contradictory tendencies always at work — on the one hand towards homogenization and on the other towards new distinctions.[11]

It is important that we move beyond seeing culture as either "exotic other" or as so inherently powerful that new distinctions will necessarily be swept away in the face of globalizing forces. All people are immersed in cultures, whether complex or simple, and much of our understanding stems from our own perspective. If we do not understand something — or it is not part of "our" culture — we may consider it "ethnic." For North Americans,

---

9. Philip Jenkins, "After the Next Christendom," p. 21.

10. Ulf Hannerz, *Cultural Complexity*, p. 252. Anthony Giddens notes that the term *juggernaut* comes from "the Hindi *Jagannath,* 'lord of the world,' and is a title of Krishna: an idol of this deity was taken each year through the streets on a huge car, which followers are said to have thrown themselves under, to be crushed beneath the wheels" (*The Consequences of Modernity,* p. 139n.).

11. Claude Lévi-Strauss, *Myth and Meaning* (London: Routledge & Kegan Paul, 1978), p. 20.

Mexican tacos are often lumped together with Indian naan or Thai tom kha kai as "ethnic food," whereas hot dogs and French fries are simply "food." Naturally, from a Mexican, Indian, or Thai perspective, the same may hold true — that is, tacos, naan, or tom kha kai are "food" and hot dogs and French fries are "ethnic" American food.[12] In addition to the sociological and cultural influences on taste, differences may in part be rooted in biological predilection as well. After all, not everybody likes chocolate. Given these differences, how do we welcome the stranger to worship? Are their gifts and talents valued within the assembly?

Christianity compels us to avoid giving "our" culture ultimate interpretive authority, even though some scholars do assign culture interpretive sovereignty, as though no extra-cultural authority exists to challenge or commend local lifeways or provide guidance about living in a pluralistic, globalizing world.[13] And the concept of culture includes both material and nonmaterial realities. For instance, the recognition that even the degree and style of emotional expressivity varies with each culture ought to challenge those of us who are tempted to connect spiritual maturity with a certain rendering of emotion (see the case study presented by Escobar and Palomino). In some cases, early missionaries introduced their own worship patterns and view of cultures to their hosts (see the case study presented by Joo in this book). Postmodern social theory valorizes the perspectival approach, as though any and all cultural vantage points are of equal value, resulting in the loss of a normative canopy that would be a guide to our common reasoning.

---

12. In fact, the origins of French fries may be in France but they were popularized by American businesses. During the First World War, American soldiers in France enjoyed eating "fried potatoes" and returned home with stories of what they called "French fries." The title stuck.

13. For example, C. Wright Mills assigns ultimate perspectival value to culture, as though it is the final court of appeal for interpretation: "For most of what he calls solid fact, sound interpretation, suitable presentations, every man is increasingly dependent upon the observation posts, the interpretation centers, the presentation depots, which in contemporary society are established by means of what I am going to call the cultural apparatus." See C. Wright Mills, *Power, Politics, and People* (New York: Ballantine, 1963), p. 406.

How Is Cultural Particularity
Both Blessed and Transcended in Worship?

In one church I attended, the pastoral staff decided to start a "contemporary, seeker-friendly" service to attract new believers. The early worship service was called "traditional" and used a robed choir, hymns, and organ, while the later "contemporary" service was led by a worship band, with words projected on a large screen that covered the stained-glass window. Even the pulpit was changed between services, from the wooden pulpit that exposed just the upper body and head of the pastor to a Plexiglas pulpit that was visually unobtrusive. Over time, the congregation appeared to be increasingly divided, with each worshiping community, "traditional" and "contemporary," believing the other was either irrelevant or spiritually immature.

This tension is also evident in the church worldwide. Some worship leaders feel free to experiment, while others believe tradition provides security and should not be tampered with. All things are permissible, but not all things are beneficial. How can there be unity in the body of Christ, both within and among congregations, if members of that body believe worship style reflects one's spiritual condition?

The biblical story exposes the speciousness of free-floating cultural relativism. It offers another vision, where culture itself, given by God, can serve as a conduit for meaningful worship, but only when it is secondary to the recognition of God as Creator, the source of diversity, and the biblical witness to that God. We do ourselves a disservice if we confuse these categories. Such skewed priorities gave rise to the early church conflict between traditional Jewish Christians, who argued for the primacy of Jewish customs, particularly circumcision, and Gentile Christians, about whom Peter said, "Truly I perceive that God shows no partiality, but in every nation any one who fears him and does what is right is acceptable to him" (Acts 10:34-35).

The Apostle Peter's own change of mind about the interpretive ultimacy of individual cultures, as he contended with the "circumcision party," gives us insight into the heart of Christian charity toward the variety of worldwide worship practices:

"I was in the city of Joppa, praying; and in a trance I saw a vision, something descending, like a great sheet, let down from heaven by four corners; and it came down to me. Looking at it closely I observed animals and beasts of prey and reptiles and birds of the air. And I heard a voice saying to me, 'Rise, Peter; kill and eat.' But I said, 'No, Lord; for nothing common or unclean has ever entered my mouth.' But the voice answered a second time from heaven, 'What God has cleansed you must not call common.' This happened three times, and all was drawn up again into heaven. At that very moment three men arrived at the house in which we were, sent to me from Caesarea. And the Spirit told me to go with them, making no distinction. These six brethren also accompanied me, and we entered the man's house. And he told us how he had seen the angel standing in his house and saying, 'Send to Joppa and bring Simon called Peter; he will declare to you a message by which you will be saved, you and all your household.' As I began to speak, the Holy Spirit fell on them just as on us at the beginning. And I remembered the word of the Lord, how he said, 'John baptized with water, but you shall be baptized with the Holy Spirit.' If then God gave the same gift to them as he gave to us when we believed in the Lord Jesus Christ, who was I that I could withstand God?" When they heard this they were silenced. And they glorified God, saying, "Then to the Gentiles also God has granted repentance unto life" (Acts 11:5-18).

The apparent hegemony of culture as a validation structure is abrogated by the weight of glory introduced by an encounter with the Gospel through the Holy Spirit. In the words of Lesslie Newbigin,

> The gentile converts were not to be Jewish *Assimilados*. And, as Roland Allen has pointed out in a vivid passage, a Jewish Christian who happened to attend a meeting for Christian worship in Corinth would probably have been profoundly shocked at something which would appear to him so appallingly pagan claiming to be the community of God's people. In spite of the shock, however, the decision was made and adhered to that conversion to Christ did not mean — for the gentile — incorporation into the existing Jewish Church as it was before the gentile mission began.[14]

Culture is set straight in relationship to the Creator in the context of worship that is teleologically inspired. Likewise, it is the grace of God that

14. Newbigin, *The Finality of Christ*, p. 103.

relativizes attempts to absolutize local culture, while at the same time reinvigorating cultural particularities, so that peripheral traditions are not subverted (see Acts 15:1-35). This is the double movement of Christian worship: worship critiques culture and culture shapes worship. These particularities can only be "blessed" by God in the context of worship. As such, Christian worship consecrates these particularities, raising them above the level of the mundane, yet resists giving them ultimate significance. They are but communicative media employable by God for God's purpose, not ours.

Can we apply satisfactorily the notion of globalization to Christianity? It would be better to disconnect the two, because the pattern of globalization suggests both uniformity and center-to-periphery communication, where Western cultures are seen as the fountainhead of cultural production and non-Western cultures as receptors. If we employ the term *globalization* to describe Christian growth, we falsely assume that culture flow emerges from particular centers (e.g., Western cultures) and overwhelms peripheral, local cultures. Challenging the "globalization" thesis, Lamin Sanneh says the worldwide Christian movement "has been occurring in societies with weak states and impoverished populations, and there has been no global orchestration of this expansion."[15]

The complexities of worldwide Christian worship would suggest an entirely different scenario than the one proffered by the globalization perspective. When Christianity takes root in a culture, interactions occur both ways. If this is so, one might well ask: what are the commonalities of Christian worship worldwide? Or is each Christian assembly entirely independent? Furthermore, what about the historical connections among Christian churches? In his periodization of the Christian movement, Andrew Walls, following a fictitious alien guest as he visits different times and places in history, suggests that the Bible and Jesus are held universally authoritative in Christian assemblies.[16] In the face of immense variety of worship practices, worshiping assemblies are shaped by a common adherence to the Bible and to Jesus Christ.

Christian worship offers a different picture of globalizing realities. Christianity is better understood as a worldwide movement, not a global-

---

15. See Sanneh, *Whose Religion Is Christianity?* p. 78.

16. See Andrew Walls, *The Missionary Movement in Christian History* (Maryknoll, N.Y.: Orbis Books, 1996), pp. 3-15.

izing religion, because of its implicit endorsement of cultural particularity. Christianity relativizes culture and worship practice in the light of Christ, but in a different way than social theorists may interpret relativism. All things are held together in Christ; we do not inhabit some fragmented universe, but one with immense variety knitted together under the banner of Christ.

How Is the Truth of Worship
Communicated through Symbols?

One of the most challenging issues when considering worldwide Christian worship practices is the use of local expressions for God, Jesus Christ, and the Holy Spirit. Christianity is unique as a world religion because it endorses the translation of the name for God in local languages. Lamin Sanneh notes that compared to Islam, which insists on the untranslated name of God as "Allah," Christianity's vitality in part stems from its affirmation of the inherent translatability of the name for God as well as nearly all other important Christian biblical concepts into vernaculars.[17] What can we learn from early Christians regarding the issue of using different names for God and other Christian notions?

Christianity is a worldwide movement of worshiping communities. The languages of those assemblies, especially in the post–Second Vatican Council period, are vernaculars. Christianity has expanded vigorously in part because of its inherent "relational validity," reflecting its essential nature as a movement of translation.[18] Reflecting on his experience in Melanesia, Maurice Leenhardt, the "pro-native" missionary in French colonial New Caledonia and anthropologist at the Sorbonne, wrote, "God speaks to a man's heart in the language he has sucked from his mother."[19] Worshiping communities worldwide employ profane languages, with the effect of relativizing access to God and denying any notion of normativeness or

17. See, for example, Sanneh, *Translating the Message* (Maryknoll, NY.: Orbis, 1989), and Walls, *The Missionary Movement in Christian History.* The term *Allah* comes from *al-ilah* ("the god"), which cannot be interpreted as anything but the singular God.

18. For a discussion of the social and religious implications of translation in Christian history, particularly in the African context, see Sanneh, *Translating the Message.*

19. "Lettre aux Pasteurs de Nouvelle-Calédonie, 11 Oct. 1938," in James Clifford, *Person and Myth* (Berkeley: University of California Press, 1982), p. 12.

exclusive control of the message by the clergy.[20] Even churches marked by high liturgies make use of mother tongues.

The earliest days of Patristic Christianity in the Mediterranean region were marked by an ongoing conflict between two fundamental orientations toward culture. Eastern church leaders, who wrote treatises in Greek, affirmed the cultural traditions of Greece and Rome. Western church leaders, who employed Latin in their formal discourses, for the most part disdained any adoption of Hellenistic culture, being convinced that pagan (secular) thought-forms or extrascriptural sources were responsible for the proliferation of heresies. The Eastern church approach is exemplified by Justin Martyr (ca. 100–ca. 165) whose doctrine of *logos spermatikos* ("seed-bearing word") suggested that God had scattered hints of truth in pagan philosophy, whereby Christ would be the final revelation. The doctrine of *logos spermatikos* affirmed the inherent goodness of culture, but it also affirmed the need for its completion in the light of Christ. The theological perspective of the Western church is represented by Tertullian (ca. 160–ca. 225), who opposed making Christian theology dependent upon pagan sources, Greek or otherwise. Tertullian's approach is best summarized by his famous rhetorical question: "What has Athens to do with Jerusalem?" According to Tertullian, secular philosophy and faith mix as well as oil and water — they are fundamentally incompatible.

Local cultural forms, with languages providing the best example, were deployed to communicate the Gospel in a meaningful way to people contemporaneous with the biblical writers. The term *Logos,* for example, was employed powerfully in John's Gospel to communicate the Divine condescension and incarnation, and the term *Lamb* conveyed the significance of Christ's substitutionary sacrifice. Such concepts functioned to announce to the Greek-speaking Mediterranean world, in the first case, and to the early Jewish Christians, in the second, the entrance of God incarnate into the world.[21] Material culture, likewise, is not neutral. Each compo-

---

20. The term *profane* is used to denote the routine and ordinary. The term does not imply a normative quality, and it is distinguished from the absolutizing of the lingua franca as exclusive carrier of sacrality. I use the term *profane* in the Eliadean sense of not referring to moral categories but to things routine, normal, ordinary, in contradistinction from something "wholly other" *(ganz andere).* See Mircea Eliade, *Sacred and Profane* (New York: Harcourt Brace Jovanovich Publishers, 1959).

21. The challenge of using a variety of metaphors when referring to the Godhead has been explored by Sallie McFague, who argues that the "*primary context,* then, of any

nent is an embodiment of meaning. And we cannot easily compare the meaning of material cultural items without understanding their context. A museum piece holds little meaning for the observer unless the original context, historical or otherwise, has been described sufficiently enough for a meaningful connection to be established. Context is important. In its early period, Christianity emerged out of its Jewish environment only to enter the Hellenistic world, adopting Greek philosophical concepts to communicate the essential affirmations of the faith, beginning with the fundamental relationship between the Son and the Father.[22]

Christian worshipers worldwide are not typically offended by the language issue. They recognize that Spanish, English, Mandarin, Quechua, Yoruba, or Kiswahili can be used meaningfully in worship. It is more unsettling for some to see the introduction of new music styles, material culture, or — perhaps most troublesome — the use of new metaphors to communicate the Godhead.[23]

---

discussion of religious language is worship," in Sallie McFague, *Metaphorical Theology* (Philadelphia: Fortress Press, 1982), p. 2. An unlimited use of metaphorical language can be tempered with Thomas Aquinas's notion of analogical predication, which points to theological language as neither univocal or equivocal but rather analogical, whether metaphorical or conceptual.

22. An early example is the Arian-Athanasius conflict over the relationship between Father and Son. The Greek terms *homoiousios* ("of similar substance") and *homoousios* ("of the same substance") were used to affirm that the Son was of the same substance *(ousios)* of the Father (Athanasius), and not merely of similar substance (Arius). Athanasius's position became orthodox and was later credalized in the Nicene Creed.

23. The dynamic relationship between language and theology is highlighted by Sallie McFague when she notes, "If we lose sight of the relativity and plurality of the interpretive context, our religious language will, as with the loss of the religious context, become idolatrous or irrelevant. It will become idolatrous, for we will absolutize one tradition of images for God; it will become irrelevant, for the experience of many people will not be included within the canonized tradition" (*Metaphorical Theology*, p. 3). Despite the disquiet some feel when introducing new images of Jesus, recently there has been a growing interest in Jesus studies, presenting various popular depictions of Jesus throughout history or cultural perspectives and illustrating the difficulty in limiting our understanding to Jesus without being sensitive to the social, cultural, and historical contexts of our perspectives. For example, see Bart D. Ehrman, *Jesus: Apocalyptic Prophet of the New Millennium* (New York: Oxford University Press, 1999); Richard Wightman Fox, *Jesus in America: Personal Savior, Cultural Hero, National Obsession* (San Francisco: HarperSanFrancisco, 2004); Jaroslav Pelikan, *Jesus Through the Centuries: His Place in the History of Culture* (New Haven: Yale University Press, 1985); Stephen Prothero, *American Jesus: How the Son of God Became a National Icon* (New York: Farrar, Straus & Giroux, 2003).

For instance, the social and religious life of the indigenous inhabitants of the island of New Guinea is centered on the pig. They use pigs for every important transaction between themselves and beings of the spirit world, and domesticated pigs hold the highest prestige and exchange value. Even today, pigs are the highest commodity item in remote regions of New Guinea. Highland Papuans keep ordinary pigs and sacrificial pigs, the latter whose blood has to be spilt during critical rituals to appease angry spirits. Moreover, the distribution of the meat of the sacrificial pig is highly formalized, similar to the way in which the bread is distributed during the celebration of the Lord's Supper and thus have missiological significance. Papuans assume that the pig's blood guarantees reconciliation and peace among the environment, human beings, and the spirit world. For Euro–North Americans, it may be meaningful to learn that the Christ is the incarnated Logos or the Lamb of God — these biblical notions hold much weight, especially for those socialized into the worldviews of Lambs and Logos. However, New Guineans have never seen a lamb, and the concept of Logos is so abstract that it is nearly impossible to make sense of it to a common villager. To many New Guineans, Christ is like a pig. Not the ordinary pig, but the unblemished one that is sacrificed and procures reconciliation.[24] He is the pig of God who takes away the sin of the world — an anathema to the ears of many Euro–North Americans. But if Christ is seen as liberator in subjugated contexts or as ancestor in tribal contexts or as a black Messiah, according to Alexander Young's "Ethiopian Manifesto," then why cannot he be seen as a pig?[25] Symbolically, that is the way the concept of Christ may function most meaningfully to pig-centered peoples.

Just how far beyond Lambs and Logos ought Christians to venture in their presentation of Christ in worship? What are the measures of appropriate usage of metaphors? Should all worship be immediately meaning-

24. It is worthwhile to note that many locally meaningful metaphors for Jesus Christ (e.g., pig) may be useful concepts in early translations, but later may be eliminated in favor of terms closer to a literal translation of the original Greek of the New Testament (e.g., Lamb), with added footnotes for clarification.

25. For a discussion of the importance of appropriate, meaning-driven Bible translation, see Eugene Nida and William Reyburn, *Meaning Across Cultures* (Maryknoll, N.Y.: Orbis Books, 1981). A general introduction to a comparative and worldwide Christology is presented by Veli-Matti Kärkkäinen, *Christology: A Global Introduction* (Grand Rapids: Baker Academic, 2003).

ful, or should some meaning be learned or become apparent through revelation? Given the pig example above, should New Guineans be made to learn about lambs before making Christ meaningful to them? These questions point to the universal-particular dynamic within Christianity and the creation of meaning itself.

Christianity is at once universal and particular. Biblical scholars and theologians exert much energy trying to unearth the significance of early Christianity so that modern readers and hearers may learn the meaning of words, experiences, and insights from followers of Jesus and the earliest commentators on Christianity. And every Sunday in churches throughout the world, good sermonizing makes sense of the biblical text for a modern audience. Often the litmus test of a good worship service is whether it communicated something meaningful to worshipers.[26] A common reason given by some Euro–North American Christians for changing churches is that worship is "irrelevant, meaningless to me."

Christian worshipers might benefit from learning the meaning of a variety of depictions of Christ, even though they might not find those initially meaningful in their own context. Jesus Christ was particular — a Palestinian Jew — yet universally recognizable. This effort to maintain a vision of the particular and universal of Jesus Christ relates to the overall culture challenge, for the same dynamic exposed when trying to make sense of the various representations of Christ can be equally applied to any other concept or material item used within the worshiping assembly. For example, what is the meaning of playing drums for Africans, and how might the use of African drums in Euro–North American assemblies be more fully appreciated or critiqued? Likewise, what about the appropriateness of using nonlocal items for the Eucharistic elements? One advantage of becoming multicultural worshipers is that we can get a glimpse of the specter of heavenly worship, where all tribes and languages will be assembled before God, and where we really will have a sense of the fullness of Christ. These questions are significant, for they can just as well be applied

26. The worship experience of Americans, which increasingly appears to be reflected in a similar pattern worldwide, is noted by Robert Wuthnow: "It was not only enough for Americans simply to visit their houses of worship once or twice a week (although, in reality, that is what most Americans did). Clergy wanted their flocks to be at home with God when they came to their places of worship. Congregations became comfortable, familiar, domestic, offering an image of God that was basically congruent with the domestic tranquility of the ideal home" (*After Heaven* [Berkeley: University of California Press, 1998], p. 33).

15

to almost any other nonlinguistic element of worship, such as architecture, use of color, style of music, or bodily movement.

How Is Worship Both Individual and Cultural?

What does worship mean to the individual? How can we understand the personal aspects of worship worldwide? Worship is personal. Human beings are capable of meaningful engagement with an abundance of cultural variety in worship. In fact, this innate ability may be related to the noble task of becoming persons embedded in communities more than it does with becoming autonomous individuals. In other words, worship may teach us to become *persons* as we praise God in community. According to Maurice Leenhardt,

> the person, in opposition to the individual, is capable of enriching itself through a more or less indefinite assimilation of exterior elements. It takes its life from the elements it absorbs, in a wealth of communion. The person is capable of superabundance.[27]

Enrichment of the person cannot be attained by simply affirming the cultural contributions exhibited in the service. That could be a form of feel-good humanitarianism. Rather, those items, hymns, and liturgies should be geared toward enriching the relationship between worshiper and worshiped — God. The difference is one that Michael Polanyi notes between fact and beauty:

> Religion, considered as an act of worship, is an indwelling rather than an affirmation. God cannot be observed, any more than truth or beauty can be observed. He exists in the sense that He is to be worshipped and obeyed, but not otherwise; not as a fact — any more than truth, beauty or justice exist as facts.[28]

Christian worship consists not in intellectual assent alone, nor in an affirmation of the facts, nor in fixity of form; rather, it entails a meaningful relationship, an encounter with the Creator.

27. Cited in James Clifford, *Person and Myth*, p. 123.
28. Michael Polanyi, *Personal Knowledge*, p. 279.

16

Christian worship necessarily brings into contact the finite believer and the infinite, at-once transcendent and immanent God. In this encounter, the personhood of the worshiper finds fulfillment. Recall that St. Paul uses the expression, "your body is a temple of the Holy Spirit within you" (1 Corinthians 6:19). Thus, Hans Urs von Balthasar suggests that the Christian experience of God involves an indwelling of a unique kind when compared to the other world religions:

> Now we can clearly see the difference between the Christian revelation (and hence Christian contemplation) and every other possible form of human religion and prayer. In the latter case the idea of an infinite "I" indwelling what is finite, taken seriously, leads inevitably to a pantheistic conclusion; the leap beyond the finite (empirical) self into the Absolute becomes, with equal inevitability, a kind of fatal yet blissful self-abdication (cf. Fichte). In Christianity this indwelling is a serious and radical feature, without needing to explode and annihilate the finite self; on the contrary, here, in the most mysterious way, the self comes to fulfillment beyond itself in God.[29]

Christian worship cannot be illuminated well without discussing what happens *to the person* in worship. This may sound strange, given that worship usually entails an assembly of people, even if only a few. Yet all people experience themselves as selves, even though some may more closely identify with a community, kinship network, or clan. Modern conditions and globalization have given rise to more diverse ways of seeing the self.[30] Among Euro–North Americans, for example, a popular metaphor for life is the "project" of constructing the self. The constructionist model of social theory suggests that the self is in the making, an unfinished project to be completed by individual and society, with robust market and ideological forces vying for allegiance. In this vein, Peter Berger has written about the use of

29. Hans Urs von Balthasar, *Prayer* (San Francisco: Ignatius Press, 1986), p. 75.

30. This is not the place to explore the issue of individual (personal) and social (corporate) selves, but it seems as though the strict dichotomy between Western and non-Western notions of self is overstated. In fact, all people experience life individually and corporately. See Anthony Giddens, *Modernity and Self-Identity: Self and Society in the Late Modern Age* (Stanford: Stanford University Press, 1991); Erving Goffman, *The Presentation of Self in Everyday Life* (New York: Doubleday, 1959); Alan Roland, *In Search of Self in India and Japan* (Princeton, N.J.: Princeton University Press, 1988); and Alan Roland, *Cultural Pluralism and Psychoanalysis* (New York: Routledge, 1996).

identity markets in shaping our self-understanding and presentation to others,[31] where the individual "is given enormous latitude in fabricating his own particular private life — a kind of 'do-it-yourself' universe."[32]

Clifford Geertz's interpretation of religion as a system of symbols gives priority to the role played by symbols as expressive and determinative of a believer's dispositions and development of self. According to Geertz, religious symbols, which he claims have inherent force and are thus intrinsically compelling, "induc[e] in the worshiper a certain distinctive set of dispositions (tendencies, capacities, propensities, skills, habits, liabilities, pronenesses) which lend a chronic character to the flow of his activity and the quality of his experience."[33] He suggests that it is specifically in the arena of ritual, with worship being the prime example, that symbolic forms, as vehicles of meaning, induce in actors the general conceptions of the order of existence.[34] As such, Geertz has a high view of worship, and compares the religious perspective with those of common sense and aestheticism to suggest that only the religious perspective "moves beyond the realities of everyday life to wider ones which correct and complete them, and its defining concern is not action upon those wider realities but acceptance of them, faith in them . . . [i]t is this sense of the 'really real' upon which the religious perspective rests and which the symbolic activities of religion as a cultural system are devoted."[35]

Geertz has made important contributions to the understanding of culture, religion, and the function of symbols in worship. However, from a Christian perspective, Geertz's portrayal of ritual life, while appealing in many ways, seems limited because of the absence of a pneumatology of

31. Peter Berger, "Social Mobility and Personal Identity," *Humanitas* 8, no. 1 (Spring 1971): 100.

32. Peter L. Berger, Brigitte Berger, and Hansfried Kellner, *The Homeless Mind* (New York: Vantage Books, 1974), p. 186. The constructionist perspective also makes sense of the smorgasbord-style of religiosity characterizing many young and older Euro–North Americans, who combine elements of various religions to create an invention suited to their individual taste and style. These religious concoctions often fail to provide systems of personal or corporate accountability — one can simply "opt out" of the religion if it is too restrictive. Among Christians, modern consumption patterns coalesce with the pattern of self-construction, giving rise to discontented selves in search of new churches that better meet their needs.

33. Geertz, *The Interpretation of Cultures*, p. 95.

34. Geertz, *The Interpretation of Cultures*, p. 112.

35. Geertz, *The Interpretation of Cultures*, p. 112.

worship. Do symbols have inherent force, as Geertz suggests? What makes symbols meaningful? Christians affirm that it is in part the Holy Spirit who draws people, revealing meaning beyond the historical interpretations of ritual practices and enabling the symbols and liturgies to function as the lens through which the worshiper encounters God.

Although a liturgy may be aesthetically appealing, it is not ultimately meaningful to the worshiper unless the Holy Spirit works to make it so. Similarly, John Calvin, following Martin Luther, maintained that the words of Scripture functioned like ordinary words until the Holy Spirit revealed the Word (Christ) through the words. For example, a rural Hindu villager may not necessarily find meaningful the celebration of the Eucharist in a large Anglican church in urban Delhi. Likewise, a secularist from Canada may not naturally find meaning in an Aladura prayer meeting among the Yoruba. Worshipers may need some education *into* the meaning of the various elements of Christian worship as well as a movement of the Holy Spirit to enliven their hearts and minds before they have a meaningful experience in that setting. Both genuineness and authenticity are marks of true Christian worship, where worshipers are neither manipulated by shallow schemes nor by counterfeit gospels (see Galatians 1:6-12).[36] In worship, as the double movement of learning and revealing takes place, worshipers are made new — not entirely by themselves, but by the power of the Holy Spirit. This is the work of worship.

How Does Worship Extend Us
beyond Self-interest to Practice Hospitality?

What is unique about Christian worship? In what ways does Christian worship worldwide stand apart from the ordinary gathering of people in

---

36. Polanyi discusses representation by distinguishing between authentic and inauthentic experiences of worship: "The worshipper strenuously concentrates on his prayer for the sake of achieving devotion to God; he may succeed or fail. Monks and nuns afflicted by 'acidia' are tormented by failure to pray wholeheartedly. Experiences can be compared in *depth,* and the more deeply they affect us, the more *genuine* they may be said to be. A person's reports of experience can be doubted even if they are correct. A person may correctly report the colours of a large number of objects, yet not really see any difference between green and red; so that when it is eventually found that he is red-green colour blind, we shall conclude that his previous reports, though correct, were not authentic" (*Personal Knowledge,* p. 202).

other social institutions? To start, we should recognize that worship is corporate. South African David Bosch notes that the Greco-Roman term *ekklesia* "normally referred to the town meetings of free male citizens of a city of Greek constitution."[37] *Ekklesia* was first adopted by the Hellenistic-Jewish Christian communities in Antioch and later employed by St. Paul to denote the church. Abraham Malherbe notes that the Pauline churches were "relatively unorganized, fraught with distress, with only rudimentary instruction in the faith, and in tension with the larger society."[38] Wayne Meeks compared Paul's use of *ekklesia* to the Greco-Roman household, voluntary associations of clubs and guilds, the Jewish synagogue, and the philosophical school.[39] Despite the similarities, the term *ekklesia* adopted by Antiochene Christians referred to a *sui generis* community, one marked neither by "free citizenry" nor special talents, but rather by kinship terminology ("brother" and "sister"), mutuality, and love.

The radical nature of the church was due in part to its boundary-breaking message that welcomed all people within its fellowship.[40] Social and economic homogeneity of the Greco-Roman guilds stood in stark contrast to the immense social and cultural variety of Christian gatherings, where immediate distinctions were relativized before God. In this sense, the "horizontality" of Christian assemblies contrasted with the "verticality" of the Greco-Roman association, where the "sense of high and low pressed heavily on people."[41] Membership in the Christian assembly neither required people to dispense of or elevate their particular trade or talents, but rather to utilize their particular God-bequeathed skills and

37. David Bosch, *Transforming Mission* (Maryknoll, N.Y.: Orbis Books, 1992), p. 165.

38. Abraham J. Malherbe, *Paul and the Thessalonians* (Philadelphia: Fortress Press, 1987), 61; also quoted in Bosch, *Transforming Mission*, p. 165.

39. Wayne Meeks, *The First Urban Christians: The Social World of the Apostle Paul* (New Haven: Yale University Press, 1983), pp. 75-84; also quoted in Bosch, *Transforming Mission*, p. 165.

40. The Apostle Paul writes, "For as many of you as were baptized into Christ have put on Christ. There is neither Jew nor Greek, there is neither slave nor free, there is neither male nor female; for you are all one in Christ Jesus" (Galatians 3:27, 28; also Romans 13:9-13 and 1 Thessalonians 4:9-12). Also see Abraham J. Malherbe, *Social Aspects of Early Christianity* (Philadelphia: Fortress Press, 1983), pp. 67-70, 94-103.

41. Abraham J. Malherbe, *Social Aspects of Early Christianity*, p. 86. The term *verticality*, which describes the tensions within Roman society, was first employed by Ramsay MacMullen, *Roman Social Relations: 50 BC to AD 284* (New Haven: Yale University Press, 1982).

gifts to uplift the community (see, for example, 1 Corinthians 12–14). The dramatic difference between Christian assemblies and Greco-Roman society was so striking that it is no wonder first-century Christians "were criticized for social rather than political reasons."[42] These early assemblies were key access points of hospitality, where travelers in an increasingly mobile society were shown warm-heartedness and generosity. The earliest "churches" had no buildings designed for worship, but met in hospitable homes, where followers of Christ would worship together.[43]

Where do we learn such hospitality that extends beyond our own self-interest? Christine Pohl suggests "hospitality begins in worship," where hospitality is first "a response of love and gratitude for God's love and welcome to us."[44] We become worshiping persons in the context of a community, and we demonstrate our transformed lives by expressing hospitality to one another and the world to which God has called us — which includes the missional feature of worship (see the case studies presented by Escobar and Palomino, Farhadian, Priest, and Wickeri). In the early church, worship invigorated personal and corporate life, which at once sustained the community and aroused believers to engage the wider society, sometimes at great risk.

How Can We Map a Spatial and Temporal Geography of Global Worship?

Christian worship is a peculiar kind of worship. The Lutheran World Federation has sought to outline the dynamic nature of worship worldwide in its "Nairobi Statement on Worship and Culture" (see Appendix). According to this statement, contemporary challenges to Christian worship include being *transcultural, contextual, countercultural,* and *cross-cultural.*[45] The transcultural nature of Christian worship recognizes the mystery that God's grace transcends all cultures even as the church exists within specific cultures and at specific times in history while remaining a worldwide communion *(communio).* The Nairobi Statement attests:

42. Malherbe, *Social Aspects of Early Christianity,* p. 21.
43. Malherbe, *Social Aspects of Early Christianity,* p. 96
44. Christine D. Pohl, *Making Room* (Grand Rapids: Eerdmans, 1999), p. 172.
45. S. Anita Stauffer, *Christian Worship* (Geneva: Lutheran World Federation, 1996), pp. 23-28.

There is one Bible, translated into many tongues, and biblical preaching of Christ's death and resurrection has been sent into all the world. The fundamental shape of the principal Sunday act of Christian worship, the Eucharist or Holy Communion, is shared across cultures: the people gather, the Word of God is proclaimed, the people intercede for the needs of the Church and the world, the eucharistic meal is shared, and the people are sent out into the world for mission.[46]

The contextual aspect of worship involves recognizing the cultural particularity of Christian worship — the use of local cultural patterns, images, materials, and terms to make worship meaningful and relevant in specific contexts. In 1989, for example, the Anglican province of New Zealand, which includes Polynesia, approved a canticle of praise as part of the eucharistic liturgy that incorporates images of the Polynesian islands into the section for thanksgiving:

> So now we offer our thanks
> for the beauty of these islands;
> for the wild places and the busy,
> for the mountains, the coast, and the sea[47]

In India, the Syrian Rite Christians "have already adopted the culture of the land from the beginning of the expansion of Christianity into India during the early centuries. They were given special privileges by the local kings and rulers, equal to the high caste Hindus, and have, in fact, accepted the gospel truth and retained the culture, customs, and ways of the land."[48]

The countercultural aspect of worship offers a countervailing force to the contextualizing logic by recognizing that "Jesus Christ came to transform all people and all cultures, and calls us not to conform to the world, but to be transformed with it (Romans 12:2)."[49] Here we hear an

---

46. Stauffer, *Christian Worship*, p. 24.

47. Stauffer, "Worship: Ecumenical Core and Cultural Context," p. 16.

48. Bryan Spinks and George Mathew, "Syrian Versus Hindu Conflict over Inculturation in India," in *Liturgical Inculturation in the Anglican Communion, including the York Statement, "Down to Earth Worship,"* ed. David R. Holeton (Nottingham: Grove Books Limited, 1990), p. 48. See the chapter by Philip Wickeri on the Mar Thoma church in this book. The chapter by Robert and Daneel in this book illustrates the continuity between an indigenous Zimbabwean (Shona) concept of space and worship.

49. Stauffer, *Christian Worship*, p. 27.

overtone of Karl Barth's "No" to the prevailing culture and Martin Luther's *simul justus et peccator* (simultaneously sinner and justified). The countercultural aspect of worship is a rejection of the idea that culture can be salvific without Christ. For instance, the Eucharist is countercultural, a meal where social relations are relativized (Galatians 3:26-28).[50] The implications of the countercultural component may be cultural as well as political, especially when subjugated Christians assemble to worship the Triune God as supreme over, for instance, the state or the powers that be.

Finally, the cross-cultural nature of worship challenges any attempt to stockpile the earthly treasures of cultures without sharing them broadly with Christian assemblies worldwide. In the words of the Nairobi Statement, "The sharing of hymns and art and other elements of worship across cultural barriers helps enrich the whole Church and strengthen the sense of the *communio* of the Church. This sharing can be ecumenical as well as cross-cultural, as a witness to the unity of the Church and the oneness of Baptism."[51] This cultural "borrowing" must be multidimensional; worship elements from non-Western settings enrich those in the West, as well as vice versa.

Conclusion

The cross-cultural nature of worldwide worship requires serious reflection on the original meaning of an adopted cultural element so as not to trivialize it within the liturgical *ordo*. Naturally, it is nearly impossible for the exact meaning of an object to be easily transferred, because contexts and cultures worldwide vary so much. Playing a cymbal holds a different meaning for a predominately German charismatic assembly in Hamburg than for a Japanese church located near the Shinto Ise Shrine in Japan.[52] In

---

50. For an analysis of the Eucharist in the New Testament, see Gordon W. Lathrop, "Eucharist in the New Testament and Its Cultural Setting," in *Worship and Culture in Dialogue*, ed. S. Anita Stauffer (Geneva: Lutheran World Federation, 1994), pp. 67-82. For an examination of Eucharist in the early church, see Anscar J. Chupungco, "Eucharist in the Early Church and Its Cultural Settings," in *Worship and Culture in Dialogue*, ed. Stauffer, pp. 83-102.

51. S. Anita Stauffer, *Christian Worship*, p. 27.

52. Shinto, the indigenous religion of Japan, employs cymbals as the way to call down the *kami*, sacred spirits in Shinto tradition. As such, cymbals play a central role in the religious life of Shinto religionists.

the words of Anscar J. Chupungco, "when we borrow a musical rhythm meant to suggest an amorous relationship, for example, for a communion song, it is possible that we are spiritualizing that type of love. But are we not thereby imposing on the musical rhythm a signification it is not meant to possess? Surely every society claims a distinct musical rhythm with which it expresses relationship with God."[53] Does cultural borrowing in worship require that the meaning from one culture to another needs to be exactly the same? In practice, adoption inevitably entails some degree of innovation. Whether a Christian assembly values high liturgical performance or simple low-church get-togethers, the affirmation that Jesus Christ is both historically particular and universally accessible makes Christian worship unique among the world religions.

53. Anscar J. Chupungco, "Liturgy and the Cultural Components of Culture," in *Worship and Culture in Dialogue,* ed. Stauffer, p. 154. Chupungco argues that "we offend cultural sensitivity when we use cultural components in the liturgy without due regard for their original meaning or purpose" (p. 154). Also, see Eugene Nida, *Message and Mission* (New York: Harper, 1960). For discussion of liturgical inculturation and the Anglican communion, see David R. Holeton, *Liturgical Inculturation in the Anglican Communion.*

PART I
Biblical Reflections

The Ephesians Moment in Worldwide Worship:
A Meditation on Revelation 21 and Ephesians 2

ANDREW WALLS

Revelation 21 is often assumed to be a representation of heaven. It is, of course, a representation of the Church. "Come," says the guiding angel, "and I will show you the bride, the wife of the Lamb." That glorious, gleaming, bejeweled city that needs not sun, moon, or building for worship, is the Church as it is in principle, and the Church that it will be in reality. You will recall that one feature of the Church, the New Jerusalem, is unlike the Old Jerusalem: it is perfectly square, with three gates in each wall, so that it is opened equally to the north, south, east, and west. The gates are never shut in any direction. The Church, that is, has no front door, no privileged point of entry. Along the roads to it we see those roads full of traffic. The peoples of the earth guided by the light that comes from the renewed Church and their rulers are bringing their wealth into it. And then an echo of a prophecy of the Old Jerusalem, where we hear the glory and wealth of the nations is being brought into the city from the north, south, east, and west. The completed, renewed Church receives the glory and wealth of all the nations, the best that they have to offer. A city so full of gold and jewels, and bejeweled gates, which we are told represent the twelve tribes of Israel, might be held to have treasure enough. But the jewels of Israel, the jewels of the nation, are not sufficient. The fullness of the Church's worship requires the glory and the wealth of all the nations in all directions. The doors of the Church are perpetually open, equally in each direction, to receive the best of the wealth of all the nations.

The image of the Church as the wife of the Lamb naturally recalls that passage in Ephesians about Christ's self-giving love for the Church, the true pattern for a Christian husband's love for his wife. This epistle, perhaps more than any other part of the New Testament, explores the relationship between cultures in the Church. Its grand theme is the place of the Gentiles — the nations, that is — in the scheme of salvation. That the Gentiles would be blessed in the Messianic Age was always apparent to anyone who read the prophets. But Ephesians reflects a sense of excitement at a new realization of just how significant that place was to be. It was a secret, a mysterion, now opened and visibly taking shape before the eyes of the readers. The nations were heirs to the promises of Israel. It was the mystery of Christ, the secret about the Messiah. Ephesians 2 declares that the nations are no longer foreigners to Israel, not even in the deuteronomic phrase "strangers within the gates," but rather fellow citizens belonging equally. They, along with members of the old Israel, are part of the building held together by Christ, a building dedicated to the Lord where God lives through the Spirit. They are being built into a temple, the appropriate place for worship. The Church is the new temple, existing for the worship of God, and the nations are building blocks within it. The passage is well known and oft expounded where the cross of Christ is represented as breaking down the middle wall of partition between Jew and Gentile. Most commonly in our own day, the new significance is seen in terms of ethnicity — that is, the abolition in Christ of the hostility between the races and the implications of this for Christians in a world of ethnic strife.

But in the first century, the middle wall is not just about two races, but about two cultures and two cultures that existed side by side within the Church. One, that of the original believers, represented the life and thought of Israel converted. Law, temple, circumcision, sacrifice, and Sabbath remained in place, perhaps more precious than ever, and certainly more fully understood in the light of the Messiah's coming. The central concern of such believers remained the same: the salvation of the nation and the hope that faithful praying people like Simeon had had for centuries, waiting for the redemption of Israel. These were people who still made a vow and kept their hair long until it was fulfilled and offered a purificatory sacrifice before cutting their hair when it was. And they could claim that the Lord himself had followed this path and that he had declared that not the smallest part of the law would be abrogated until the time of fulfillment. Certainly they could point to the example of his brother James, brought up in the same household, who now presided over the church in Jerusalem and was respected throughout the Jewish community as "James the Righteous," who was righteous in Jewish terms, heart-felt, humble, and an adherent to the law. The temple that Jesus cleansed and called his Father's house remained at the heart of the worship of these early believers. All that they believed about Jesus, all that they believed about the work of Jesus, made perfect sense in terms of Jewish history, Jewish thought, and Jewish destiny. The Messianic Age had dawned with all the prophetic signs of that age, the pouring out of the Spirit of God. They did not even realize that they were Christians. This was a name not bestowed in Jerusalem, but to the mixed believing community in Antioch. They did not need a name; they were Israel. They were the restored, morally renewed Israel that the prophets foretold would appear in the Messianic Age. They were Israel converted, turned back, turned around to face the Messiah. Their characteristic lifestyle, with its shared property, its care for marginalized groups like widows, its meals shared from house to house, showed a Jewish society transformed from that exploited and selfish society revealed by Isaiah and Amos.

But the first-century Church also included another culture group, marginal at first, but steadily gaining in significance until it became the majority. An attack on believers in Jerusalem, we remember, led to the exodus from the city of many believers, with people naturally gravitating to the Diaspora communities, where many doubtless had relatives. The word about the Messiah was thus spread in the Diaspora communities right across the eastern Mediterranean. But in Antioch, some bold religious entrepreneurs presented Jesus to pagans, and some responded. Antioch became the first bicultural church. It became also the base for a mission to the heart of the Hellenistic world.

The nature of its biculturalism is worth reflection. If we follow the accounts in Acts and Galatians with all the jigsaw difficulties that are present, we find that the old righteous believers of Old Jerusalem, the apostles and elders of the Church, came to a remarkable decision about the new believers in Antioch and its mission (see Acts 15). It would have been easy, almost natural, to treat them as Gentiles who came to worship the God of Israel. Gentiles who saw the light had always been welcomed in Israel, but they were proselytes receiving the sign of adoption into Israel by circumcision and undertaking as Israelites to obey the law of Israel. Even the prophecies, which spoke of flocks of Gentiles coming to worship Yahweh in the Messianic Age, spoke of them coming to the mountain of the Lord's house in Jerusalem. All agreed that faith in the Messiah of Israel brought people into Israel. Yet the apostles and elders took a different path. They explicitly declared that the requirements of circumcision and Torah were unnecessary, and new believers could enter Israel without becoming Jews. Paul went further. He would not even allow it as an option that a Hellenistic ex-pagan should adopt a Jewish lifestyle, even if it was the lifestyle of an apostle. They were not proselytes copying an existing lifestyle from their teachers. They were converts determining their own way of life towards Christ.

The apostolic decree of Acts 15 builds cultural diversity into the Christian church forever. In the first instance, however, it established in that church two sharply different ways of being Christian. One was well established, built on ancient foundations and embodying law, temple, circumcision, Sabbath, food laws, ritual purification, and festivals. For the other group, temple, the heart and center of worship for the old community, was out of balance. Circumcision alone would have opened the temple to them, and now circumcision was laid aside. The new believers, free of the law, did want to perform the worship, and could not perform it. For the most part, they were not able to keep the Sabbath. They could copy the Jerusalem believers' custom of frequent communal meals, but, as we gather from the Corinthians, this custom could get out of hand for good cultural reasons in Hellenistic societies and had to be abandoned. The surprising thing about the decree of the Jerusalem council is that, outside of fairly narrow limits of dietary and sexual conduct, it left the question of lifestyle, and in effect that of worship, completely open. Hitherto, there had only been one way of being a Jesus believer, and that way started with the life of an observant Jew. Hellenistic believers were left under the guidance of the Holy Spirit to find a Hellenistic way of being Christian.

Substantial portions of the New Testament (1 Corinthians is an excellent example) show that construction process going on, constructing a Hellenistic way of being Christian where believers could do what the apostles had never done — for instance, going to dinner with a pagan and talking about Christ at a pagan dinner table. Peter and John had never done that and never would. It becomes a necessary part of the new Christianity. Hellenistic social and family life was not to be replaced; it was to be converted.

It is clear from the New Testament that Christian biculturalism caused trouble, and it was at the table that it caused the most trouble. The common meals united Jewish and ex-pagan believers in Jesus. As the latter were now within Israel, there was every reason to eat with them. They were no longer Gentiles. But for many it was hard to swallow that they were not still Gentiles. Even Peter, who was theologically convinced of the position, found it prudent not to let visitors from Jerusalem see him actually eating with Gentile Christians in Antioch. As Galatians shows, there were Gentile Christians to whom the idea of proselyte status was attractive, perhaps as a sort of higher Christian life. The new Hellenistic way of being Christian must necessarily be risky, with endless opportunities for things to go wrong. If any conservative-minded Jewish believer were to read 1 Corinthians, we can imagine him crying out, "I told you so! This is exactly what happens if you allow more pagans to go without the guidance of the Torah!" And perhaps there were Hellenistic Christians (there is a hint of this attitude in 1 Corinthians, too) who despised the scruples of their Judaic brethren, and who would not or could not participate in cosmopolitan culture.

In the Ephesian picture, the wall between the two cultures is broken down. It is not that they become one culture; it is not that they are assimilated one way to the other. That way was explicitly rejected by the Jerusalem council. Jew and Gentile believer did not become one culture. I recognize, of course, that many Jews were, in different degrees, already participating in Hellenistic culture. I do not think this affects the point. They are negotiating the culture from the outside and from the security of their own Jewish identity — Jewish and Gentile, or more properly, ex-Gentile — because they are no longer Gentiles but rather citizens of Israel. Jewish and ex-Gentile believers, each group converted but differently converted lifestyles, were brought into the same structure: a new Temple that existed for God's worship, the abode of the Spirit, who in each case led the process of confession. Believers with converted lifestyles were the bricks that built the Temple, and both sets of bricks were needed. The epistle then goes further: Jewish and ex-Gentile believers with their converted but distinct lifestyles are part of a single functioning body with Christ as the head, the directing brain that moves all of the organs.

And then we come to the most staggering statement of all. We have not yet realized the full height of that body, the full stature of Christ. But that is the goal — that we all come together to the full stature of Christ. Notice that together, in the full context of the argument that has been built up so far, the two diverse distinct expressions of Christianity are equally necessary to realize the fullness of Christ. One on its own is defective. In the Ephesian picture, Hellenistic Christianity was not a soft option for benighted heathens, as some Old Jerusalem believers undoubtedly thought it to be. Nor was Judaic Christianity a sort of legalistic bondage that later Gentile Christians thought it was. Nor, in postmodern fashion, does the epistle suggest that these are alike, valid forms of expression that are equally acceptable — alternatives, as it were. There is no trace in Ephesians of two churches. There is only one Church that depends on the union of the two. There is one body of Christ, needing both Christianities for its proper functioning.

When Ephesians was written it was a question of two major cultures and two ways of life and worship arising out of them. Now, the number is legion, but the Ephesian principle applies still. Each converted entity is necessary for a single functioning body of Christ in the world. We will not reach the fullness of Christ without them. There is no generalized humanity any more than there is a generalized language. Just as one must speak a particular language, there is only culture-specific humanity. It is culture-specific humanity that has to be converted. But conversion means turning towards Christ what is already there. Conversion is not substituting something new for something old. That is the way of the proselyte, which the apostolic church could have adopted, but explicitly abandoned. Nor is it a matter of adding something new, a new element to what is already there. Conversion is turning what is there, turning hearts and minds in culture-specific segments of humanity. If Christ is indeed perfect humanity, that is, complete humanity, then all of the culture-specific bits or fragments are necessary to the fullness of Christ. The Church must be diverse because humanity is diverse. The Church must be one, because Christ is one, embodying in himself all of the diversity of culture-specific humanity.

Christian faith is embodied faith, embodied in thought as well as in living. It cannot be carried without a lifestyle that forms a casing for it. It is like a hospital oxygen supply that has to be carried in a cylinder. The cylinder itself is useless for the purpose of sustaining breathing, but there is no way of carrying the oxygen without it. From one point of view, therefore, oxygen and cylinder are inseparable, both for the transmitters and the recipients. But the experience of the two groups is different. Transmitters who carried the cylinders over long distances cannot easily think of the oxygen without mentally envisioning the cylinders in which they brought it. Recipients think of the effect of the oxygen itself as they take it into their bodies, and eventually they may store it for use in cylinders of their own.

Sometimes the gas escapes in the course of transmission or the tap comes loose, or the casing breaks. When this happens, the recipients can separate the idea of the gas from the idea of the cylinder much more quickly and have little interest in the cylinder.

In the more recent cross-cultural diffusion of the faith to the non-Western world, the one in which Western missionaries played a part, the gospel oxygen was necessarily conveyed in cylinders of Western culture. There was no other way which people of Western culture could carry it. None of us can take in a new idea except in terms of an idea that we already have. This principle applies both to those who transmit the faith and to those who appropriate it. The circumstances of transmission varied greatly.

Of all the heresies that have affected the Church, the most persistent and the most recurrent has been the earliest one: Judaizing, the desire to turn converts into proselytes, copying the lifestyle of others rather than turning their own existing life to Christ. The Ephesian moment was a brief one. The wonderful time of the broken wall of partition soon passed. The Jerusalem church, the church of the apostles and elders disappeared. Gradually, the bicultural church in the Hellenistic world faded. (It seems to have lasted rather longer in the Syriac world.) Christianity in the eastern Mediterranean became as overwhelmingly Greek and Gentile as it had once been overwhelmingly Jewish. In the few references we have in mainstream Greek, writers to the remnants of old Jewish Christianity regard them not as the spiritual descendants of James the Just and the apostles and elders, but as legalistic eccentrics who practice circumcision or as heretics dangerously defective in Christology.

Still worse was to follow. Western Europe in the 1490s finally enforced the logic of Christendom. In Spain, the Jewish and Muslim communities were forced to convert to Christianity. Conversion, however, was not enough. It was not enough to be baptized, to confess sincerely the faith of the Church and the creeds, to attend regular Mass. The suspicion of keeping the Sabbath, of avoiding pork, of observing a Jewish festival was enough to bring the accusation that the conversion was hypocritical or pretended. The main business of the Inquisition in Spain was testing the authenticity of Jewish and Muslim conversions, authenticity that was determined by the closeness of the cultural Gentile modes.

The principle of apostolic plurality was abandoned. Paul would urge that if you are a Hellenistic Christian, you should not try to be a Jewish disciple, even if the apostle Peter was. And if you are a Jewish believer in Christ, you should not give up your Jewishness. But Europe through the centuries knew only of one way of being Christian and only one way by which Jews might become Christian. Whether voluntarily or by compulsion, they must be made not simply Christians, but Gentile Christians.

The Ephesian moment faded, but now it has returned. It may not be irrelevant to our purpose here to consider the effect of five centuries, even if I do so briefly. Until some time in the second millennium, Europe was only one of the regions of the world where Christians were to be found in substantial numbers. The Western European tradition of Christianity was only one expression of a faith that could be found from the Atlantic to East Asia, from Siberia to East Africa. By 1500, the situation was different. European Christendom was still expanding, the Baltic lands recently brought within it. Muslims were driven from Spain after centuries of Islamic presence there. On the other hand, most of the other Christian communities elsewhere had gone into eclipse. Some disappeared altogether. The form of Christianity now dominant was the product of several centuries of interaction with the languages and cultures of the European peoples.

It is at this point that the great European migration began, and the ocean-based migration that lasted for four and half centuries, during which millions of people left Europe for the worlds beyond. They were a diverse crew of adventurers: the destitute and unwanted, religious and political refugees, younger sons frustrated by European inheritance laws, discharged soldiers, convicted felons, solid people looking for a better life or a fairer society than Europe afforded. The Americas were the first and always the most favored target areas, but of course there were other areas too. Generally speaking, the migrants from Europe sought to maintain their ethnic and cultural identity. They also sought to establish political control of the areas to which they moved, and where this was not possible, to get exemption from indigenous political structures. By the early twentieth century, the migration process had produced a series of new nations. Several of them were vast in extent or population or both. Huge maritime empires fell to Britain and France, a huge land-based one in Russia, and other ones to Western powers. Western economies were reoriented to incorporate the human and material resources available to them in the non-Western world. Competition among the Western powers thus engendered helped to destroy the world order that they helped establish. In the middle and second half of the twentieth century, the maritime empires were dissolved, leaving two large nations to compete for hegemony. One of these, the United States, was essentially created by migration; the other, the Soviet Union, took its shape from migration. The outcome of the latter's withdrawal from the competition, I leave aside.

Before migration began, Europe was more Christian than it had ever been before, and Christianity more European than it had been before. The natural instinct of the Christian Europeans at the beginning of the migration was to seek to extend Christendom by bringing the lands now known to them into the territorial complex where the rule of Christ was acknowledged. Blasphemy, heresy, and idolatry were proscribed. The instrument was at hand, and successfully employed in the recent cleansing of Spain from Muslims. The Spanish migration to the Americas was, in its religious aspect, the last of the Crusades. The Spanish American territories were brought into Christendom, their populations baptized, and their tradition of worship proscribed. Mexico became New Spain, with the faith and glory of Old Spain.

But the experience of Spanish America could not be replicated in Asia, nor often in Africa. Outside small, well-defined enclaves, conquest was impossible and the existing religious traditions refused to lie down and die. The result is that the power-wielders in Christendom, once committed to the worldwide propagation of the Christian faith, now saw the lands beyond Europe in essentially economic and strategic terms. Radical Christians inside Christendom could not be satisfied with less than the proclamation of the gospel in these lands and had to find another way of achieving it, and so the missionary movement was born from the frustration of the crusading instinct. A new sort of migrant appeared — the missionary sent to persuade, to demonstrate, to offer, but without the power of compulsion.

The most striking result of the Great Migration was a huge accession to the Christian faith among peoples in the non-Western world. Most surprisingly of all, the period of the Great Migration and its aftermath saw the decline of Christianity in the West. By the end of the twentieth century, Christians of the non-Western world outnumbered Christians in the West. The reason lies not only in the great accession to the faith in the non-Western world, but also in the accelerating recession in the West. It is the largest recession from Christianity since the first rise of Islam, and much faster than that one. The end of the great European migration came in the mid-twentieth century with the final dissolution of the Western empires.

Europe's imperial dreams faded and it became absorbed in intra-European constructions or defining the relations with the two new superpowers.

And then the Empire struck back. Britain and France found they had acquired substantial new populations from their former residual colonies. Other European nations found flows of people from troubled areas.

The great new factor of our time, with momentous consequences for Christian worship, is that the Great Migration has gone into reverse. There has been a massive movement, which all indications suggest will continue, from the non-Western to the Western world. But the Great Migration left a curious legacy — a post-Christian West and a post-Western Christianity. Christianity, once the religion of confident technological advance and rising affluence, and sometimes seeing these things as a mark of God's favor, is replaced by a Christianity that will increasingly be associated mostly with moderately poor and very poor people, and with some of the poorest countries on earth. And peoples from the non-Western world will be the principal agents of Christian mission across the world. It is in the non-Western world that representative Christianity will now be found. And even in the Western world, they will have a significant place. For it may be that in some areas of the Western world at least Christianity will be increasingly associated with immigrants.

The United States has more of this world Christian diaspora than any other country. Recent studies show just how important these are. In this country it is possible to find congregations and networks of Somali Christians, which is impossible in Somalia. The immigration legislation of the 1960s has brought about the most important feature of American religious life today. The fact is that in the United States, more than anywhere else in the world, all the present Christian discourses are to be found. The rich diversity of the diaspora, all too often unknown to national traditional mono-cultural congregations, has the capacity to advance Christian mission in the Western and the non-Western world. It also opens the dazzling possibility that the fullness of the stature of Christ can be realized as new ethnicities and cultures are united within the body of Christ within our own time.

It is the Ephesian moment come again and with a power, complexity, and diversity that brings to mind the excitement of the epistle's second chapter. Here is the mystery of Christ, the secret of Christ kept hidden for centuries and now revealed, revealed to us. The third Christian millennium presents a greater diversity than the faith has ever known before.

That means a greater capacity for blessing and perhaps more capability for disaster. The great issues of contemporary Christianity are ecumenical in the true sense of the word: worldwide. The greatest issues will be how African, Indian, Chinese, Korean, Hispanic, North American, and Eastern and Western European Christians can make real the body of Christ. It offers the prospect of a new era of creative theology as the biblical tradition interacts with the ancient cultures of Africa and Asia, as it once did with those of the Hellenistic world, when the classical doctrines of the Trinity and the incarnation were forged from the local intellectual materials of middle-period Platonism, and in the Western world, where the atonement of Christ was explored using the traditions of Roman and Germanic customary law. It will raise hard questions, not least about language, for English has become the new Latin of the Christian world. I suspect in some areas of the world we are seeing what, in effect, are new sacraments emerging where the traditional sacraments have become misdirected. The Christian mixture is overwhelmingly rich. It is Ephesians 2 on the way towards Revelation 21. The body of Christ cannot be realized simply by pick-and-mix methods, as though we were sampling items of cuisine from around the world. Christian faith is embodied faith. It is converted segments of social reality. There is no realization of the body of Christ without fellowship, fellowship across the broken middle wall of partition, until we all come together to the measure of the stature of the fullness of Christ.

PART II

Case Studies

Editor's Introduction

The following seven case studies of Christian worship worldwide illustrate the variety of expressions of worship in rural and urban locations of the non-Western world. We look at under-represented areas of study among Roman Catholic, Protestant, and Evangelical congregations in the non-Western world. The case studies do not focus narrowly on hymnology and liturgy, but rather offer a wider perspective on worship that takes the context of worship seriously by considering the architecture, material culture, socio-political realities, and even traditional myths of the people represented in the assembly. It is important that readers pay keen attention to the social and cultural realities that influence worship. Note especially how each assembly utilizes space, music, and bodily movement.

These case studies present contemporary Christian worship in a variety of Asian, Africa, Latin American, and Pacific contexts. Why are there no North American case studies? The focus of this book is on the diverse practices of Christian worship in the non-Western world. Rather than focusing on historical trends, or the experience of worship in the West, the authors illuminate specific current expressions of Christian worship in the non-Western world. As you read each case study, look for the ways in which worship practices interact with specific social and cultural contexts, and the ways that new social relationships are formed in the worship assembly.

Here are some questions you may want to ask yourself as you read these chapters: What are the non-local cultural items in the worship assembly? How and why are these adopted into the assembly? In what ways do these non-local

39

cultural items change in the context of the worshiping assembly? It is fascinating to recognize that in the face of such cultural diversity there are some significant similarities to Christian worship worldwide. Can you recognize some of these commonalities? Another noteworthy aspect of worship is the use of space: How is space significant in each case study? How would you describe the understanding of space in each case study — for example, sacred or mundane? Look for any hints about the relationship between the worshiping assembly and the larger community surrounding it. In what ways is the worshiping community similar and dissimilar to the community in which it is a part? For instance, how representative is the worshiping assembly of those that make up the surrounding community?

Some things are non-negotiable — that is, that people have been bequeathed a schema (such as for baptism). All use water. All affirm the Trinity. How do these non-negotiables get transmitted in worship? Are they transmitted through missionary encounters, through the Bible, or through social carriers of new knowledge? How are these non-negotiables worked out in a particular setting? And what motivates specific worship practices? Ecclesiastical connections? Historical connections? Traditional elements? Modern elements? For instance, how does denominational affiliation affect what is accepted and not accepted from culture? And how does worship unite or divide people? Finally, what is the relationship between worship and the renewal or conservation of culture? And what are the political implications of worship — is liturgy politically suppressive? Just as the early church was political ("Whom do you worship, God or Caesar?"), today's worship is not simply ornamental. What is the relationship between worship and the political order? The case studies suggest that local problems and issues are inseparable from worship.

Here are seven broad questions that can help students of worship to understand the relationship between worship and cultures. First there is a question that on the surface seems simple but when reading the case studies becomes more complex: **what is worship?** Is worship getting together with two or three good friends in a living room or workspace and praying together? What is the goal of worship? Can you recognize the purpose of worship in these case studies?

Second, **where is worship done?** We must take the context of worship seriously. Where do people worship? Do people worship at home, outdoors, in a football stadium? How does worship space affect the worshiping community? There is a church in California whose pastor and congregation together hike up a high mountain each Sunday morning. When they reach the top of the mountain, they sing together and the pastor speaks encouraging words to them. After the service, they descend the mountain together. The flora and fauna make up their sanctuary. What *needs to be there* for worship to occur? Icons? Pews? A building? Where do people worship and why do they worship there?

Third, **what are the politics of worship?** In other words, who attends worship, what personal or corporate risks do people take when gathering together in an assembly? Economically, ethnically, racially, do worshipers reflect the larger community or do they stand apart from it? Is worship a place for everybody, or just the wealthy or just the poor? What are the psychological, theological, economic, or social constraints that exclude some and include others? How is it possible to be a witnessing assembly even to those outside the walls of the church?

Fourth, **what are the economics of worship?** That is to say, how many of the resources of the church community go toward the worship service? Furthermore, what kinds of gifts and substances are presented for tithes and offerings? Money? Food? Time? What does the kind of offering we give communicate about the worship assembly, about our own culture, and about our understanding of God?

Fifth, **who are the worship leaders** — the educated, lay, ordained, men, women, children? Along these lines, how are various age groups (e.g., children, young adults, elderly) incorporated into the service? How do authority structures of the surrounding society impact our understanding of worship? That is, who leads, and why? What roles do church leaders play in the wider society?

Sixth, **what is the focus of the worship service?** Often churches have particular focuses in worship, such as on healing, deliverance, praise singing, biblical exposition, remembrance. What appears to be the heart of worship as presented in these case studies? If certain themes are given priority, then what appears to be the secondary themes of the worshiping assembly? How might the social, cultural, and economic conditions of a region impact the focus of worship? As you read the case studies, what are the differences that distinguish the case studies from one another? How does the assembly utilize time and space, and what makes the use of time and space different or the same across cultures?

Seventh, **what are the commonalities among the worshiping communities presented?** What seems essential and what seems non-essential to Christian worship worldwide? How are particular cultural elements renewed in the context of worship? What are the non-verbal components of worship and what role do they play in the assembly? For instance, what role does body movement (or just hand or head movement) play in the worship service — that is, when and why is there bodily movement, and who moves?

Christian worship worldwide is an embodied relationship in the widest sense, for it involves not only the individual believer but visible solidarity with fellow believers in the context of social and cultural realities that are in some ways different from the experiences of Western Christians. Whether they are evangelical Aguarunas from the Amazon, Roman Catholic Samoans from Leauva'a, or Presbyterian Koreans from Seoul, worship assemblies consist of a gathering of all kinds of people, from all walks of life, regardless of race, ethnicity, economic or educational background, for the purpose of honoring God. And worship is much more than that. As you read the following case studies I encourage you to imagine yourself among the worshipers, where you may get a glimpse of the fullness of the body of Christ and the future of the church worldwide.

Worship among Apostles and Zionists in Southern Africa

Dana L. Robert and M. L. Daneel

Editor's Introduction

The case studies begin with a distinctive glimpse of a worshiping community in the African Initiated Church in Zimbabwe. In the twentieth century, Dana Robert and M. L. Daneel write, the AIC was seen as the epitome of "the assimilation or contextualization of Christianity into traditional African contexts." But as the authors note, worship in the AIC has been subject to little study, in part because the AIC produces a meager paper trail. Its worship thrives on informality, spontaneity, and recitation rather than written documents and orders of worship.

The authors bring a unique reservoir of years of study and teaching about the AIC, and so their account reflects years of wisdom rather than initial observations. Their contribution is one of the most comprehensive reports ever on AIC worship.

This case study illustrates worship that is visibly contextual; outdoor worship, worship garments, spontaneous song, ritual cleansing, and exorcism of evil spirits all evince a distinct cultural flavor in worship. However, there are subtler cues that transcultural, counter-cultural, and cross-cultural elements are also present in AIC worship. How are these three elements evident, and how do, in the authors' words, "worship, healing, and communal fellowship together create a seamless whole of acceptance and well-being"?

✦   ✦

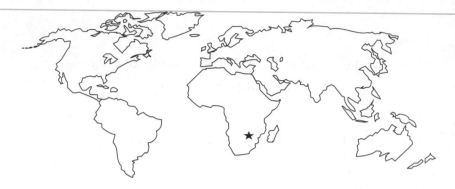

Every weekend in Zimbabwe and South Africa, thousands of people can be seen walking alongside the roads, on their way to worship services. Men and women are wearing white robes and head coverings, others their colorful Sunday best, and still others their khaki uniforms or shirts displaying a five-pointed star. These are members of African Initiated Churches (AICs), defined as churches founded in Africa, by Africans, primarily for Africans. The sound of singing reverberates across the granite rocks and tall grasses, and through the townships of tin shacks, as clusters of worshipers gather under the largest trees. Outsiders are drawn to the singing and dancing, the neat clothing, and the sermons, prayers, and testimonies that emanate from the sanctified circle of worshipers.

The administrative headquarters of the larger AICs also function as healing centers, some of them called "Zion." People are drawn to Zion in hopes of being healed. They remain for weeks or even months, residing in huts on the premises, as they pray to be restored to health and to healthy relationships by the prophets in residence. Every Sunday the hymn summons people to the Zion City of church founder Samuel Mutendi:

> Come and see what Jesus does,
> Come and see what Mutendi here performs,
> Come and look from the East
> You from the West, come and observe what Zion does.
> You who are sick, to Zion City for treatment come,
> Come and see!
> You with epilepsy, come and be healed,
> Come and see what Jesus does.

The other day we were with him [the prophet Mutendi],
Last night we were in his sight,
Last year we were with him
Even today he's with us.
Come and see what Zion does![1]

In the hymns that call people to weekly worship at Zion City, it becomes apparent why approximately fifty percent of black Christians in Southern Africa had become members of African Initiated Churches by the late twentieth century. In the AICs, worship, healing, and communal fellowship together create a seamless whole of acceptance and well-being, using African cultural forms. The holistic worship life of AICs is a major manifestation of their unique identity as African movements, and a sign of independence from "mission church" structures.[2]

Early AIC leaders in the early to middle twentieth century crafted new forms of worship that integrated their understanding of Christian practices with reinterpretations of traditional African beliefs. While the innovations of AIC leaders and their separation from mission churches at first caused them to be labeled "separatist sects" and "heretics," by the late 1960s a more sympathetic understanding of AICs was emerging among some mission scholars. Rather than being seen as "bridges back to heathenism," AICs represented the assimilation or contextualization of Christianity into traditional African contexts. Over the past thirty years, the sympathetic scholarly literature on AICs has expanded to the point that researchers today often view them as the most "authentic" form of African Christianity.[3]

---

1. Quoted in M. L. Daneel, *Old and New in Southern Shona Independent Churches,* vol. 2: *Church Growth* (The Hague, Netherlands: Mouton, 1974), p. 201.

2. AICs are usually distinguished from "mission churches," also known as "mainline churches" or "historic churches." Mission churches are the African branches of denominations that originated in the West and were originally brought to Africa by western missionaries, such as Catholics, Methodists, Presbyterians, and Anglicans. By the late twentieth century, the vast majority of mission churches had become indigenous institutions run by Africans, though with historical connections to western churches.

3. The South African Missiological Society keeps a database of materials on AICs and on AIC researchers, run by researcher S. Hayes. The web address of the database is http://www.geocities.com/Athens/Parthenon/8409/aic.htm. The issue of "authenticity" can be a hotly contested debate between supporters of mission churches and supporters of AICs. Recent historical research on so-called "mission churches" demonstrates how these churches

Despite the centrality of worship as a marker of AIC identity, the fascination with AICs by anthropologists, scholars of religion, and missiologists has not extended to liturgical scholars or practical theologians. This is probably because of the complexity of gaining access to materials on AIC worship — especially among the group of AICs known as "Spirit-type" movements.[4] In Southern Africa, Spirit-type AICs focus on the charismatic manifestations of the Holy Spirit rather than on written liturgies; they use African rather than western languages; and they usually consist of poor and unlettered people in rural areas or townships.[5] Access to AIC worship requires gaining the trust of the leaders, learning the appropriate African language, and participating rather than conducting research in libraries. Because of the difficulties of gaining information about AIC worship, and their relative isolation from scholarly or ecumenical circles, the substantial accomplishments and innovations in Christian worship by AICs have not been adequately appreciated.

The purpose of this chapter is to describe and to analyze weekly AIC worship among Spirit-type AICs in Southern Africa, more specifically in Zimbabwe. Since Spirit-type churches constitute roughly 80 percent of all AICs, their importance for understanding African worship is obvious. The number of AIC denominations was estimated at between 5,000 and 6,000

---

have self-consciously wrestled with issues of African culture and promoted African leadership. The characterization of AICs as "authentic" and mission churches as "inauthentic" is therefore a misleading stereotype.

4. Typologies of AICs usually divide them into two major categories: Spirit-type (Aladura, Zionist) and Ethiopian-type churches. Ethiopian churches originated as break-offs from mission churches over issues of racism, predominantly from 1890 to 1920. Spirit-type churches emphasize the high role of the Holy Spirit, a prophetic leadership, and faith healing. Their greatest period of origination was the twentieth century, beginning in the 1920s. For discussion of AIC typology, see M. L. Daneel, *Quest for Belonging* (Gweru, Zimbabwe: Mambo Press, 1987), pp. 38-42; Allan H. Anderson, "Types and Butterflies: African Initiated Churches and European Typologies," *International Bulletin of Missionary Research* 25 (July 2001): 107-13.

5. It should be noted that Pentecostal worship forms among the AICs are a product of indigenous cultural practices and are not organically related to the now international Pentecostal-charismatic movement. In many places, the AICs are in competition with the newer Pentecostal movements, who tend to see AICs as old-fashioned and steeped in traditional culture, rather than modern and more urban. For a study that traces the relationship among AICs and Pentecostals in South Africa, see Allan Anderson, *Zion and Pentecost: The Spirituality and Experience of Pentecostal and Zionist/Apostolic Churches in South Africa* (Pretoria: Unisa Press, 2000).

Shona Worship
from the authors'
personal collection

in 1968, and around 10,000 by 2003. It is therefore impossible to provide a blueprint that characterizes all AIC worship. Rather, each congregation or group of churches has its own traditions that have emerged in dialogue with its particular theological and cultural context. Similarities nevertheless exist across ethnic and denominational lines, especially among the largest groups of AICs in South Africa, Swaziland, and Zimbabwe, namely the Zionists and the Apostles.

The primary data on which this paper is based are nearly forty years of empirical observation and participant observation by missiologist

M. L. Daneel, who has conducted the most complete study of AICs in any one cultural group in Africa.[6] Although trained in theology and comparative religions, Daneel also has been since 1991 a bishop among the Ndaza (Holy Cord) Zionists in Zimbabwe. His perspective thus includes both "insider" (emic) and "outsider" (etic) insights. Other data include ten years of intermittent worship experiences in South Africa and Zimbabwe by missiologist Dana L. Robert, as well as scholarly material gleaned from Daneel and Robert's years of teaching and research in African Christianity and African traditional religions. This case study of worship within Spirit-type AICs in Southern Africa is a construct based on years of experience and reflection, rather than a description of a particular worship service. We will describe the basic elements of weekly worship among Apostles and Zionists, discuss the seasons of the liturgical year, and comment briefly on their relationship with both African traditional religions and missionary practices.

Apostles and Zionists — Who Are They?

Of the many groups of AICs, the Zionists and Apostles were the two most successful in Zimbabwe. The Zion Apostolic Church (ZAC) originated in South Africa in 1908, as a multiracial group of pentecostals who practiced speaking in tongues, healing by laying on of hands, and other charismatic manifestations. As the movement grew among the African population, it expanded through division and the migration of followers, many of whom were migrant laborers. Offshoots took on different names, such as Zion Apostolic Faith Mission, Zion Sabbath Church, and Zion Protestant

6. For an overview of the work of M. L. Daneel, see G. Cuthbertson, H. Pretorius, and D. Robert, *Frontiers of African Christianity: Essays in Honour of Inus Daneel* (Pretoria: Unisa Press, 2003). The other great pioneer researchers into the AICs in the mid- to late twentieth century were Bengt Sundkler, Harold Turner, J. D. Y. Peel, Marie-Louise Martin, and G. C. Oosthuizen. Of these pioneer researchers, Peel, Daneel, and Oosthuizen are still alive. For an anthropological study of the political and cultural significance of the Zionist movement, see Jean Comaroff, *Body of Power, Spirit of Resistance: The Culture and History of a South African People* (Chicago: University of Chicago Press, 1985). For a participant-observational study of the Apostles, see Bennetta Jules-Rosette, *African Apostles: Ritual and Conversion in the Church of John Maranke* (Ithaca, N.Y.: Cornell University Press, 1975). For a partial list of younger AIC researchers, see the AIC database at the South African Missiological Society website.

Senior Ndaza Zionist official, the Rev. Guruveti, preaching at consolation/ordination ceremony at Gavure homestead from the authors' personal collection

Church. Migrant workers including David Masuka, Moses Makamba, John Mtisi, Samuel Mutendi, and Andreas Shoko spread the movement into Rhodesia (Zimbabwe) in the early twentieth century. Zionist churches tended to found headquarters called "Zion Cities," in which leaders lived, and to which people came for assistance. Samuel Mutendi's Zion Christian Church (ZCC) became the largest branch of Zionists in Zimbabwe because it attracted more chiefs, based on Mutendi's reputation as a miracle worker, provider, and leader, as well as his descent from the royal Rozvi clan. Members wear uniforms to worship, and the five-pointed Zionist star pin on their lapels when not in uniform. Other groups of Zionists wear long, flowing, colorful robes for worship, and a sacred rope *(ndaza)* around their waists. They are thus called *vaZioni veNdaza* — Zionists of the holy cord.

Whereas Samuel Mutendi drew many of his early members from the large Dutch Reformed mission in central Rhodesia, the African Apostolic Church *(vaPostori)* emerged from the Methodists in Umtali (now Mutare). Johane Maranke was from a prominent early Methodist family when in 1932 he heard a voice telling him he was John the Baptist. The voice commanded him to go into the world, preaching and converting people, and commanding them "not to commit adultery, steal or become angry."[7] Maranke began a new life as an itinerant evangelist, roaming as far as the Congo, baptizing people and organizing them into churches. Like Samuel Mutendi, Maranke healed people through the laying on of hands. To join the Maranke Apostles means being baptized in a river (known as "Jordan"), and donning a white robe. The highlight of the year for Apostles is when they gather in *Pendi* (Pentecost) centers for preaching, baptisms, teaching, and the celebration of communion. Annual Pentecost celebrations commemorate the gift of the Holy Spirit to Maranke at the time of his conversion. The *vaPostori* have many ranks of male leadership. They are also one of the most patriarchal of all AICs, as they practice polygamy, conduct virginity examinations of girls, and do not have separate women's organizations that can facilitate the emergence of female leaders. But both the Apostles and the Zionists are great missionary organizations among the grassroots people. Johane Maranke spent thirty years itinerating throughout southern and central Africa, and his movement remains one of the most widespread in the region. It is also the largest AIC in Zimbabwe.

Weekly Worship

Spirit-type AICs typically have one central worship service a week, either on Saturday or Sunday. Worship usually takes place outside, under the shade of a large tree, and lasts from late morning throughout the afternoon. The site of the service is made holy by frequent use as a worship spot, and sometimes the perimeter is marked by stones. Although African

7. M. L. Daneel, *Quest for Belonging,* p. 56.

Holy
Communion
from the authors'
personal collection

traditional religions (ATR) have traditions of sacred trees, or holy groves, in which dwell ancestral spirits, the choice of a tree under which to worship appears to be more pragmatic than spiritual. The tree is chosen for its shade and convenient location by people who lack the resources to build a building. Some AICs worship in large huts, but most worship outside. Even when Zionist church buildings exist, they prefer to worship indoors only in bad weather. Apostles have no church buildings, as that does not coincide with their perception of discipleship in Christ, in which believers compose a vibrant evangelistic movement on the move rather than a settled establishment.

Many leadership roles are available in AICs, most of which are confined to males. The hierarchy of leadership varies in the different churches, and the following description is most typical of the Ndaza Zionists: the bishop[8] is at the top, and he leads the worship service and designates other ministers and evangelists who also preach. Prophets of varying ranks play major roles throughout the service, as do healers. Elders and "policemen" keep order, and the secretary handles financial issues. More than one role can be held at once, as greater responsibilities come with seniority. For example, bishops were often prophets and/or ministers before they were bishops. Prophets and healers are often the same person. Just as in the traditional religion a chief might have particular spirit mediums or diviners attached to him, so in the AICs an important bishop might work in alliance with a particular healer or prophet. After his death, a major leader will still relate to people from the spirit world, by bringing spiritual renewal to people who make pilgrimages to his grave, and appearing to his followers in dreams.[9] Leading worship is the most important task of a bishop, as he is considered to be the elder who is closest to God and who consequently has the most spiritual power.

Preparation

Preparation is a vital part of worship in Spirit-type AICs. Unlike in western churches in which people file into their pews as individuals and wait for the service to begin, preparation for worship is a communal cleansing of the congregation so that it appears worthy before God. Prophets form the gates into the holy terrain. People file barefooted into the sacred space between the "gates." With the help of the Holy Spirit, the prophets diagnose and observe the sins of the people who are entering the sacred space. They encourage them to confess their sins in a process of internal cleans-

8. The *vaPostori* call the bishop the "high priest."

9. Pilgrimages to the graves of deceased leaders are part of popular African Christianity both in AICs and mission churches. See Janet Hodgson's article on the Sotho prophetess Mantsopa, "Mantsopa: Popular Religion in the Anglican Church in South Africa," in Cuthbertson et al., *Frontiers of African Christianity*, pp. 210-35.

ing. Since the AIC congregation usually consists of a local community, rather than the western pattern of people driving from miles away to attend the church of their choice, the prophets already have a good idea of the sins and weaknesses of the congregation. Through the act of confession, people reveal what is not right in their lives, and they improve themselves through the inner cleansing provided by the act of confession.[10]

Since ritual cleansing is a big part of African traditional religions, it appears that the extensive preparation ritual in AICs is an adaptation of both traditional and biblical patterns of ritual cleansing. The communal process of ritual cleansing extends throughout the service. Prophets continue with the process of communal purification by counseling and praying with persons seated along the edges of the congregation. Cleansing of life problems and of evil spirits continues throughout the afternoon. Menstruating women must sit on the outer fringes, because their condition would cause defilement of the worship service. The practice of marginalizing menstruating women is consistent both with traditional African practices and with levitical instructions in the Old Testament, and current practice among Orthodox Jews.

Another aspect of preparation besides ritual cleansing is the wearing of garments or uniforms into the service. Shoes are removed when standing in holy space. To don a worship garment is to leave the ways of the world and to enter an alternative space of purity and holiness. Uniforms also witness to non-believers by providing a visible symbol of one's commitment. Apostles wear white robes for worship, and the women also keep their heads covered with white scarves. Women Apostles thus resemble Catholic sisters in the garb in which they always worship. In their white garments, Apostolic women also resemble African American women in the "sanctified church," who wear white clothing to affirm their dignity despite the menial jobs and exploitive socio-economic context in which they often live.[11] The white garments of Apostolic women help them to maintain their purity before God.

Male leaders in most Zionist churches wear long, flowing, colorful robes that twirl outward when they dance. When they put on their beauti-

---

10. Preparation before special religious events can be elaborate and lengthy, with extensive fasting and other observances.

11. Cheryl Townsend Gilkes, "'Together and in Harness': Women's Traditions in the Sanctified Church," *Signs: Journal of Women in Culture and Society* 10, no. 4 (1985): 685-86.

**Apostolic
Evangelist**
from the authors'
personal collection

ful robes over the drab and often torn clothing of everyday life, and they enter the sacred worship space, Zionists make a transition from poverty and hardship to hope and joy. The decision to invest in a worship robe is itself an indicator of religious commitment, and is often a sign of a man's suitability to enter one of the offices of the church. Zionist men receive the color of their robes in a dream. While color symbolism is not a matter of hard and fast association, certain colors typically represent important realities. Green is a very popular color, as it represents life, prosperity, and well-being. White represents purity and sanctity. Red is the color chosen by prophets, for it represents spiritual danger. Red also represents the presence of the Holy Spirit, who is a danger to evil forces and sinners. Blue is often a color of well-being, of water, and of fertility. In Zionist services,

**Apostolic
Prophet**
from the authors'
personal collection

women keep their heads covered with scarves. Some women, typically the wives of church leaders, have special scarves with crosses on them, or scarves of a certain color. In the Zion Christian Church, leaders wear military-type uniforms as signs of their authority and dignity.

Even outside the worship services, AIC members are often recognizable because they wear symbols of their membership, such as the ZCC star-shaped pin. Male Apostles wear their hair shaved or short, and grow pointed "goat" beards. Bishops in the different AICs will sometimes carry distinctive staves as emblems of their authority and spiritual power. The staves of those of higher rank carry more spiritual power than those of lower officers. Apostles may be counseled to wear their robes in public as special protection from evil forces. Such visible symbols of group allegiance set AIC members apart from the world, and mark them as God's people. Preparation is not only a major aspect of AIC worship; it is an ongoing process in AIC life.

Singing and Dancing

After the people have assembled in the worship space, they usually begin the service with singing and dancing. Men and women gather opposite from each other. Women and small children sit on the ground, and men and older boys sit across from them, sometimes on stools. The practice of women sitting on the ground, while the more important men sit in higher places, is common in many patriarchal cultures and is not confined to African AICs. Among Ndaza Zionists the people make a circle, with space in the center kept open for the preacher and for other activities. Drummers and those who blow on the kudu horns sit to the side within the circle. The Maranke Apostles sit in long rows of males and females, with a passage in the middle in which the preachers can walk up and down. The main worship leader guides the rhythm of worship with his staff.

Singing and dancing play extremely important roles in Spirit-type churches, as through them people work themselves up into higher spiritual states. People enjoy the singing and dancing, and it continues throughout the service between the sermons. Singing is an especially strong aspect of worship among women. Since males are the preachers, women can respond to the sermons with song, and even interrupt them if they go on too long. If people appear to be bored or sleepy, someone will break out in a song and then the singing, dancing, clapping, and ululating ends the sermon.

The main instruments besides the human voice are drums, rattles, and kudu horn trumpets. The musicians sit to the side within the circle. The Ndaza drums consist of five gallon tins with two pieces of skin stretched over the ends. On one side, the skin has been put into water, which gives it a deep and thick sound. The other skin is thinner and is kept near the fire to give it a higher tone. Some groups use hollowed-out tree trunks with skin stretched over the top. Both men and women can be

**Shona
Drumming**
from the authors'
personal collection

drummers and shake rattles, though usually the drummers are men. Men also blow into kudu horns intermittently throughout the dancing. Drums are essential to the dancing, as they set the pace. One cannot help but feel the spirit lift in anticipation when the drummers begin.

Among Ndaza Zionists, men dance in a circle, with their colorful robes flowing as they whirl. A senior bishop leads the dancing or designates a leader. Men step around to the drum beat and then every few steps raise their knees in a hop. Sometimes individual men leave the group and go pirouette in the field, making their garments billow. Not to be left out of the fun, women dance together in a line on the side by taking three steps and then a quick turn. The line proceeds back and forth. As the pace quickens, the women dip lower and lower during the turns. Although sometimes women dance with babies on their backs, they often hand their children over to other women who choose not to dance. Youths are free to join the adults in their dancing, but they often do not.

While all AICs enjoy music, the attitude toward dancing differs. Zionists are famous for their dancing. While Ndaza Zionists use traditional instruments and dance in a circle, the Zion Christian Churches (ZCC) prefer modern drums and band instruments. ZCC dancers stomp in various rhythms that resemble the old hunting dances in which warriors called up their *shavi* spirits to give them a successful hunt. With their khaki uniforms, ZCC men give a more militant appearance than Ndaza Zionists in their flowing robes, and the warlike quality of the dancing represents a transformation of traditional practices. The Maranke Apostles, in their white gowns, do not dance. They do, however, sing in choirs with harmony. Perhaps the Apostles' condemnation of dancing symbolizes a break with traditional religion as well as continuity with the strict piety of the Methodist missionaries who first influenced the Apostles' founder.

Prayer and Exorcism

Singing and dancing are chief ways in which Spirit-type AICs create a heightened state of spiritual consciousness that helps worshipers approach God in fervent prayer. The worship leader, who is seen by the worshipers as close to God, whips up the group with his holy staff in the air. Singing and dancing often lead to prayer, and the supplicants together fall to their knees and pray simultaneously, their heads prostrate on the ground in a posture of submission to God. The murmured prayers rise and increase in volume, in a scene that resembles "praying in the Spirit" in pentecostal churches. People break out in speaking in tongues, and loud praises to God. The pentecostal prayer languages have different rhythms depending on the type of church, whether Ndaza Zionist, ZCC, or Apostolic. Apostles sing and pray while facing East, because that is the direction from which Jesus Christ will come when he returns. Singing in harmony and praying jointly, they lift their hands to the East. Singing and prayer are intermingled. When the prayers and praise songs reach a crescendo, the worship leader brings his staff to the ground and the people become quiet and sit down. Throughout the prayer sessions of supplication and praise, the congregation follows the staff of the worship leader, as an orchestra follows the baton of a conductor.

Sometimes services are interrupted by evil spirits. In the midst of prayer or during singing and dancing, someone will cry out in a loud voice and fall to the ground in an act of spirit possession. Intense and driving music can provoke the evil spirits to appear. Prophets immediately surround the affected person. In the Ndaza services, prophets tie up the victim with holy cords while they admonish the spirits to drive them out. They lay hands on the afflicted and begin shouting and cursing at the evil spirits manifested in the disturbance of worship.[12] Not being allowed to swear in regular life, the prophets shout and swear at the evil spirits with gusto as the congregants dance around them. Swearing and shouting at evil spirits provides a needed release of emotion for prophets, who drive away the evil spirits and then laugh at themselves in comic relief.

Sermons and Testimonies

Sermons and testimonies are one of the main features of regular Sabbath worship among Spirit-type AICs. Men are always the preachers. While some AICs allow women to preach, they are only allowed to preach to all-female gatherings at meetings of the Mothers' Union or women's prayer meetings. Since AICs are characterized by a multitude of leaders, preaching is spread among the male leadership rather than confined to the main bishop or worship leader. In the Zion Christian Churches, a few ministers are chosen ahead of time to lead worship, and they prepare a few main texts. Among Ndaza Zionists, the main bishop selects a theme and several illustrative texts, and chooses about eight or so preachers for the day. He may distribute the texts at the beginning of the service, and

12. Rituals for dealing with evil spirits are not confined to Sabbath services. A key moment for expelling evil spirits is baptism, during which evil spirits are driven out through repeated immersions. Other ceremonies provide protection from evil spirits at people's homesteads, such as pegging off the area and treating it with holy water. Some AICs also have all-night prayer services during which people struggle against evil spirits. See Daneel, *Old and New in Southern Shona Independent Churches*, vol. 2, pp. 240-43; Titus Presler, *Transfigured Night: Mission and Culture in Zimbabwe's Vigil Movement* (Pretoria: Unisa Press, 1999).

the preachers are expected to be able to reflect extemporaneously on the underlying theme.

In all Spirit-type churches, an official reader stands and reads the text to a point the preacher directs. Even if the reader stops at a comma, or interrupts a pericope, the preacher will preach up to that point of the text. Among the Ndaza Zionists, preachers address the same theme in a given service, even if they use different texts. Since Bibles are scarce and not all preachers can read, the text is often recited from memory. Song, dance, prayer, and testimonies are alternated with the sermonizing. Sometimes there are dialogue sermons. Popular texts are chosen repeatedly, as the AICs do not follow a lectionary. When compared with western homiletical practices, AIC sermons seem to be fragmented rather than structured.

Sermons begin with a preamble, during which the preacher greets the people and sets the occasion. "Peace be with you" is a frequent interjection by the preacher during the course of his reflections. Preachers draw direct connections between biblical figures and practices to the worshipers and issues that concern them. For example, the biblical "Men of Judah" become the local worshipers (e.g., Men of Gutu, Men of Bikita, etc.), Paul and Barnabas become local church leaders, and the Egyptians ("heathens") become the practitioners of African traditional religion, and so forth. Biblical texts are preached literally without regard to the distance between rural Africa and biblical Palestine. The themes that emerge from the texts are applied to the living situations of the congregation. Preachers are not concerned about the social context of the biblical passage, as they are not aware of higher criticism or western methods of exegesis. The preacher uses African cultural forms to explain theological and moral teachings: for example, to rest in Christ is to sit with one's legs outstretched; the idea of church unity is for believers to share one totem; hatred can be expressed as argument between first and second wives. The direct transposition of biblical commands to the African context is completely believable to the hearers.

The content of sermons ranges from immediate political and social issues, to recurring themes such as testimonies of healing, and ongoing spiritual warfare against evil forces. The sins of the community are addressed, such as the temptation to frequent beer halls and neglect one's family, the temptation to worship the ancestors or consult a *nganga* (traditional healer/diviner) when ill, and exploitative gender relationships. Men are warned against the evils of city life, such as taking on a mistress or "woman of the pots." A random survey of AIC sermons preached in rural

Masvingo Province during the 1980s reveals a variety of theological issues addressed, including the nature of God as Creator and protector, the Holy Spirit as the source of power and purity of heart; and Jesus as the source of blessings and peace. Even the most spiritual topics rely on earthy and colloquial language, and employ the imagery of peasant society or township life. For example, in a particularly memorable image from the 1960s, Bishop Samuel Mutendi, founder of the Zion Christian Church, and a polygamous father of over sixty children, preached sermons on the meaning of salvation. He often indicated that the assurance of one's salvation after conversion was as certain as urination after sexual intercourse.

A sermon preached in rural Masvingo Province in 1986 on 1 Corinthians 2:14 had as its message that "sin destroys the sinner." The illustration used by the preacher drew from the daily lives of his listeners: "There was a mother who visited her daughter. The daughter boiled maize grain. She then gave some to her mother before she left to fetch water from the well. The mother felt that the grain she was fed with was too little. Then she was offended and she decided to kill her daughter by putting poison on the traditional grinding stone. She then left for her home before her daughter came back from the well. When the daughter came back she decided to grind her sorghum on the traditional grinding stone where poison was rubbed. The daughter unknowingly took the mealie-meal to her mother a few days later. This mealie-meal was consumed by the mother who had previously rubbed poison on her daughter's grinding stone. The lesson from the teaching is that the sin destroys the sinner. The daughter said, 'Mother, here is your sin. You had put poison on the grinding stone to destroy me and my children.' This means a sinner is destroyed by his sins."[13]

As the afternoon lengthens, attention to the Word of God becomes more intense and the sermons more concentrated. Long-winded intensity by the preacher, however, can result in being interrupted by a woman in song, a signal that draws people to their feet for more singing and dancing. The preacher then knows that his time has run out. The prerogative of the male preacher must give way to the active worship of the congregation, according to the movement of the Holy Spirit.

Testimonies often alternate with preaching on the Word of God. People witness to the group as to what God has done for them during the

13. Sermon excerpts are translated from the Shona, from the transcribed sermon collection of M. L. Daneel.

week. Women give thanks for their children, or for health restored. Since barrenness is the greatest curse for women in traditional African societies, and a woman's social status relies on whether she bears children, the gift of children is a major cause for thanksgiving for African women. For women, difficulties in family life include barrenness, illness, spousal quarreling, enmity between wives in polygamous households, lack of money for school fees, and problems with children. Not all prayers are answered, and sometimes the testimonies witness to God's grace despite the apparent lack of answer to years of prayer.

In response to visions, prophets will address congregants by name during the course of the afternoon. For example, Apostolic Bishop Nyasha of Pentecost Church is known for his prophetic powers. In 1986, in Gutu, he prophesied to his congregation as follows, "Peace be to you! I have been looking in a cloud. It spoke into my ears. God's continual speaking to me worried me very much. He told me that Never must go and confess his problems. Mr. Mudodo must go and confess as well." Turning to a woman cursed by barrenness, Nyasha said, "Mother, I see a naked woman before you, fighting against your life. She will put hair in your stomach. Mother, I do not see you succeeding in bearing a child. So if you wish to repent and be a godly person, the better for you. But if you repent, someone will come to you later, discouraging you from worshiping God." The power of Bishop Nyasha's prophecies stemmed from their relevance to the physical, spiritual, and relational problems of his congregants.

The pattern of sermonizing and testimony in Spirit-type AICs shows that theologizing is the task of the congregation as a whole. In western Protestant churches, with their educated ministerial professionals, the congregation expects the preacher to deliver the theology through the Sunday morning sermon, and to bring his or her extensive education into play in the interpretation of biblical texts. In many western mainline churches, the "pastoral prayer" substitutes for the audible prayers of the congregation. But among the Zionists and Apostles, theology emerges in the interplay of numerous interlocutors, each of whom brings a different piece of the meaning to the group. With their power of interruption, with their testimonies, and with their songs, the worshipers discipline the preachers and shape their messages. Because the sermons interact with prayer, healing, testimonies, singing, and dancing, they are part of a comprehensive worship event rather than an isolated feature of the service.

The location of the preacher also illustrates the communal nature of theologizing among Spirit-type AICs. Apostolic preachers walk up and down between two long rows of people separated by gender. Zionist preachers stand in the circle amidst them. In neither case does the preacher reflect the western Protestant tradition of ascending into a high pulpit in the front of the congregants, as if his control of the Word of God is a special revelation born of his educational attainments. Rather, preaching takes place as an integral part of a total worship experience in which the authority of the preacher is granted by the affirmation of the people. Preachers in Spirit-type AICs are not professionals. Rather, they are men of the community who hold ordinary jobs during the week, but who on the Sabbath are respected for their ability to voice the aspirations and needs of their communities, as well as share their wisdom derived from being closer to God than the average worshiper.

Healing

In Spirit-type AICs, special prayers for healing are the concluding portion of the weekly worship service. Other denominations emphasize healing as well. Across Africa, church-related healing centers have sprung up as alternatives to western medical care. Black Methodists in South Africa invite people with special prayer needs to remain after the service. In recent decades, liturgical mission churches like Catholics and Anglicans have begun holding special healing services that may or may not follow the conclusion of the main worship service.[14] But in AICs, healing is a central aspect of the main worship service itself. Spirit-type AICs have made prayer for

---

14. For insightful work on healing as a major theme in African churches of various denominations, see G. C. Oosthuizen et al., eds., *Afro-Christian Religion and Healing in Southern Africa* (Lewiston, N.Y.: Edwin Mellen Press, 1989); J. P. Kiernan, *The Production and Management of Therapeutic Power in Zionist Churches within a Zulu City* (Lewiston, N.Y.: Edwin Mellen Press, 1990); Chris O. Oshun, "Healing Practices among Aladura Pentecostals," in Daneel, ed., *African Christian Outreach*, vol. 1 (Pretoria: South African Missiological Society, 2001), pp. 242-53; Lilian Dube-Chirairo, "Mission and Deliverance in the Zvikomborero Apostolic Faith Church," in Daneel, ed., *African Christian Outreach*, vol. 1, pp. 294-311; Stuart C. Bate, "Inculturation in Process: Influence of the Coping-healing Churches on the Attitudes and Praxis of Mainline Churches," in D. L. Robert, ed., *African Christian Outreach*, vol. 2: *Mission Churches* (Pretoria: South African Missiological Society, 2003), pp. 177-207; Tabona Shoko, "Mainline Church Healing in Zimbabwe," in Robert, ed., *African Christian Outreach*, vol. 2, pp. 208-35.

healing a marker of their identity. This emphasis expresses their faith in the power of the Holy Spirit and their knowledge that Jesus was a healer. Healing also is a central model for mission in AICs, as being healed is one of the main reasons people leave more westernized churches to join them.[15] One AIC member after another testifies to how healing could not be found in either the mission churches or in traditional religion, and that relief could only be found in the AICs. For example, Apostolic healer Torera shared his own story of how the illness of his son brought him into the *vaPostori:* "I became a Christian through my son who was critically ill. . . . When the Apostles came they prayed for the child. They rose from their knees and addressed me as follows: 'We must baptize you in order to obtain the power of praying for your child.' I told them that I had no objection if they started by baptizing my wives, so that I could first stand and watch the procedure and make up my mind. Thereupon they asked me: 'Don't you want your child?' I told them, 'I want my child!' We quarreled until they said that they would stop praying for the child. At this stage I consented. So I took my whole family [*musha wose*] with me to the Jordan. We were all baptized and then returned to the homestead. There the praying for my son was resumed until he was healed."[16] The AIC focus on healing also reflects the almost total lack of western medical care available to poor rural people in Africa. In this day and age in which the AIDS epidemic is decimating the working-age population of Southern Africa, healing as a feature in AIC worship retains a central, if not dominant, role.

During the worship service, prophets counsel needy people. Toward the end of the service, they may bring some of these people forward, tell their stories, and invite the congregation to sing and dance around them. Persons share the details of their condition, including confessing sins that have made them ill, or telling of dreams that have haunted them. Individuals with prayer needs come forward and kneel. Bishops and prophets go from person to person, laying hands on them and praying. The laying on of hands can be a matter of quiet individual prayer, or it can be a public exorcism, in which several prophets place their hands on the head of the afflicted and pray to drive out the evil spirits that are afflicting him or her.

---

15. AIC members frequently mention being healed as a central reason for joining the church in the first place. See the chapter on healing as a recruitment technique in Daneel, *Old and New,* vol. 2, pp. 186-260.

16. Quoted in Daneel, *Old and New,* vol. 2, p. 195.

**Ordination of
Bishop**
from the authors'
personal collection

Healing in the context of AIC worship encompasses all of life — the need for rain, jobs, work, sound family relations, and physical health. People often attribute their problems to being bewitched by others, and thus witchcraft detection and eradication remain big parts of the healing process.

Usually only male prophets and bishops are allowed to lay hands on persons of both sexes during the main worship services. Some women receive special calls to be healers, but they usually work with women, or they work through mediating objects such as injections of holy water, driving

65

evil spirits into inanimate objects, binding the afflicted with cloths, or other methods. Both male and female healers work in healing colonies affiliated with the Zionist and Apostolic movements, and there female healers might touch their patients. Healers make ample use of holy water, which they sprinkle on people to protect them from evil forces and from illness. Since healing is a holistic matter that involves human relationships as well as what westerners would define as medical care, the healing present in the main worship service is only the tip of the iceberg in the healing process. Whether or not the healing process has been medically successful, the main accomplishment of healing is in lifting up people's needs before God, calling upon the divine spiritual power mediated by the church leaders to bind the forces of sickness and darkness, and re-integrating alienated persons into the community. Making one's needs known to the community during the church service is a powerful means of obtaining help and understanding from a supportive group.

The healing process among families and neighbors continues even after the Sabbath service has finished. People leave the worship space and take off their special garments. As is the practice in Christian communities around the world, worshipers disperse and then take their main meal of the day with their families or others in the village. Healing continues in the *koinonia,* the acts of fellowship, that take place during the week after the services have ended.

Seasons of Worship and the Liturgical Year

While AICs do not observe the events of the Christian year in the way that Anglicans, Catholics, and other more liturgical mission churches do, they have special seasons of celebration. They also have other kinds of worship events such as mid-week prayer meetings, baptismal ceremonies, ceremonies to remove evil from people's homes, funerals, and ceremonies that accompany the deceased to heaven *(runyaradzo).* For the *vaPostori,* Pentecost is the biggest special worship event of the year. Apostles come from across the country to celebrate the giving of the Holy Spirit to their founder Johane Maranke and his brothers.

Most Spirit-type AICs celebrate the paschal feast, the Lord's Supper, three or four times a year: July (optional), October, Christmas, and Easter or Pentecost. The most important one for Zionists coincides with Easter and is the major worship event of the year. At Easter, Zionists converge on their Zion City. In South Africa, the Easter celebrations of the Zion Christian Church near Polokwane (formerly Petersburg) attract three to six million people, and in post-apartheid society have become a prime destination for ambitious politicians. The other communion celebrations take place in areas in which large churches are active. In the Zion Apostolic Church, members meet at the headquarters for the October seed conferences. Among the purposes of these communion festivals is to cement the authority of the leader and to keep each movement together. Reaffirmation of connections in a personal manner, rather than by long-distance control, is essential in traditional cultures.

In the Zion Christian Church in Zimbabwe, the paschal celebrations can be used for big outreach campaigns. Following the communion service as a launching point, teams of revivalists are sent into different parts of the country to visit other congregations, to sing and to preach, and to recruit new members. During two weeks of intense evangelization, church members conduct healing sessions, visit potential members, and assist the needy. On the last weekend of the campaign, new members are baptized in a river and incorporated into the community.

In the Zion Apostolic Church, one of the communion feasts takes place sometime between July to September, toward the beginning of the rainy season. While in the Northern Hemisphere springtime fertility festivals were incorporated into Easter, in the Southern Hemisphere the reverse of the seasons means that spring occurs in October. The Easter celebration thus lacks the trappings of European pre-Christian religion such as eggs, bunnies, and other signs of fertility. In African traditional religion the onset of the spring rainy season was the time in which the high god Mwari was called upon to bring rain. During the rain conference *(ungano yemvura)*, people ask for rain and hear sermons on the importance of rain, good harvests, and plentiful livestock as signs of salvation. Selected prophets are sent to climb a mountain and seek visions from God about the anticipated rainfall. Prophets spend the night in fasting, prayer, singing, speaking in tongues, and prophesying. Prophets share their visions with each other, and then descend the mountain to share what they have learned. The following is a typical example of a prophetic vision from a rain conference in the late 1990s: "I have been lifted up into the air to view the whole country. I observed a clear and cloudless sky. I took time observing it and suddenly I noticed a tiny object moving across the sky. The object then grew to cover the whole eastern sky. Then a voice said to me, 'There is plentiful rainfall. But tell the bishop to take a red and a green cord and use them in praying over a cup of water, which should be sprinkled at the four points of the compass."[17] Petitioners for rain bring their offerings to God, and the rain conference ends with a communion service.

Samuel Mutendi, founder of the Zimbabwe Zion Christian Church, called the October paschal celebration a "seed conference" *(ungano hwembeu)* during which people ask God's blessing on the planting of their crops. While the Zion Apostolic Churches often have separate rain and seed conferences, the ZCC combines these functions into one large October event. Zionists pray for rain and bring their seeds to be blessed. The October (spring) seed festival and communion service represents a contextualization or transformation of the traditional rainmaking ceremonies at the cult headquarters of the Shona high god.[18] October also tends to be vacation month for those with jobs, and so people travel to see their families at the time of spring planting. During the seed conferences, people prepare themselves to be blessed. Once the people — the first seeds — are themselves cleansed and blessed, then their seeds are blessed. The bishop lays hands on the small containers of different kinds of seeds. People take home containers of holy water with which to sprinkle their domestic animals and to guard the perimeter of the *kraals* (homesteads). By linking the communion celebration to the earth's springtime cycle, the Zionists draw a link between African traditional religion and the theology of the New Testament, just as early Europeans drew connections between their own fertility traditions and the celebration of Jesus Christ's death and resurrection.

Another connection with African Traditional Religion can be seen in the annual Thanksgiving conferences *(matapona)* held in some Zion Apostolic Churches, during which people bring the first fruits of their crops to be blessed. They also donate portions to the church granary, which is then used during the year to feed the needy. The harvest conferences are smaller and less significant than the October seed conferences.

In addition to roots in agriculture-based peasant society and African traditional rituals involving rain, and the planting and harvesting of crops,

17. Quoted in Solomon Zvanaka, "Salvation in Socio-Economic Perspective," in Daneel, ed., *African Christian Outreach*, vol. 1, pp. 225-26.

18. On the Shona high god, see M. L. Daneel, *The God of the Matopo Hills — An Essay on the Mwari Cult in Rhodesia* (The Hague, Netherlands: Mouton, 1970).

Procession of Bishop   from the authors' personal collection

the several communion festivals of Spirit-type AICs probably also owe their origins to the quarterly meetings and camp meeting traditions of the missionary churches from which their founders broke away. According to Dickson Bruce, the apex of the American frontier camp meeting was a huge interdenominational communion service. People poured in from the rural areas and camped out for a length of time, while attending preaching and testimony sessions, singing frontier hymns, and recruiting and baptizing new members. The culmination of the frontier camp meeting was the communion service.[19] Leigh Schmidt has written on how periodic Scottish communion fairs were a predecessor to the American camp meeting.[20] Johane Maranke was the product of a pietistic type of Methodism, and had undoubtedly attended extensive revival services, including the great revivals of 1918, remembered in Zimbabwean Methodism as the "year of the holy spirit." It is fair to speculate that the *vaPostori* communion festivals

19. Dickson D. Bruce, Jr., *And They All Sang Hallelujah: Plain Folk Camp-Meeting Religion, 1800-1845* (Knoxville: University of Tennessee, 1974).

20. Leigh Eric Schmidt, *Holy Fairs: Scottish Communions and American Revivals in the Early Modern Period* (Princeton: Princeton University Press, 1989).

owe their origins to the contextualization of American camp meeting religion, and its merger with transformed traditional rural African practices.

Conclusion: Worship, Mission, and the Eschatological Community

As the largest group of African Initiated Churches in Southern Africa, the Spirit-type churches possess rich worship lives that attract millions of followers. With their focus on ritual purification, singing and dancing, preaching, exorcism, prayer, and healing, the worship practices of the Zionists and Apostles grow from the realities of their everyday lives and culminate in day-long, weekly worship services. The evolving worship traditions of these churches represent creative assimilation of the Protestant Christianity from which their founders broke, with traditional worldviews as embodied in African traditional religions. The paschal celebrations of the Spirit-type AICs are the high point of the liturgical year, and represent both innovation and continuity with Christian tradition, as well as integration with the earth's seasonal cycles. Even more than in many western churches, the worship that one experiences among AICs resonates with the biblical themes of purification, prophecy, healing, and commentary on the Word of God.

Worship among Zionists and Apostles is clearly a missionary event, for more than anything else the worshiping community is what attracts non-members. By the celebratory singing and dancing under the trees, the distinctive uniforms, the opportunities provided for grassroots leadership, and the visible victories over evil spirits and illness, AIC worship bears testimony to a holistic gospel. AIC worship life should be a model for other churches around the world as to the effectiveness of worship itself as a form of missional outreach.

Above all, worship among Zionists and Apostles is the enactment of their theology, in which they replicate the world of the Bible in the African context. In the course of a worship service, the African worshipers place themselves into the biblical story, and an African Jerusalem, or holy city, becomes manifest and takes shape. As an eschatological process, worship is a sign of hope that God's kingdom is concrete here and now: hope becomes real, the wizards and the demons flee, the complexities of life become manageable, and the promises of rain and good crops are revived for people in a precarious subsistence economy. Through worship, hope in a future afterlife is sustained, and God's kingdom draws near on earth.

The Mar Thoma Christians of Kerala:
A Study of the Relationship between Liturgy
and Mission in the Indian Context

PHILIP L. WICKERI

Editor's Introduction

It sounds like a liturgical experiment: take a church with deep roots in Syrian Christianity and put it in India. A church with Orthodox affiliation but Reformed Protestant influences. A church with a distinct identity in a pluralist social context. A church in one of India's most densely populated yet smallest states. What would such a worshiping community look like?

As Philip Wickeri shows, this is no hypothetical exercise; it is the defining question of the Mar Thoma Church in Kerala, India, a place Wickeri calls "one of the most beautiful places on earth." His evocative opening description of Mar Thoma worship in the melodious tongue of Malayalam, and his image of shoes waiting at the door for their wearers, who have abandoned them in reverence for the worship space, sets the scene for his sketch of Mar Thoma's complex liturgical history and rich cultural context. In Kerala, Wickeri shows, worship arises out of ancient tradition but is given unique expression.

•   •

St. Mary's Mar Thoma Church is located in the small town of Rubber Board, Kerala, not far from the city of Kottayam. The town is so named because it is the site of the state government's rubber authority. St. Mary's is a medium-sized church, about fifty years old, and has eighty-five families from the surrounding parish, many of whom work in the rubber industry. The nave of the church is simply designed, with woven mats covering the aisles and the area before the communion rail, simple wooden pews, and

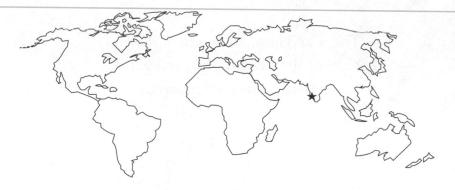

ceiling fans. Here, as in other parishes, the choir consists of a few stalwart adults and a dozen or so young people. Malayali people wear sandals or shoes that can be easily slipped on and off, and they are left on the concrete apron at the main door or one of the side doors. As in all Indian places of worship, no one wears shoes in church, out of respect for being in a sacred place. Inside, the women in colorful saris or the traditional Syrian Christian white sit on the right side of the church and the men, in their distinctive *mundus* and *kurtas,* on the left.

I arrive with a colleague from the Mar Thoma Theological Seminary who will celebrate and preach today at the main service. The priest-in-charge serves a mission parish on alternate Sundays. All seminary faculty are ordained priests, and they are expected to fill in on Sundays because of the shortage of clergy.

Prayers are said, hymns are sung, the Bible is read and a sermon is preached. But the center of the service is the *Holy Qurbana* or Eucharist. A light gauzy curtain with sequined church emblems closes off the sacristy before worship. Just before the service begins, candles are lit behind the curtain which opens to a Syrian Christian altar covered with embroidered red cloth, flowers, candlesticks, and a gleaming gold chalice and paten. The celebrant's plain white cassock is covered by an elaborate chasuble and cape in the same style and color as the table dressings. He is assisted by a seminary student in training and three deacons.

It is a sung service, and the melodic resonance of the Malayalam language makes it particularly beautiful. The same liturgy is used in Mar Thoma churches all over the world. In the Syrian Christian culture, this is what gives religious meaning, provides continuity, and enriches the faith-

**Mar Thoma
Seminary
Church,
Kattayam**
from the author's
personal collection

ful. The priest faces east to the altar for much of the service, yet turns to include the people in his prayers as he asks them to pray for him. The censers are filled and refilled, and they are passed between the priests and the deacons, who bow to one another, censing the altar, themselves, and the people. The congregation sings the prayers and responses. The deacons and many of the older people know the entire service by heart. The people come forward for the Eucharist distributed by the priest; a small wafer and wine in a small communion spoon are given to each person. At the end of the service, the curtain is closed once more.

As soon as the service ends, the children gather in the front pews for Sunday school. (There is no church hall; everything is held either in the

Mar Thoma Seminary Grounds, Kattayam   from the author's personal collection

church or at a parishioner's home.) The youth group meets in the same place after the children. At St. Mary's, the youth group is both large and well organized. The priest attends their meeting, listening to and initialing the previous week's minutes, encouraging participation, speaking briefly, and offering a prayer. A group leader calls on the others to report on activities, read Bible passages, sing, and pray. After Sunday school, I am told, some of the young people go off to attend a Pentecostal youth gathering.

When the Sunday school is concluded, I am taken to the elegant home of a well-to-do parishioner, who has recently returned to Kerala after establishing his business in the Persian Gulf state of Dubai. He and his wife have graciously invited us to lunch. When I enter the house with the priest, he offers a prayer for the family and for the food. One of our fellow guests is the brother-in-law of our host, a Communist Party worker in the state government. All three Kerala power centers are represented here this Sunday: the Party, the Church, the Gulf. But this is a day for the church.

Introduction

The liturgy and mission of the Mar Thoma Church is a unique case in world Christianity. Mar Thoma is a distinctively Indian church that traces its roots to the Syrian Christian community of the first centuries of the Christian era. It is a church with a deeply rooted sense of Christian tradition in the multi-religious reality of India. Mar Thoma is a church that combines an Orthodox form of worship with a kind of Protestant mission and practice, standing between the Oriental Orthodox and the Protestants in a relationship not unlike that of the Anglicans between Roman Catholics and Protestants. Mar Thoma is a church that has literally been formed through its mission and through the nineteenth-century reforms in its liturgical practice. It is an Indian ethnic church with a strong commitment to ecumenism and social justice.

There are useful and important comparisons to be made with the Christian Church in China, and its re-emergence since 1979. China and India are the two most populous countries in the world, and both have growing Christian minorities. The Christians of the two countries also face serious challenges in the areas of church-state relations. The national government of India is controlled by the Bharatiya Janata Party (BJP), while China is under the leadership of the Communist Party of China (CPC). In recent years, the BJP has been telling Indian Christians to follow the example of the Three-Self Patriotic Movement in China, to mute "Western" influences and to become more identified with Indian culture. But Mar Thoma has in fact been an Indian church for two millennia, and, like the China Christian Council, it is a self-governing, self-supporting, and self-propagating ("Three-Self") community.

Kerala and the Syrian Christian Community

Kerala, the land of "lakes, latex, and letters," is one of the most beautiful places on earth, "God's own country," according to its people. It is situated on the southwest coast of India on the Arabian Sea, with a range of mountains in the east separating Kerala from the neighboring states of Karnataka and Tamil Nadu. Historically, it has been a trading center for spices and agricultural products, and even today the economy continues to be dependent on its production of rubber, coir, coconut, spices, and other commercial agricultural products. There is also significant revenue from tourism, but relatively little industry. Many people from Kerala work in the Persian Gulf states, and others have emigrated to Southeast Asia, Europe, and North America, and they contribute to the regular inflow of hard currency. Kerala has maintained a sense of independence from the policies of the national government in Delhi during critical periods of Indian history. The Communist Party came to power in Kerala in 1957, and it has been a significant force in the state ever since. One writer has observed that society is based on the interaction of "the Party, the Church, and the Gulf,"[1] and this is part of what makes Kerala unique.

The demographic and social indicators are also unique. The population of Kerala is almost 32 million people, with an area of 39,000 square kilometers that is divided into 14 districts. The capital is the southern city of Thiruvananthapuram (or Trivandrum).[2] Kerala is slightly smaller than Switzerland, but it has more than four and a half times its population. Kerala is also one of the smallest but most densely populated states in India, with 1.18 percent of the total area but 3.43 percent of the population. The per capita income is comparable to other parts the country, although the poverty rate is slightly below average. Yet it is the literacy rate of Kerala that makes it unique in India and all over the Third World. Kerala has the highest rate of literacy in India: 91 percent overall and 88 percent for women. Nationally, literacy is only 65.4 percent and 54.2 percent for women, respectively.[3] Life expectancy, access to health care, and education levels are also higher. The higher literacy rate and education levels have been attributed to the influence of the church and the Communist Party in Kerala, undergirded by the long literary tradition in Malayalam, the language spoken by the majority of the population.

According to *The Hindu*, an important national newspaper, 43 percent of Kerala's population are minorities, mostly Christian and Muslim.[4] Christians are far more numerous and much stronger institutionally than Muslims. Unlike many parts of North India, there is little friction among religious groups in Kerala, which has a long history of religious tolerance. This may help explain why there are more Christians in this small state

1. Vijay Nambisan, "The Thief of Memories," in *Where the Rain Is Born*, ed. Anita Nair (New Delhi: Penguin Books India, 2002), p. 264.

2. *Manorama Yearbook: 2002* (Kottayam: Malayala Manorama, 2002), p. 656.

3. *Manorama Yearbook: 2002*, p. 528.

4. "Dangerous Games," *The Hindu*, 26 July 2003.

than in any other part of the country. According to the 1991 religious census, Christians in India numbered about 2.3 percent of the population,[5] but the Christian population of Kerala is estimated by some to be more than 30 percent — about the same percentage as in South Korea. In Kerala, the vast majority of Christians are from Syrian traditions, which includes the Mar Thoma Church. (Appendix I provides estimated figures on the number of Syrian Christians in Kerala today.)

It is difficult to be precise as to what the term "Syrian" Christian really means. It certainly indicates the ancient connection between India, Antiochian Christianity, and the missionary work of the Church of the East since the fourth century, but it means a great deal more than that. According to the Anthropological Survey of India, Syrian Christians are a distinct, endogamous ethnic group, in many ways similar to a caste. They have a history of close to two thousand years, and in language, religion, and ethnicity, they are related to Persian as well as to West Syrian Christian traditions. Traditionally, the Syrian Christians of India have had distinct customs, dress, and religious beliefs. They associate themselves with the tradition of St. Thomas, as discussed below, and consider themselves of high-caste descent. The main function of the various social divisions within the Syrian Christian community is to maintain their distinctive social grouping, propagate Christian beliefs, and regulate marriage.[6] Syrian Christians of Kerala are very well-educated, and as a group they have extensive landholdings and wealth, both personally and in their churches. This accounts for their power and standing in society, and, as we shall see below, their difficulty in reaching out to other ethnic groups, particularly the Dalits.

---

5. *Manorama Yearbook: 2002*, p. 547. The reliability of these figures are open to question, and of course the number of Indian Christians has grown since 1991, particularly among the Pentecostals and in tribal areas. Because conversion is a sensitive issue in India, there has certainly been an under reporting of the number of Christians. However, I still find the Indian estimates more credible than the exaggerated figures in D. B. Barrett, George T. Kurian, and Todd M. Johnson, eds., *World Christian Encyclopedia: A Comparative Survey of Churches and Religions in the Modern World* (Oxford and New York: Oxford University Press, 2001). They claim a figure of more than 62 million Christians in mid-2000, which includes 21.5 million "crypto-Christians" (vol. 1, p. 360). The highest estimates I was given for the total number of Christians from Indian Christian sources was 25 million.

6. See T. Madhava Menon, Deepak Tyagi, and B. Francis Kulirani, eds., *People of India: Kerala*, Vol. 27, Part III, *People of India*, gen. ed. K. S. Singh, Anthropological Survey of India (New Delhi: East-West Press Private Ltd., 2002), "Syrian Christians," pp. 1349-1360.

The Mar Thoma Church: Born in Mission and Liturgical Reform

Christianity in India has a much longer continuous history than any other part of Asia east of the Indus River. According to tradition, the church in India was founded by the Apostle Thomas in the year 52 C.E. Although there is no historical evidence to prove this conclusively, there is reliable evidence of continuing Christian communities along the Malabar coast and in northern India related to the tradition of the Apostle Thomas. These communities had irregular communication with the Church of the East from the fourth century onward.[7] From the eighth until the late fifteenth century, the Indian Christian community developed in relative isolation from Christians elsewhere, save for irregular contact with Christian prelates and emissaries from Persia and Syria.

The Portuguese arrived in India in 1498, and early relationships between the Roman Catholic missionaries and the Syrian Christian community were open and friendly.[8] But tensions grew as the missionaries, supported by the Portuguese colonial authorities, challenged both the independence and orthodoxy of the Syrian Christians. Finally, at the Synod of Diamper (1599) the Portuguese hierarchy in India brought the entire church over to Rome.[9] Although Indian Christians were allowed to retain their Syriac liturgy and some local liturgical rites, they were no longer an independent church. Syrian Christians from many parts of Kerala resisted the heavy-handed practices of the Portuguese, and in, 1653, a large group gathered at one of the churches near Cochin and swore a Christian oath to reject Roman authority. This revolt is known as the "Coonen Cross" incident, for some of the protestors hung themselves on the cross piece that bent as a result. From this time forward, the church became di-

---

7. The standard source for this early period is A. Mathias Mundadan, *History of Christianity in India*, Vol. 1: *From the Beginnings up to 1542* (Bangalore: Church History Association of India, 1989). See also L. W. Brown, *The Indian Christians of St. Thomas: An Account of the Ancient Syrian Church of Malabar* (Cambridge: Cambridge University Press, 1980).

8. See A. Mathias Mundadan, *Indian Christians: Search for Identity and Struggle for Autonomy* (Bangalore: Dharmaram Publications, 1984).

9. George Nedungatt, S.J., ed., *The Synod of Diamper Revisted* (Rome: Pontificio Instituto Oriental, 2001). After the Synod, Catholic missionaries destroyed almost all the documentary evidence from the pre-Portuguese period, as well as many churches and artifacts.

vided between those who remained loyal to Rome and those who were once again independent.[10]

Ten years after the Coonen Cross incident, the Dutch replaced the Portuguese as the colonial power along the Malabar coast, and they ordered all the Portuguese priests to leave India. This worked to the advantage of the non-Roman churches, who were now freer to develop on their own. They established contact with the Jacobite patriarch in Jerusalem, who sent his representative to India to consecrate a new metropolitan. From that time forward, the independent Syrian Church began to elect their own bishops and metropolitans and develop in the Jacobite tradition related to the patriarch. Mar Thoma historians maintain that the Jacobite Church was already "corrupt" by the early eighteenth century. There was little theological education; boys as young as ten were ordained as deacons; the liturgy was in Syriac, a language which no lay people knew and few priests knew well; church power was in the hands of a few families; and clergy depended for their income on prayer services said for the dead.[11] Their theology was not orthodox, according to the standards of Chalcedon and Nicea. The church, according to Mar Thoma historians, was already in need of reform. It should be noted at this point that there is little documentary evidence from the period between 1653 and the early nineteenth century, and it is difficult to establish what the real situation was. Catholic, Orthodox, and Mar Thoma scholars continue to debate this period, for it has important implications for their legitimacy and identity today. (See Appendix II.)

By the early nineteenth century, British imperial power was ascendant all over India, including Travancore and Cochin, the central region of present-day Kerala. In 1806, Rev. Claudius Buchanan, chaplain of the British East India Company, was impressed by his visit to the Syrian Christians there, and he encouraged the Church Missionary Society (CMS) to help this church.[12] The second British Resident (the colonial administrator) Col. J. Munro was a devout evangelical dedicated to the mission of the church. He arrived in Travancore in 1810 and was determined to help the

10. C. P. Matthew and M. M. Thomas, *The Indian Churches of St. Thomas* (Delhi: ISPCK, 1967), p. 37.

11. Juhanon Mar Thoma, *Christianity in India and a Brief History of the Mar Thoma Syrian Church* (Madras: K. M. Cherian, 1968), p. 19.

12. See Claudius Buchanan, *Christian Researches in Asia with Notices of the Translation of the Scriptures into the Oriental Languages*, 3rd ed. (Edinburgh: J. Ogle and Manners & Miller, 1812).

Jacobite Christians. He asked the CMS to send a "Mission of Help," and in 1816 their first missionary arrived in the city of Alleppey. Over the next few years, CMS missionaries were sent to other parts of Kerala and welcomed by the Syrian Christians. They established a theological seminary for the training of clergy in Kottayam; translated the Bible and other literature into Malayalam; built schools and offered advice about church and liturgical reform. Initially, they were very careful in respecting the church and its leadership, according to their motto: "not to pull down the ancient church and build another, but to remove the rubbish and repair the decaying places."[13] The church was to be brought back to its own liturgy and discipline, rather than to adopt an Anglican liturgy.

In time, however, tensions developed between the missionaries and the Indian church leadership. Who was to decide what was "rubbish" and where were the "decaying places"? How should the work of removal and repair proceed? The CMS missionaries were evangelical and iconoclastic, and some of the missionaries who came later were less sensitive and more doctrinally rigid than those who went initially on a "Mission of Help." These later missionaries saw in the liturgy and beliefs of the Jacobite Church similarities with the Catholic reforms of the Oxford Movement in England, which they detested. M. M. Thomas, the most prominent Mar Thoma theologian of the twentieth century, used to suggest that the relationships with missionaries might have been significantly different if they had been from the "high church" United Society of the Propagation of the Gospel rather than CMS. In any case, by the early 1830s, the relationship had deteriorated to the point of open hostility between the missionaries and the Orthodox Metropolitan Mar Dionysius IV. The Anglican Bishop Daniel Wilson of Calcutta visited Travancore in 1835, seeking to make peace. After meeting with the metropolitan, he suggested six points of church reform for his consideration. Bishop Wilson's suggestions were not well received, even though most of them were subsequently adopted by reformers in the church. Mar Dionysius saw Bishop Wilson as interfering and heavy-handed. He called a Synod the following year, which rejected the proposal *in toto*. With this action, the CMS "Mission of Help" to the Orthodox church came to an end.[14]

13. Mar Thoma, *Christianity in India,* p. 20.

14. CMS remained in Kerala, but after 1837 they worked on their own. In 1878, the CMS missionaries established the Anglican Diocese of Travancore and Cochin, which became part of the Church of South India seventy years later.

Nevertheless, the CMS missionaries had introduced the idea of reform in the Orthodox church. Those in the Indian Syrian community who continued to be interested in reformation had no desire to work under the British, much less to join the Anglican church, but they did see the biblical and theological importance of what the missionaries had been saying. In 1836, twelve priests under the leadership of Abraham Malpan and Kathayal Gervase, both teachers at the seminary in Kottayam, issued a twenty-three point call to reform.[15] Because the British Resident still maintained jurisdiction over church properties, they submitted their proposal to the same Col. Munro who had initiated the "Mission of Help." All of the reforms were liturgical and theological:

> All prayers for the dead and invocation of saints were removed. The following words which the officiating priest used to utter on taking the Bread into his hands were also removed: "Thee I am holding Who holdest the bounds; Thee I am grasping Who orderest the depths; Thee O God, do I place in my mouth." In another prayer of the priest, "We offer Thee this unbloody sacrifice for thy Whole Church all over the world," the words "unbloody sacrifice" were replaced by "prayer." The epiclesis, or prayer of consecration of the elements, was changed into "May the Holy Ghost dwell on this bread (or the wine in this cup) and make it the body (or the blood) of our Lord the Messiah for the remission of sins and for life eternal unto those who receive it." The words "unto those who receive" are a significant addition. A rubric for the blessing of the censer was deleted, but the use of the censer was continued. In the old liturgy, the priest at one place, when removing the veil or the covering, addresses it as follows: "Thou art the hard rock which was set against the tomb of our Redeemer." This prayer was changed by Abraham Malpan to one addressed to our Lord himself: "Thou art the tried and precious stone which was set at naught by the builders." Certain changes in practice were also initiated by Malpan. The communion was to be administered in both kinds, and was not to be celebrated when there were no communicants. The service was to be conducted in the mother tongue (Malayalam).[16]

---

15. The 23 points are listed in K. K. Kuruvilla, *The Mar Thoma Church and Its Doctrines* (Madras: The Christian Literature Society of India), pp. 15-17.
16. Matthew and Thomas, *The Indian Churches of St. Thomas*, pp. 75-76.

These were radical innovations, and the first such reforms proposed in an Oriental Orthodox church. The reforms could not be accepted by the church as it was then constituted. The metropolitan rejected all the proposed changes and removed Abraham Malpan from his post at the seminary. Abraham returned to his parish in Maramon, and there, in 1837, he acted. He took an image from the church that he regarded as idolatrous, and cast it down into a well. Then, with the support of the lay leaders of the church, he celebrated the liturgy in Malayalam for the first time, eliminating prayers for the dead, prayers to the Virgin Mary, and what they saw as a "magical view" of the sacraments. He called on the church to initiate a full-scale reform. With these actions, the Mar Thoma reformation had begun.

M. M. Thomas has described Abraham Malpan's initiatives as a threefold reformation. It was a reformation of *doctrine,* implied in the changes in theology and liturgical practice. It was a reformation that brought a new *evangelical vision* to the Syrian Church, encouraging individual repentance and spiritual renewal by the grace of Jesus Christ. Finally, it was a reformation in *society and culture* that was part of the whole movement of change and reform in the nineteenth-century Kerala "renaissance." Abraham Malpan instilled in his church a love of liberty and a sense of creativity, and it was this that contributed to the Kerala renaissance.[17] The evangelical awakening in the church was thus related to democratic renewal in society. In the church, this involved a democratization of church governance and greater participation of the laity on the one hand, and a commitment by the church to work for justice on behalf of the poor and the oppressed on the other.

The history of contestation between reformers and traditionalists in the Orthodox Church between 1837 and the establishment (or reformation) of the Mar Thoma Church (1889) is extremely complex. Both sides appealed to both the British Resident and to the Jacobite patriarch. Their battles were fought in the churches as well as in the courts, and they divided families and parishes. Abraham Malpan died in 1846, but his cause was kept alive by other reformers, and the legal and theological disputes continued. Finally, in 1889, after many court battles and church struggles, the split between the reformers and the traditionalists was finalized by a decision of the High Court in Trivandrum that recognized the claim of the

---

17. M. M. Thomas, *Toward an Evangelical Social Gospel* (Madras: Christian Literature Society, 1977), pp. 7-8.

Jacobite Metropolitan to be head of the church, and granted the Jacobites control over most church properties, seminaries and schools, and bank accounts. Thomas Mar Athanasius, the reformist metropolitan, relinquished the control of his properties, but rejected the decision of the court in all other matters. He and other reformers established the newly independent Mar Thoma Church, unrelated to the Jacobite Patriarch, a church with a new name but which claimed to be built on the foundations that had been laid in the first century.

> Left with practically nothing in 1889, the Mar Thoma Church developed rapidly over the next decades. The church was born with a sense of reforming mission, and it reached out to Malayali people in parishes up and down the Malabar coast. Today, the Mar Thoma Church has an estimated membership of 750,000 in India and all over the world. It is concentrated in Kerala where there are an estimated 450,000 communicants in six dioceses, and seven of the nine Mar Thoma bishops. The headquarters of the church is in Thiruvalla, where there are also several church-related mission organizations. In addition to the seminary in Kottayam, there are church schools throughout the state, as well as a women's Bible College in Thiruvalla. The Mar Thoma Church was one of the founding members of the World Council of Churches in 1948, and it has played an important role in the ecumenical movement in India and internationally.

The earliest Mar Thoma migrant churches were in Malaysia, where Indians from Kerala went to work on rubber plantations in the 1930s. In the 1950s and 1960s, parishes were established in the Persian Gulf states for Malayali immigrants and business people, and in several major American cities for the same reasons. There are also parishes in Canada, New Zealand, Australia, and Great Britain. All of these parishes continue to provide funding and support for Mar Thoma mission initiatives in India. The growth of indigenous (non-Malayali) parishes in India is a relatively new phenomenon related to the church's evangelistic outreach. There are parishes in Karnataka, Andhra Pradesh, and Tamil Nadu worshiping in their own languages. In the church as a whole, there are also almost 180 Dalit parishes.[18] For a church with a total membership of less than one

18. Statistics on Mar Thoma parishes may be found in the *Mar Thoma Sabha Diary*, issued yearly.

million, the Mar Thoma Christians have an enormous social and missionary impact.

Liturgy and Mission in the Mar Thoma Church

According to Juhanon Mar Thoma, perhaps the most influential metropolitan of the twentieth century, there are four cardinal features of the Mar Thoma Church: ecclesial autonomy; biblical faith; Eastern forms of worship; and evangelistic vision.[19] It is the latter two that most concern us in this chapter, but all four are closely related.

From the CMS missionaries, the Mar Thoma Church inherited an evangelical theology and a strong emphasis on mission and evangelism. The Mar Thoma Evangelical Association was founded in 1888, the year before the church itself was established. This evangelical emphasis gave the whole church a sense of responsibility for mission, and it came at a time when the church was threatened by financial disaster due to its losses in the High Court. Because of this concern for mission, laymen and -women play a much more important role in the leadership and governance of the church than they do in other Oriental Orthodox churches. The Maramon Convention, a weeklong revival, was begun on lay initiative in 1896 and it has continued to meet every year (in February) to this day. It meets in the town where Abraham Malpan began his liturgical reforms, the home of the church now regarded as "the cradle of the reformation." The focus of the yearly convention is preaching, and it attracts huge numbers of people from other churches (and even other religions). Local parishes and dioceses have their own conventions throughout the year. The mission emphasis for the church is reflected in the motto attributed to Juhanon Mar Thoma that appears on the church emblem: "Lighted to Lighten."

The Mar Thoma Church practices the West Syrian (or Antiochan) liturgy of St. James, which was developed from the Jacobite liturgy, but with significant changes. The center of worship is the Holy *Qurbana*, a Syriac word meaning "offering." Services of worship are much the same in all Mar Thoma parishes, using the standard liturgy which is said or sung in Malayalam and other vernacular languages.[20] After opening prayers and a

19. Juhanon Mar Thoma, *Christianity in India*, p. 44.
20. For an English translation see *The Mar Thoma Syrian Liturgy: A Translation into*

hymn, one or two Bible lessons are read, followed by a sermon. Unlike many Orthodox services, the sermon is very important in the Mar Thoma Church, and it is a vehicle for teaching and inspiring the congregation for mission.

The second half of the service is the *Qurbana,* which remains the highpoint of the liturgy. It ends with a final blessing, the last of four given in the service. Depending on the size of the church and the number of priests officiating, services tend to be about one and a half hours in length.

Like other Orthodox churches, the Mar Thomites observe seven sacraments: baptism, confirmation, confession, marriage, the Eucharist, ordination, and extreme unction. A North American Protestant worshiping in a Mar Thoma Church might think he or she is part of an Eastern Orthodox liturgy, but this would be so only in comparison with the "free church" worship of Protestantism or the Western liturgy of Roman Catholics. The Mar Thoma Church, the Church of South India, and the Church of North India enjoy mutual recognition and the reconciliation of ministries with one another, a rather unique relationship in the ecumenical world. Although Mar Thoma does not yet ordain women priests, this relationship helps to keep the issue alive in the church. In its *theology* of liturgy, the Mar Thoma Church is closer to the Protestants than it is to the Oriental or Eastern Orthodox. Indeed, there has been some debate over how Protestant Abraham Malpan's reforms were, and to what extent they really differed from the liturgy that was introduced by CMS missionaries. Despite the theological underpinnings, however, the liturgical *form* is definitely Eastern and Orthodox.

The shape of worship and liturgy in the Mar Thoma Church must be understood in the context of its relationship to the broader Syrian Christian tradition. Although a full consideration of the development of the Mar Thoma *Thaksa* (or liturgy) is beyond the scope of this paper, several of the changes that have been noted above require further elaboration:

English, trans. and ed. George Kuttical Chacko (New York: Morehouse and Gorham, 1956). The church also has its own version of the liturgy in English and other Indian languages for use in churches. For English, see *The Mar Thoma Church: Order of Worship, Prayers & Hymns* (Merrick, N.Y.: The Mar Thoma Diocesan Sunday Schools for the Diocese of North America and Europe, 2000).

1. The Jacobite liturgy gave great importance to the use of *incense*, giving the impression that its use somehow effects reconciliation with God. The invocation, "Accept our incense out of Thy mercy, O Lord," was changed into "Accept our worship, O Lord," and "be reconciled to us through the incense offered by Thy priests" into "Attend unto the prayer of Thy priests."

2. The word *sacrifice*, wherever it expresses the idea that the sacrifice of Christ is being repeated in the *Qurbana*, is either dropped or clarified. It was replaced by the expression "the bloodless sacrifice of grace, peace and praise."

3. With regard to the words of institution in communion, Christ's words as given in the Gospels are alone retained (Luke 22:19; Mathew 26:28). Also, the word *mystery* was dropped from all places where it occurred, as it was feared that this word might encourage the worshipers in the belief that some magical change took place in the bread and wine during the Communion Service. In the *Epiclesis* (the prayer of invocation of the Holy Spirit) the following prayer was accepted: "May the Holy Spirit sanctify this bread and wine to be the body and blood of our Lord Jesus Christ." The words "transform" and "descend on" are omitted.

4. With regard to the *Person of Christ* all passages suspected of Monophysitism were dropped from the liturgy. For example, the statement "Emmanuel is one and the same after the indissolvable connection; He is not divided into two natures" was removed. Christ is seen as being fully human and fully Divine, as he is in other churches which accept the Chalcedonian formulation.

5. Regarding the *priesthood* and *priesthood of all believers,* in all prayers that the priest offers in his own name for the people, the first person singular is deleted and either the first person plural or the second person plural signifying the congregation is substituted. This change was made in order to emphasize the priesthood of the laity (1 Peter 2:5; Rev. 1:6). It also affirms that Christ alone is our Mediator, for the church does not recognize the "mediatorial priesthood."[21]

21. These five points are drawn from Alexander Mar Thoma, *The Mar Thoma Church: Heritage and Mission*, 3rd ed. (Tiruvalla, 1993). Compare Matthew and Thomas, *The Indian Churches of St. Thomas*, pp. 75f.

All of these changes were also made in Protestant liturgies in Europe after the sixteenth-century Reformation. But liturgical reform in the Mar Thoma church emphasized not only *theological* change, but continuity *in form* with the Orthodox. For example, the opening words of the Jacobite liturgy are "Mary who gave birth to Jesus and John who baptized him, pray for us." This was changed to: "O Lord Christ, born of Mary, and baptized by John, have mercy upon us." The names familiar to worshipers — Mary, John, and Jesus Christ — were retained, but the prayer became a prayer to Jesus Christ. The form of the service was the same, with the continued use of liturgical vestments, candles, and incense, but the message of the service was reforming.

In Eastern and Orthodox traditions, the formulation of doctrine in confessional statements or dogmatic theologies has never been common. The Orthodox are not a confessing tradition, in the way that this would be understood by Protestants, nor do they advance systematic church teachings, as this would be understood by Roman Catholics. Instead, doctrines are expressed through the church liturgy, prayers, teaching. In the Mar Thoma reformation, therefore, no attempt was made to define doctrinal beliefs. However, a new emphasis was given to preaching and the exposition of the Bible, neither of which had been prominent before. This has served to underscore the church's commitment to mission. Mar Thoma is not a "Word alone" church, but there is a great emphasis on the Bible in preaching, the conventions, seminary education, and Bible study. In this way, mission and liturgy are connected in both the service of the Word and the service of the Sacrament.

As noted above, lay people, both men and women, play an important role in the mission of the church and in preaching. The Evangelistic Association, the Women's Association, and the Bible Institute have all been organized by and for the laity. The fact that the Bible and liturgy had been translated into Malayalam was already a step towards greater participation of the laity. There are prominent lay preachers in Mar Thoma churches. Although the church does not yet ordain women, more than eighty women have graduated from the seminary in Kottayam, and they are active in the mission of the church. Women play a more active role here in the Mar Thoma Church than in any other Syrian tradition. Service ministries and mission and evangelism beyond the Syrian Christian community are primarily the responsibility of lay people. In comparison to other Syrian traditions, Mar Thoma is a Bible-centered church that emphasizes individual piety, ministry of all the laity, and social justice in its mission outreach.

Orthodox in liturgy and worship, reformed in mission and theology, the Mar Thoma Church has encouraged spiritual and mission formation through liturgy and Bible study. This has been the history of the Mar Thoma Church from the beginning, and it is reflected in the practice of the Mar Thoma Church today. Within the church, there is a deep emphasis on personal salvation, Bible reading, and *individual* devotion alongside the formal sung liturgy that is celebrated every Sunday and on feast days for the *community* as a whole.

An Exploratory Contextual Analysis

The dual emphasis on liturgy and mission is reflected in the practice of the Mar Thoma Church today. My own research on contemporary Mar Thoma liturgy and mission in Kerala was confined to the Kottayam diocese in central Kerala. Kottayam is a very old city, and it has long been a center for the Syrian Christian community and the Mar Thoma Church. It encompasses a medium-sized district in the state, with a total population of 3.1 million people, 26 percent urban.[22] The Kottayam Diocese of the Mar Thoma Church has 113 parishes, and more than 100,000 communicants, including children. Church size is usually calculated according to the number of families.

The Mar Thoma Church is organized hierarchically, with a threefold order of ministry centering on the priesthood. In greeting the people, the bishops habitually bless them, and great deference is shown to the bishops from all the Syrian churches in the society as a whole. Mar Thoma bishops, unlike priests, are unmarried, and so the whole church becomes their family, as I was told time and again in churches. Kerala in some sense is an Indian version of Christendom, and, because of the power and influence of the church, bishops are listened to as much as any other public figure.

The church hierarchy is reflected in the liturgy. One distinctive aspect of this is the passing of the peace, which begins with the priest or bishop with closed hands who embraces the hands of other priests and then deacons. They in turn pass the peace to the rest of the congregation.

22. *Malayalam Manorama Yearbook: 2002*, p. 67.

The Mar Thoma worship service is centered on the actions of the priest and deacons, but lay participation is enhanced by virtue of the liturgy in Malayalam. Laypeople assist the priest, and they may read the scripture or offer prayers. The liturgy is actually a dialogue between the priest and the people. It is known by heart by older members of the parishes, who also know many of the Malayalam hymns inherited from the nineteenth-century reformation. Several priests and laypersons told me that they did not want to see any major changes in the liturgy, for this was what had formed the church and what kept it strong. The hymns are changing in some parishes — an influence of contemporary Western praise music, I am told — but the liturgy remains the same. The fact that the liturgy is sung in Malayalam provides an important sense of identity for the Mar Thoma Syrian Christians.

The liturgy of the Mar Thoma Church is also well suited for the Indian religious context. Any Indian, steeped in the country's rich religious traditions, would recognize what was going on as an act of devotion. Even if he or she did not understand the words that were spoken, the service would convey the feeling that one was in a sacred place, beginning with the removal of shoes before entering the sanctuary and continuing in the use of candles, incense, and colorful vestments. Most Protestant and Catholic services appear stark in comparison. The Mar Thoma liturgy continues to be Oriental Orthodox in form. It appeals to all the senses: sight (although no icons are used, the altar and the vestments are quite colorful and elaborate); sound (chanting, singing, and reading); smell (the incense); taste (the bread and wine) and touch (the passing of the peace, the texture of the vestments). Although the "magical" elements were removed in the reformation, the mystical aspects of the liturgy remain. A curtain is used to keep the sacramental elements hidden before and after the service. The priest faces the altar as he says the eucharistic prayers, but he also turns around for the response of the people. The bowing, the prostrations, the use of incense, the movements of the hands, the singing, all reinforce the sense of sacred time and place that is expressed in the sensual nature of devotion in other Indian religious traditions.

The liturgy itself is an expression of the mission of the church in the Mar Thoma understanding. The heritage of liturgy is precious, but so too is the concern to make Christianity new through mission and evangelism. I heard no reference in Kerala to the often quoted Orthodox idea of mission in the ecumenical movement as the "liturgy after the liturgy,"[23] but mission is a frequent subject of preaching both in weekly church services and in the conventions. Liturgy and worship are understood as a means of revival and empowerment for mission, a link between the historical witness of the church and its calling in mission. Liturgy provides the roots and the reach for the mission of the Mar Thoma Church.

But it is precisely at this point and in this relationship that we encounter a fundamental problem. Just as the liturgy helps situate the Mar Thoma Church in the broader Syrian context, so the Syrian tradition and use of the Malayalam language inhibit the full participation of non-Syrian Mar Thoma Christians in the life of the church. As a recent study of the Mar Thoma Church has clearly demonstrated, there is discrimination against Dalit converts in particular.[24] Syrian communalism and ethnic exclusivism serve to marginalize the Dalits in both church and society in Kerala. Within the Mar Thoma Church, the attitude of church members tends to be patronizing at best and actively excluding at worst. There are Syrian Christians who will not receive communion with Dalits or from a Dalit priest, and who will not even enter a Dalit church. In every Mar Thoma diocese, there are separate churches for Dalits, although there are also churches that have mixed Dalit-Syrian congregations. The church has made special efforts in recent years to work for greater inclusion of Dalits in the life of its worshiping communities, and greater outreach to Dalits in their mission.[25] But these efforts have not gone very far, and the issue of caste and ethnicity remains an obstacle to a more inclusive understanding of mission and community. The basic question is the extent to which Syrian ethnicity is central to the understanding of the Mar Thoma Church. The "Syrian" in "Syrian Christian" has been described as a remnant of the caste system in Christian dress. What Ninan Koshy wrote about in the late 1960s is still problematic today: "The caste system forms the basis of social organization, and is arranged in a hierarchical order from the highest to the lowest in terms of sacredness and

23. Ion Bria, *The Liturgy After the Liturgy: Mission and Witness from an Orthodox Perspective* (Geneva: WCC Publications, 1996).

24. Kurian Thomas, "A Study of Biblical Dal and Indian Dalit Theology: Its Implications for the Mission of the Mar Thoma Church" (D.Min. dissertation, San Francisco Theological Seminary, 2004). I had the honor of serving as the supervisor of Rev. Thomas's dissertation.

25. Thomas, "A Study of Biblical Dal and Indian Dalit Theology," pp. 250f.

caste pollution."[26] Although the Mar Thomites may be ahead of other Syrian churches in matters of mission and inclusion, the issue is one that the church continues to struggle with.

A strong commitment to ecumenism has helped the Mar Thoma Church address issues of caste and inclusion. Ecumenism is integral to mission in the Mar Thoma Church, not just an incidental "add-on," for ecumenical outreach has been part of its history from the beginning. For the Mar Thomites, ecumenism is related to the historical relationship with other Syrian churches in matters of liturgical form and church order on the one hand, and to the evangelical vision and reformation understanding inherited from CMS on the other. Mar Thoma is a bridge church, in the same sense that the Anglicans are, but theirs is a bridge connecting both Orthodox and Protestant as well as Indian and non-Indian traditions. The combination of evangelism and social justice is an expression of Mar Thoma ecumenism, and this is what compels many in the church to struggle for greater Dalit inclusion. The Mar Thoma Church has learned about issues of mission and inclusion through its involvement in the wider ecumenical fellowship, just as it has contributed to ecumenical understandings of liturgy, contextualization, and concerns for Christianity and culture.

Mar Thoma is committed to ecumenism, but it has always been a self-governing, self-supporting, and self-propagating church. It is autocephalic in terms of church order, and it does not rely on foreign missionaries or mission support from abroad. Direct funding for new mission initiatives comes largely from the Mar Thoma worldwide communion, particularly from wealthy churches in Kerala, North America, and the Gulf. In an age of globalization, the Mar Thoma Church has come to rely heavily on churches overseas for the construction of new churches and church institutions. In the years to come, this may pose problems for the churches of Kerala. Globalization increasingly separates the rich from the poor, even in the same churches, and the structure of church funding is a looming challenge for the mission of all churches. To what extent does the globalization of church giving, with the expectation of wealthy churches and the vulnerability of the poor, challenge the integrity of independent churches like Mar Thoma?

26. Ninan Koshy, *Caste in Kerala Churches* (Bangalore: CIRS, 1969), p. 11.

Concluding Observations

The mission and liturgy of the Mar Thoma Church provides an outstanding example of the way in which contextualization in worship is related to reformation in mission and evangelism. In most studies of world Christianity, the Oriental Orthodox churches have been neglected, but on the basis of my research, I believe that this has been an unfortunate oversight. The Mar Thoma Church provides a fruitful source of further investigation into the contextualization of Christianity in the religiously and culturally pluralistic situation of South Asia, and it affords important opportunities for comparison with churches in other parts of the world, particularly China.

In some ways, it would be more fruitful to compare the Christian experience in India and China as a whole, but this is beyond the scope of this essay. Because my reading of the Mar Thoma Church was inevitably informed by my more than twenty years of work with the China Christian Council, my concluding observations are a modest attempt to make the comparison explicit. My purpose is to be suggestive rather than comprehensive in identifying possibilities for future areas of study, research, and exchange.

The Mar Thoma Church and the China Christian Council have visited one another over the last twenty years, but they have not had extensive conversations. Both are churches with dedicated leaders who are overly committed to their work at home, so the opportunity to learn from one another has been extremely limited. But the similarities between the two churches are notable. Both are indigenous churches rooted in their national cultures and committed to principles of self-government, self-propagation, and self-support. Both are churches whose worship has been influenced by their cultural environment and the missionary heritage. Both are churches deeply committed to mission and evangelism. Both are tiny churches in overwhelmingly non-Christian contexts, in which political realities weigh strongly on their witness.[27]

There are also significant differences in the history and experience of

27. Both churches have produced leading ecumenical theologians in the second half of the twentieth century, K. H. Ting in China and M. M. Thomas in India. The two were friends in the World Students' Christian Federation, and in their writings they addressed similar theological and socio-political concerns, from two very different contexts. I am now at work on a study comparing the two.

the two churches, not to mention vast differences in the Chinese and Indian historical, cultural, and political contexts. The Mar Thoma Church has a much more deeply rooted sense of history and tradition than the Christians of China, many of whom are first generation believers. Mar Thoma Christians tend to be more literate and better educated than Chinese Christians, especially in rural areas. Christianity in China is growing more rapidly than in India, in part because it is not tied to a particular tradition or dependent on a well-defined church order. The spread of informal and non-institutionalized Christian communities, particularly in rural China, presents a very different pattern from that of the well organized Mar Thoma mission churches. Mar Thoma is primarily an ethnic and regional church, whereas the congregations of the China Christian Council are spread all over the country.

We have seen how "high church" liturgical tradition in the Mar Thoma Church helps to foster Christian identity, cultural rootedness, and mission, but the tradition is at the same time limited in its outreach by its "Syrian" ethnic character. "Low church" post-denominational Chinese Protestantism has no such limitations, and like evangelical churches everywhere, it is open and accessible to all. But the China Christian Council has yet to discover a sense of church formal unity, embodied in institutions and an accepted church order. It is desperately short of trained clergy and theological educators.

The strengths and weaknesses of the two churches are complementary. The liturgy and mission of the Mar Thoma Church can contribute to the discussion of Christian unity in China, just as the Chinese experience of post-denominationalism and informal community can enliven the ecumenical discussion in the Mar Thoma Church. The possibilities for mutual learning and exchange between the two communions are many, and they can enrich the broader ecumenical discussion of the relationship between worship and mission for churches everywhere.

Appendix I
Syrian Christians and Other Churches in Kerala

Oriental Orthodox Churches

Malankara Orthodox Syrian Church (Metran Kashi)* (autocephalic in spiritual communion with Antioch)	2,200,000
Malankara Syrian Orthodox Church (Bara Kashi)* (jurisdiction of the Patriarch of Antioch and All the East)	1,300,000
Malankara Syrian Knanya Church* (jurisdiction of the Patriarch of Antioch and All the East)	100,000
Independent Thozhiyur Syrian Church (Antiochan rite)*	20,000
Chaldean Syrian Church of the East in Trichur (Nestorian)*	30,000

Roman Catholic Churches

Syro-Malankara Catholic Church*	350,000
Syrian Knanaya Catholic Church*	150,000
Syro-Malabar Catholic Church (Chaldean rite; 12 dioceses)*	3,000,000
Other Latin Rite Catholics*	220,000

Protestant Churches, including Mar Thoma

Mar Thoma Church (6 Kerala dioceses)*	450,000
St. Thomas Evangelical Church of India*	20,000 (?)
Church of South India (4 Kerala dioceses)*	400,000
Travancore-Cochin Anglican Church (5 dioceses)	300,000
Other Protestants and Pentecostals	unavailable

*indicates churches that are predominantly or overwhelmingly Syrian Christians

Figures in this table are taken from A. K. Thomas, *The Christians of Kerala*, 2nd ed. (Kottayam, 2001).

Appendix II
The Syrian Christians of India

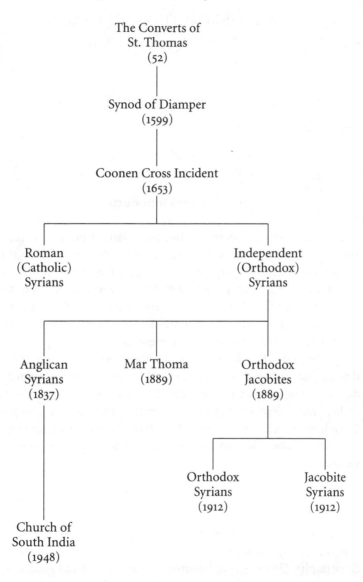

The Converts of
St. Thomas
(52)

Synod of Diamper
(1599)

Coonen Cross Incident
(1653)

Roman
(Catholic)
Syrians

Independent
(Orthodox)
Syrians

Anglican
Syrians
(1837)

Mar Thoma
(1889)

Orthodox
Jacobites
(1889)

Orthodox
Syrians
(1912)

Jacobite
Syrians
(1912)

Church of
South India
(1948)

Adapted from Susan Visvanathan, *The Christians of Kerala: History, Belief and Ritual Among the Yakoba* (Madras: Oxford University Press, 1993).

A Traditional Thanksgiving Festival
in South Korea: Chusok

SEUNG JOONG JOO

Editor's Introduction

Rituals can lose their resonance when transplanted into a new cultural context. This is true of Thanksgiving in Korea, where the Christian church practices Thanksgiving worship in November, as taught by Western missionaries, says Seung Joong Joo. A Korean festival of thanksgiving is available to Korean Christians: the traditional Chusok celebration, observed in September or October. During this nationwide festival, Koreans dress in traditional silk clothing and commemorate their ancestors with offerings of the harvest.

Although Chusok has greater cultural resonance with Koreans, and although Thanksgiving worship in late November seems anticlimactic and redundant to worshiping Koreans, the Christian church has yet to adopt Chusok as its primary ritual of Thanksgiving worship. Here Seung Joong Joo explains Chusok, summarizes the history of the Protestant thanksgiving worship in Korea, and describes the potential synthesis of Chusok and Christian thanksgiving worship.

•   •

The Korean church has been growing rapidly in the number and size of congregations, making it a rare case of robust growth in the history of Asian Christianity. However, Christianity in Korea is still not rooted in the hearts of the people, as many Koreans see Christianity as having been imported by foreign missionaries. For this reason, Korean Protestant Christianity does not yet have a harmonious relationship with Korean traditional culture.

From the beginning, the relationship between Christianity and Korean culture has not been positive. Early Protestant missionaries who came to Korea at the end of the nineteenth century contributed considerably to the conflict, since they had a negative view of Korean culture. Most early Protestant missionaries called Korean culture pagan, and taught that American culture was a genuine Christian culture. To become Christians, Koreans had to eliminate their own culture and traditions from their lives. To this day, there is a great disconnect between their lives as Christians and their lives as Koreans.

Most nations, whether developed or not, celebrate harvest in one way or another. For instance, when Americans give thanks, they recall the first Thanksgiving held by Puritan settlers in New England. In Korea, the great traditional thanksgiving festival day is called *Chusok,* the harvest moon festival held on the fifteenth of August on the lunar calendar. Koreans call it the Full Moon Festival or the Harvest Moon Day, and it usually falls in September or October on the solar calendar.

The problem is that the Korean Church keeps its thanksgiving day on the third Sunday of November, as introduced by early American missionaries to Korea. This "foreign" festival prevails in Korean Christianity, although a small number of congregations have begun having the Thanksgiving service on the Korean Moon Festival. The discrepancy between the cultural and the Christian thanksgiving celebrations is one of the reasons Christianity has not been rooted in the hearts of the Korean people.

Chusok: The Traditional Thanksgiving Day Celebration

Chusok, the Harvest Festival, is the Korean Thanksgiving. This great national holiday of the year falls on the fifteenth day of the eighth lunar month, usually September or October on the solar calendar. As this date marks the harvest time, it is regarded as the traditional Thanksgiving Day and is celebrated as enthusiastically as the lunar New Year's Day. This holiday is observed nationally to celebrate the new harvest, cherish the memory of one's ancestors, and renew family ties. Today, Chusok is officially observed as a three-day traditional holiday; in practice, most Koreans spend almost a week celebrating this festival.

The origin of Chusok lies far back in the history of Korea. In fact, Chusok is one of the oldest Korean holidays. According to *Samguk-sagi (The History of the Three Kingdoms),* the Harvest Moon Festival started during the reign of King Yuri (24-56) of the Shilla Kingdom.[1] Meanwhile, it is said that the ancient people selected the fifteenth day of the eighth moon for their thanksgiving celebration because of shamanistic beliefs. They were afraid of the shadows at night. Because of the shadows, they could not see anything, such as the approach of wild animals or the attack of enemies. On the other hand, early Koreans were delighted when there was a bright full moon, so they had a festival on bright moonlit nights. This led to shamanistic rituals related to celebrations of the harvest moon, which is the biggest and brightest moon of the year. Many folklore scholars think these rituals may be the origin of the Full Moon Festival (Chusok) in Korea.

Chusok denotes a time when Korean people offer homage to their ancestors with freshly harvested grains and fruits. It also has the seasonal peculiarity of being neither too cold nor too hot, as well as the availability of a bounty of newly ripened crops and fruit. Thus, all farmers and the whole nation enjoy this day as a thanksgiving day, with wine, cakes, and other food made with the new grain. All delicacies of the season are made from the newly harvested crops and fruits, and *songpyeon* (a moon-shaped rice cake) is probably the season's most popular delicacy.

There are three types of important sacrificial rites performed by a family on behalf of their ancestors in Korea. These rites include "tea rites"

---

1. Seung-Gee Hong, "*Chusok:* The Korean Version of Thanksgiving," *Asian Culture Quarterly* 17, no. 4 (1989): 1.

(charye), "household rites" (kijesa), and "seasonal rites" (sije).[2] The tea rites are ancestral sacrifices held during the daytime on such important holidays as lunar New Year or Chusok. On Chusok, all members of the family, after washing up in the morning, wear beautiful traditional silk clothes (hanbok) and gather in the house of the head of the family. They hold a memorial service praying for the souls of four generations of ancestors and for blessings on the family.

After the ceremony at home, families visit their ancestors' graves (Seongmyo) in the mountains. Visiting a grave is a time-honored custom. Family members line up before the grave and express their love and respect. The eldest member of the family tells the youngsters about the proud achievements of their ancestors and stresses their filial duties. This ancestral rite, which is deeply embedded in Korean tradition, is one of the most important customs practiced on Chusok. For example, one of the filial duties is to mow wild grasses on the graves. Even today, if any grave is left untended, the descendants are scorned for their lack of filial piety.

Chusok combines the traditional ritual of ancestor worship with the fruitfulness of the season to inspire homecoming and family reunions. One folklore scholar argues that "to the modern society of Korea, the significance and function of Chusok are in reuniting families separated by urbanization and recovering family unity through the ancestral ceremony, rather than a 'harvest festival.'"[3] Another scholar suggests that "Chusok is an occasion to pay homage to one's ancestors and thus to strengthen the bonds not only among the living members of a family but also with all who have gone before. . . . Therefore, Chusok plays an important role in reuniting families separated by the exigencies of modern life."[4]

Chusok is essentially an agricultural holiday. With the harvest completed, each family makes rice cakes, wine, and other foods with the newly harvested crops. After prayers for their ancestors and visits to their graves, each family exchanges gifts of food with its neighbors. The Korean people still think of Chusok as a festive time to share food, wine, and fellowship with relatives and neighbors. Therefore, Chusok has been

---

2. Kwang-Kyu Lee, "The Practice of Traditional Family Rituals in Contemporary Urban Korea," *Journal of Ritual Studies* 3, no. 2 (1989): 173

3. In-soo Sohn, *Educational Annual Customs of Korea* (Seoul: Moon Um Sa, 1991), p. 227.

4. Seung-gee Hong, "*Chusok:* The Korean Version of Thanksgiving," p. 5.

observed with sincerity and pleasure by sharing in human fellowship and good neighborliness.

A History of the Thanksgiving Service
in the Korean Protestant Church

The first Christian Thanksgiving service in Korea was held in 1901. The report of the Presbyterian Mission (Northern) gave an account of this first thanksgiving worship service:

> In *Chung Wha* district was inaugurated this year the harvest festival of first fruits. A letter was sent to each group of the *Chung Wha* and *Sang One* Magistracies asking them to meet at *Chung Wha* on July 21st and spend the day in a service of praise and thanksgiving, asking each to bring as a thank offering a measure of barley or wheat from the recent harvest. The letter received a most hearty response, every group sending representatives. All day Saturday they kept coming in, each with his measure of wheat or barley on his back, and on Sabbath morning those living near came in until 210 had gathered. Everybody came in the best of spirits, and a most inspiring meeting was held. After a testimony meeting, during which each group told of the blessings they had received, we had a solemn communion service, which was appreciated by all present.[5]

This report contains several interesting observations. First, the Thanksgiving worship was observed on July 21. Since that region cultivated mostly barley or wheat, the worship service was held in July, when barley and wheat are harvested. Thus, the first Korean Thanksgiving service had no relation to American Thanksgiving, which is in November. Second, the service included a "testimony meeting" in which worshipers shared their blessings of the past year. Third, this Thanksgiving worship concluded with a solemn communion service.

The first Korean Presbyterian Council of 1901 resolved to adopt Thanksgiving as an official holiday. "After one of the conferences, a discussion on 'Thanksgiving Day,' it was decided to adopt a day, and a committee was appointed to consult with other denominations, and see if a common

5. Annual Report of the Board of Foreign Missions of the PCUSA (1901), p. 208.

day could not be agreed upon. November 10 (Sunday) was adopted for that year only."[6] Finally, in 1906, the Presbyterian Council set November 19 (Sunday) aside as Thanksgiving Day.[7]

Thus, by 1906, there were two kinds of thanksgiving days. One was the official day in November, and the other was the unofficial day in July. The latter gradually came to be called *Maekchu Kamsajol* (Thanksgiving Day for the Harvest of Barley), whereas the former was named *Chusu Kamsajol* (Thanksgiving Day for the General Harvest). These two kinds of thanksgiving days are still observed today.

In 1908, Thanksgiving Day was set as the last Thursday in November. In the 1914 General Assembly, Thanksgiving Day was changed to the Wednesday following the third Sunday in November, to coincide with the date of the first missionary's arrival in Korea. However, this changed date for Thanksgiving appears to have its origins in the American Thanksgiving tradition, despite the supposed rationale. According to a famous church historian, "we do not even know who that first missionary was."[8] Therefore, it is generally believed that the November Thanksgiving Day in Korea was based on the American Thanksgiving introduced by the early Protestant missionaries.

The Problem of Contextualization for the Korean Church's Thanksgiving Day Festival

Today, Protestant churches in Korea celebrate Thanksgiving Day on the third Sunday of November. The problem is that by late November, it is already winter in Korea, and there is no spirit of thanksgiving among most Koreans. Thus, when a minister preaches on the subject of thanksgiving on that day, most congregations feel awkward, for the great thanksgiving day, Chusok, is already two months passed. Thus, keeping Thanksgiving on the third Sunday of November is problematic among Koreans and the church.

To make it more meaningful, the current Christian Thanksgiving should be moved to the traditional Korean thanksgiving day. Recently, a

6. C. A. Clark, *Digest of the Presbyterian Church of Korea (Chosen)* (Seoul: Korean Religious Book & Tract Society, 1918), p. 19.

7. Clark, *Digest of the Presbyterian Church of Korea*, p. 26.

8. L. George Paik, *The History of Protestant Missions in Korea, 1832-1910* (Pyengyang, Korea: Union Christian College Press, 1929), p. 378.

small number of congregations have initiated a Thanksgiving service on Chusok, using folk drama and traditional songs with traditional musical instruments. This movement should be encouraged to contextualize the Christian festival in the Korean church.

If the Protestant churches of Korea would have a Thanksgiving Sunday near Chusok with the character of a family reunion, then it might be more appealing to Korean Christians. As I mentioned earlier, Chusok is the day not only for thanksgiving but also for homecoming and family re-unions in Korea. Thus, if the Korean church could adapt the notion of homecoming to the Sunday celebration near Chusok, then the church's thanksgiving celebration will be more meaningful to Korean Christians. The church could then celebrate thanksgiving with the whole congrega-tion, a new family in Christ, the communion of the saints.

This new family in Christ is much larger than a biological family and includes not only the living members of the family but also faithful ances-tors. Thus, in addition to moving the Thanksgiving service to Chusok, it needs to have the character of a family reunion in terms of the commu-nion of the saints, the reunion of the whole faith community in Christ. In this way, Korean Christians can naturally thank and worship God with their whole hearts and minds without losing their cultural identity.

The Eucharistic Meal and the Ritual Meal of Chusok

If the Protestant churches of Korea celebrate a Thanksgiving Sunday near Chusok, the Eucharist should be given on that day. Since Chusok is the thanksgiving feast, the meal plays an important role in this festival. The Korean people offer homage to their ancestors with freshly harvested grains and fruits on Chusok. After that, they enjoy the thanksgiving family feast and each family exchanges gifts of food with its neighbors. Therefore, the ritual meal on Chusok could be another point of contact between Ko-rean culture and Christianity. The eucharistic meal on a Thanksgiving Sunday near Chusok would become a meaningful Lord's Supper for the Korean Christians in the context of the distinctive cultural value attached to the tradition of the ritual meal.

Unfortunately, however, the Protestant churches of Korea share the Lord's Supper only twice — or at most four times — a year. Twice a year is most common, usually Easter and Thanksgiving Sunday in November, although some churches have communion on Christmas instead. In other words, Easter, Christmas, and Thanksgiving Sunday are the only times when Korean churches celebrate the eucharistic meal.

Nobody knows either why or how long the Korean churches have celebrated the Lord's Supper on these occasions. It may be due to the influence of the theology of John Calvin, the Reformed theologian who has had the most influence on the Protestant churches of Korea. Even though John Calvin declared that the Lord's Supper ought to be celebrated "every Sunday," he eventually agreed to a monthly communion. And later on, he agreed to celebrating the Lord's Supper only four times a year, on Easter, Pentecost, Christmas, and the first Sunday of September. Even though the Korean churches have never held the Lord's Supper on Pentecost, they do serve it on Thanksgiving Sunday. If these churches were to celebrate the Lord's Supper on a new Thanksgiving Sunday near Chusok, then it would be more in agreement with Calvin's first Sunday of September.

One further aspect to consider is the meaning of the Lord's Supper if it were held on Thanksgiving Sunday near Chusok. According to "Baptism, Eucharist and Ministry" (BEM), which was produced by the World Council of Churches in 1982, the Eucharist has five meanings: as thanksgiving to the Father, as memorial of Christ, as invocation of the Spirit, as communion of the faithful, and as meal of the kingdom.[9] BEM explains the most important meaning of the Eucharist: "Eucharist is the great thanksgiving to the Father for everything accomplished in creation, redemption and sanctification, for everything accomplished by God now in the Church and in the world in spite of the sins of human beings, for everything that God will accomplish in bringing the Kingdom to fulfillment. Thus the Eucharist is the benediction by which the Church expresses its thankfulness for all God's benefits."[10] Indeed, the church's experience of God's self-giving in the Lord's Supper is that of joyful thanksgiving. Through the celebration of the Eucharist, the church gives thanks to God for everything that God has made, is making, and will make. And, as we have seen, the ritual meal is one of the most important features of Chusok. Thus, on this day, if the Korean church could have the eucharistic meal with thanksgiving for everything God has done, is doing, and will do, then

---

9. For the five meanings of the Eucharist from the World Council of Churches, see *Baptism, Eucharist and Ministry* (Geneva: World Council of Churches, 1982), pp. 10-17.

10. *Baptism, Eucharist and Ministry*, p. 10.

Korean Christians could truly celebrate this new Thanksgiving Sunday with joy, gratitude, and meaning in the context of Korean tradition.

The Contextualized Thanksgiving Service of Myung Sung Presbyterian Church in Seoul, Korea

Myung Sung Presbyterian Church in Seoul is one of the biggest Presbyterian churches in Korea. The church has more than sixty thousand members and has seven worship services on every Lord's Day. Rev. Sam Hwan Kim is also interested in Korean traditional culture and always encourages the congregation to praise God by using Korean tunes and traditional musical instruments in worship services throughout the year. The Thanksgiving service at Myung Sung Presbyterian Church exemplifies the adoption of traditional Korean culture.

Here is the order of the Thanksgiving Service of October 27, 2002.

Opening Call to Thanksgiving . . . . Worship Leader
Hymn of Praise (Korean Tune) . . . . Children & Singers
Offertory Song . . . . Choirs
Offering with Harvest . . . . Congregation
Corporate Prayer . . . . Congregation
Hymn: "We Plow the Fields, and Scatter" . . . . Congregation
Scripture Reading: 1 Kings 16:8-10 and 25-29, Colossians 3:15-17 . . . . . Reader
Hymn of Thanksgiving . . . . Elders
Anthem . . . . Choirs
Sermon #1: Give Thanks to the Lord . . . . Rev Kim
Hymn of Thanksgiving: Classical Liturgical Dance
    & Praise with Traditional Song . . . . Liturgical Dance Team
A Skit Drama with Praise . . . . Parishioners
Sermon #2 . . . . Rev Kim
Sharing Thanksgiving Cake . . . . Congregation
A Skit Drama with Praise . . . . Parishioners
Offering with Tithes: "O, the Help that God has given" . . . . . . Congregation
Prayer for Offering . . . . Rev Kim
Fellowship and Welcoming . . . . Rev Kim
Hymn: "Give Thanks with My Spirit" . . . . Congregation
Blessing . . . . Rev Kim
Postlude . . . . Choirs

Many Korean cultural elements are reflected in this Thanksgiving worship service. First, the purpose of the worship service is to express gratitude and to respond thankfully to the gracious initiative of God. Because of the grace so richly bestowed upon them by God through Christ, worshipers do everything with thanksgiving in this service. However, it is frustrating that the worship does not include the Eucharist. The word *Eucharist* means "thanksgiving"; what could be more appropriate than for Korean Christians to celebrate the great thanksgiving represented by the Eucharist on their traditional thanksgiving day? Second, Chusok is the festival of family reunion; thus, the church needs to summon the whole family of God to celebrate this festival with thanks. Leaders at Myung Sung Presbyterian Church always encourage the congregation to invite people who have not been to church for some time and anyone else who can come to the church, so that the whole family of God may participate in the Thanksgiving service and give thanks to God. Third, Chusok is the time for sharing. Thus, after the service, the whole congregation is invited to participate in the fellowship meal. They even share the traditional Thanksgiving traditional cakes *(songpyeon)* during the service. By sharing a meal and the traditional cakes together, the whole congregation reaffirms that they are the family of God and the body of Christ in the context of their traditional meal. Fourth, it is recommended that the minister, worship leader, and choir members wear *hanbok* (traditional clothing) and *dooroomagi* (a traditional gentleman's coat) as vestments. Rev. Kim always encourages people to come to the Thanksgiving service in traditional clothes, and he himself always wears a white *dooroomagi* to this service. Fifth, some traditional Korean musical instruments, such as a brass gong, a drum, a bamboo oboe, a *kayakum* (a Korean harp with twelve strings), and an hourglass-shaped drum, are used in the Thanksgiving service. The drum and an hourglass-shaped drum are played with organ accompaniment during the congregational hymns and Psalms. Many traditional Korean tunes are also used for the congregational hymns. Sixth, the minister, the elders, and choir members process, accompanied by the appropriate signs of the harvest, which include various baskets filled with fruits and grains that are brought to the altar.

Many traditional festivals still greatly affect the lives of the Korean people as well as most Christians in Korea. Korean Protestant Christianity, however, does not have harmonious relations with these traditional festivals. One of the basic laws of communication is that no message is meaningful or comprehensible unless it is communicated in understandable cultural forms, for "human beings are tied to culture and cannot be evangelized unless they are addressed in terms of their own culture."[11] Thus the gospel message, to become meaningful to human beings, has to be incarnated in the cultural forms of the people for whom it is intended. In this sense, the gospel message, including the worship service, requires an integral method for effective communication: contextualization.

Contextualization has been defined as the "process of incarnating the Good News in a particular cultural context"[12] or "the process by which indigenous cultural forms and ideas are utilized to communicate Christian truth within a given cultural milieu without changing essential biblical meanings."[13] I would suggest that the process of contextualization applies to all dimensions of human life and development. Within contemporary Christianity, contextualization signifies the movement that takes local cultures and their values as the basic instrument and a powerful means for presenting, reformulating, and living Christianity. Within this process, an effective dialogue between Christianity and the local culture could be carried out. Therefore, I suggest that the adoption of Chusok by Protestant churches in Korea would be a significant example of contextualization and encourage these churches to consider ways in which contextualization of Christian worship can be implemented throughout the rest of the year.

11. Aylward Shorter, *Toward a Theology of Inculturation* (Maryknoll, N.Y.: Orbis Books, 1992), p. 77.

12. Dean S. Gilliland, "Contextual Theology as Incarnational Mission," in *The Word Among Us,* ed. Dean S. Gilliland (Dallas: Word Publishing, 1989), p. 12.

13. Gilliland, "Contextual Theology as Incarnational Mission," p. 13.

Worship and Culture in Latin America

MIGUEL A. PALOMINO AND SAMUEL ESCOBAR

In the last two decades, new models of worship have emerged in the midst of deep religious changes in Latin America. The proliferation of a wide variety of groups has given birth to an assortment of worship expressions that observers regard as the natural result of the process of pentecostalization taking place in the region. This process becomes another part of the ongoing cultural amalgamation that turns ever changing Latin American cultures into "hybrid constructions."[1] The struggle for legitimacy in the religious field might be considered as part of that process. The hybrid nature of the resulting movements in Latin America makes it difficult to classify them, but we could use the distinction Vinson Synan makes between classic Pentecostalism, also known as "Popular Protestantism," "neo-Pentecostalism" present in several older denominations, and "Third World Indigenous Groups."[2] The latter have an atypical constitution that does not necessarily follow the Latin American evangelical tradition brought by the missionary movement rooted in European Pietism and the nineteenth-century American revival, which is the kind of Protestantism that first arrived on this continent.

Intentional efforts to study the worship expressions in the life of the Latin American churches began in the 1970s.[3] One of the first studies was

1. See Néstor García Canclini, *Culturas híbridas: estrategias para entrar y salir de la modernidad* (Buenos Aires: Fondo de Cultura Económica, 1997).

2. For a discussion of Vinson Synan's classification and other approaches to the issue see Karl-Wilhelm Westmeier, *Protestant Pentecostalism in Latin America* (Cranbury, N.J.: Associated University Presses, 1999), pp. 15-21, and Samuel Escobar, *Changing Tides* (Maryknoll, N.Y.: Orbis, 2002), pp. 77-84.

3. We will not review all the literature published by Latin authors on the subject. We

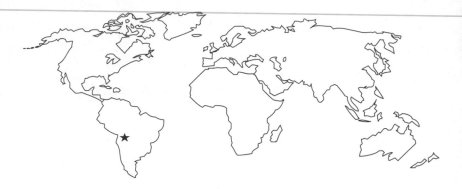

about the meaning of worship among the historic Protestant churches of Argentina and Uruguay, published in 1972 by the Centro de Estudios Cristianos under the title of *Culto: Crítica y Búsqueda*. This work analyzes, among other things, the influence of Catholicism and the immigrant churches on evangelical Christians. In 1974 missiologist Orlando Costas wrote about worship in the Pentecostal church, a piece that proved to be groundbreaking research that not even Pentecostals had attempted until that point.[4] Two valuable chapters about Latin America appeared in a volume that came out of a global study sponsored by the World Evangelical Fellowship. While Felicity Houghton offered a reflective phenomenological piece appreciative of Pentecostal patterns, Guillermo Méndez outlined a theological chapter about the traditional evangelical position.[5]

Another effort is that of the quarterly *Misión* edited by René Padilla from 1982 to 2001. From its first edition it dedicated a section to liturgy, where Eduardo Ramirez developed several models of worship to be used in evangelical churches. *Casa Bautista de Publicaciones* did the same through *Preludio,* a periodical that included music for worship, and which provided

---

will limit ourselves to works that only deal with worship in non-liturgical churches. For those interested in other confessions, see Edilberto Márquez, *Is There a Peruvian Liturgy in the Evangelical Church?* (Tayport, Escocia: Mac Research, 1995), and Nelson Kirst, *Culto Cristiano: Historia, Teología y Formas* (Quito: CLAI, 2000).

4. See René Padilla, *Fe Cristiana y Latinoamérica Hoy* (Buenos Aires: Certeza, 1974).

5. See Felicity Houghton, "Some Reflections on the Meaning and Practice of Worship from Inside South America," and Guillermo Méndez, "Worship in the Independent Free Church Congregational Tradition," in D. A. Carson, ed., *Worship: Adoration and Action* (Grand Rapids: Baker — Paternoster, 1993), pp. 158-77.

ideas and popularized Latin composers. Two books that deserve our attention are Miguel Darino's *La Adoración* (1992), where he reflects on biblical and historical patterns of worship from the perspective of the Latino communities of the United States, and *Adoremos* by Marcos Witt (1993), singer and composer whom many regard as the initiator of the praise renewal movement in Latin America. In his book Witt defines worship, taking into account the Scriptures and his own experience as a music minister.

When referring to Latin American worship, Witt is actually talking about *culto,* which both in Spanish and Portuguese conveys the idea of any meeting where prayer, Bible reading, preaching, and other liturgical components are performed both formally and informally. These gatherings can take place in church buildings, homes, or any other location that people might find suitable. It is here where praising God is expressed with deep intensity. Therefore, the Christian *culto* is the key to understanding worship, because the church materializes itself in it.[6]

This chapter is an account of the way the *culto* is carried out in the context of contemporary worship in Latin American evangelical and Pentecostal churches. We will begin by reviewing its development in the past years; then we will analyze its structure and components; and will conclude with particular reflections that may lead us to elaborate a theology of the *culto.*

Culto in Historical Perspective

To understand worship in Latin America — that vast territory that goes from Cabo de Hornos in Chile to the Río Grande in Mexico — it is important to bear in mind that traditional *culto* was shaped by the three Protestant streams that arrived on the continent originally.[7] The first stream came with the European immigrants in the late nineteenth and early twentieth centuries. They settled mainly in Brazil, Uruguay, Argentina, Chile, Venezuela, Mexico, and Paraguay, and scholars describe the

6. See João Ferreira, "Compreendendo o Culto Cristão: Uma Perspectiva Bíblica," *Revista Teológica* 61, no. 52 (July-Dec. 2001): 9.

7. For a discussion of the typologies of Protestantism in Latin America see Samuel Escobar, "The Promise and Precariousness of Latin American Protestantism," in Daniel R. Miller, ed., *Coming of Age,* Calvin Center Series (Lanham, Md.: University Press of America, 1994), pp. 6-7, and Westmeier, *Protestant Pentecostalism in Latin America,* pp. 15-21.

churches they established as "transplant churches." These churches were the place where their native language and culture was preserved, and where they continued practicing the same liturgical patterns they performed back home. As time passed and new generations came, these immigrant churches tended to isolate themselves from the rest of the community, a pattern still clear today.[8]

The second stream came with missionaries from Great Britain and the United States, strongly influenced by pietism, the nineteenth-century revivals, and the Holiness movement. These missionaries emphasized individual conversion understood as an emotional crisis, literalism in the interpretation of the Bible, and a minimal commitment of the believers to the secular world. This approach to Christianity was reflected in worship services where the main goal was preaching the gospel to evangelize the lost. Worship patterns of the missionaries reflected the worldview of the lower middle classes in Great Britain or the United States, with an emphasis on order, propriety, and dignity; they were translated and adopted with little or no reflection about the context, and almost no instruction to the congregants about appropriate theology and practice of worship.

The third stream came with the Pentecostal movement at the beginning of the twentieth century. This movement brought a new worldview translated into a particular pneumatology, personal ethics, and music. The fact that the movement was born among the poor classes in the English-speaking world, including African Americans, should be taken into account to understand its worship patterns. Pentecostal churches rapidly immersed themselves in Latin American culture, and ventured to incorporate native tunes, guitars, and tambourines in their services. Though severely criticized by other evangelicals, Pentecostal worship would find good soil mainly among the poor, who seemed more responsive to this type of *culto* — where miracles and other manifestations would happen and there would be less concern for propriety — perhaps because the poor are open to believe in the supernatural more readily than others.

The influence of these traditions had a threefold effect on Latin

8. This phenomenon was already recorded and studied years back in the Río de la Plata area (Argentina, Uruguay, and Paraguay), where, according to Ronald Maitland, these churches had been aware that their liturgies did not respond to the necessities and expectations of the population, and therefore they had to look for ways of being relevant to the people. See Carlos Valle, *Culto: Crítica y Búsqueda* (Buenos Aires: Centro de Estudios Cristianos, 1972).

American worship. First, it delayed its development and the formation of an identity. Traditionally, churches, no matter what their denominational background, have displayed for years a similar pattern of *culto:* organ prelude, invocatory prayer, hymns, offerings, reading of Scripture, preaching, and doxology. Songs, more than anything else, reflected a kind of spirituality that was not rooted in Latin America but in cultures from other latitudes, which were loaded with individualism and a pessimistic view of the world.[9] This situation began to change with the publication of music written by Latino authors that had both indigenous rhythm and lyrics, which certainly served to create a propitious atmosphere of worship in accordance with the cultural context.[10]

Second, this early worship tradition placed the directing of the *culto* mainly in the hands of the clergy, which limited the participation of the congregation in the service. Generally speaking, people would go to church just to listen to the sermon and sing a few hymns. As in the Catholic mass, only the minister would perform, and the believer would watch whatever happened on the stage. This passive participation created an attitude of "receiving" rather than "giving," which made the service monotonous. This eventually hindered the core value of worship: that is, to express with acts and words recognition of God as Lord.

Third, early worship patterns encouraged the improvisation of the *culto* where everything, including sometimes the sermons, would seem not to have been well prepared. Numerical growth and the lack of adequate ministerial training gave way to uneducated leadership that tended to improvise, especially at the more popular levels. Although improvisation is an important skill for Latin Americans, it is also likely that this can be perceived as chaos and lack of reverence.

9. See "Cantos Comunes de Algunas Iglesias" in Valle, *Culto,* where Pablo Sosa analyzes some hymnbooks and comes to the conclusion that there is still not an indigenous hymnody on this continent.

10. It is worth mentioning *Cancionero Abierto* published by ISEDET (1970s), and the series *Corazón y Voz* by Casa Bautista de Publicaciones (1970s). Today *Celebremos Su Gloria* (Texas: Celebremos/Libros Alianza, 1992) is perhaps one of the few songbooks widely used in Latin America that has made the effort to include Latino composers in its collection.

Development of Contemporary Worship

Changes began to take place during the decade of the 1960s, as radio station HCJB, broadcasting in Quito, Ecuador, and Evangelism In Depth, a Costa Rica-based evangelistic program, developed missionary strategies that aimed to reach the whole region, anticipating a kind of evangelical globalization that would affect denominational bodies as well as local churches. Let us reflect on some of the key elements that eventually brought worship to the point where it is now.

The Sixties: Traditional Worship

Until the 1960s the evangelical church had basically kept the same worship service scheme that for many years had been the model to follow, with the sermon as the centerpiece. In the late 1950s, evangelistic teams of Youth for Christ and HCJB started to promote Latin American composers such as Guatemalan Alfredo Colom, whose hymns became popular throughout Latin America. Following the American revivalist tradition, these evangelistic teams included "song leaders," and Latin Americans were chosen for that purpose. Subtle changes came because of the new church music that HCJB and other local stations broadcasted widely in Latin America. Short, upbeat songs — known as *coritos* — pioneered by Manuel Bonilla, Brus del Monte, and others, soon made their way to evangelical congregations, attracting mainly young people regardless of denomination. Subsequently, U.S. composers such as Ralph Carmichael, Andraé Crouch, and the Gaither Brothers would become familiar names as their music was translated into Spanish and sung as *coritos*. These songs were played with the guitar, an instrument that some churches, mainly Pentecostal ones, had started using, although in many circles it was still considered an inappropriate instrument for worship. Young people favored the guitar over the organ because it lent itself to playing local tunes and making the services more lively, and it was less costly and easier to learn to play and to carry around. The *culto* then had two parts: one at the very beginning, in which only *coritos* were sung in a kind of warming-up time waiting for latecomers to arrive; and the second part that was carried out in the conventional way. It soon became evident that far more *hermanos* (brothers and sisters from church) preferred the first part that was informal, joyful, and more open for them to express their praises to God.

The Seventies: Contemporary Worship

Two movements that developed in Latin America during the seventies affected the church in many ways. One was the Renewal Movement that spread very rapidly from Argentina to other countries, radically influencing the concept of worship through new *coritos* that emphasized the kingdom of God rather than personal testimonies as traditional hymns did.[11] The other movement was a wave of strong nationalism related to some military regimes and populist movements that spread through practically every nation of the region. This brought a renewed search for the indigenous as well as the old Spanish roots of culture. It was an effort to recover the Latin American identity, reflected in the rise and growth of a strong revival of folkloric music and poetry. It connected with renewal trends in the Catholic culture as a result of the Vatican II Council, with its emphasis on a liturgy in the language of the people. In places such as Argentina, Mexico, and Nicaragua, contextual versions of the Mass and folkloric paraphrases of the Gospels became popular even among people who did not affiliate with a church.

Within the frame of this recovery of folklore, the School of Music of Union Seminary (ISEDET) in Buenos Aires fostered research and the creation of worship materials. Ecumenical theologians such as Mortimer Arias and Federico Pagura wrote lyrics for which Latin American tunes were created or arranged by musicians such as Pablo Sosa, Homero Perera, and Alejandro Núñez. This material was collected in *Cancionero Abierto,* a series of songbooks published between 1974 and 1979. This trend made churches appreciate folkloric tunes and lyrics that would speak of worship and Christian commitment in a manner not conceived of before. Folk groups like *Trío Mar del Plata* of Argentina, *Oasis* of Chile, and *Kerygma* of Peru undoubtedly helped change the conception of the use of indigenous music in worship and evangelism. As a result, traditional duets, trios, and quartets that dominated church music in the past decades had to give way to new bands that began to emerge everywhere. Because of this phenomenon, the *culto* experienced a renewal, since leaders sought greater participation by lay people, and worship became more spontaneous and informal, and therefore much longer than services in the past. Later, worship

---

11. See Samuel Berberián, *Dos décadas de renovación en Latinoamérica, 1960-1980* (Guatemala: Ediciones Sa-Ver, 1986).

came accompanied by modern music, with drums, bass guitar, electric guitars, and other instruments that had not been part of the evangelical *culto* before.

The Eighties: Entertainment

It was during the eighties that the electronic church made its presence felt in Latin America.[12] The television format of shows like PTL and the 700 Club were reproduced in some churches, while others began to buy and rent movie theaters to convert them to church buildings, a phenomenon that today is characteristic of the region.[13] Social communicator Rolando Pérez rightly points out that in this type of liturgy there is a conscious appropriation of the show business world that can hardly be ignored. In his words,

> From the moment you enter a church, particularly in those of the upper and middle classes, the physical make-up of the place shows a significant adaptation of television's aesthetic structure. In fact, many churches have found that cinemas in Latin America are quite suited for holding church services. In the church itself, the decor, the placing of electronic equipment, the equalising sound — controlled from an electronic room — the use of electric musical instruments, are not only direct adaptations of media technology but of the symbolic codes of mass culture as well. Even poor churches have incor-

12. See Hugo Assman, *La iglesia electrónica y su impacto en América Latina* (San José, Costa Rica: Departamento Ecuménico de Investigaciones [DEI], 1988), and Dennis Smith, "The Impact of Religious Programming in the Electronic Media on the Active Christian Population in Central America," in *Latin American Pastoral Issues* (formerly *Occasional Essays,* San José, Costa Rica, Year XV, No. 1, July 1988).

13. In Lima, Peru, where this trend started at the beginning of 1980, Cuban Rodolfo González, pastor of *Casa de Dios Puerta del Cielo* church, bought the *28 de Julio* cinema located in one the most deprived and dangerous areas of the Peruvian capital city. Soon afterwards American preacher Jimmy Swaggart purchased the *Teatro Azul* for the Assemblies of God, and in the last few years several charismatic churches have been meeting in cinemas situated in the middle-class sectors of Lima. Similarly, Brazilian churches such as *Igreja Universal do Reino de Deus* have also shown interest in movie houses. However, behind this interest for cinemas another strategy is carried out quietly: the purchase of X-rated cinemas as a way of terminating pornography and other associated social ills.

porated elements of mass culture. Their sound equipment and musical instruments may be less sophisticated, but they are still there. In addition, one finds that the brightly coloured banners, the way the pastor leads the congregation, the service, and his carefully rehearsed movements speak of a staged ritual which modifies the traditional ceremony associated with the church building. The solemn services, the ceremonial or circumspect preachers, have been replaced by the pastor-entertainer, by the high-pitched voice, by the applause, and by the extremely rhythmic chanting.[14]

Pérez's observations seem to touch what has become the brand-name of entertainment liturgy: "show-biz" *culto* having the song leader as "master of ceremony." In a service like this almost anything goes. That is why observers would say that in this type of *culto* even personal testimonies and miracles that were part of Pentecostal church services in the past are manipulated to achieve a dramatic and emotional appeal to the audience.

The Nineties: Praise Renewal

During the nineties, churches began experiencing an unparalleled phenomenon with the influence of the praise and worship movement. The David Fisher International Symposium of Praise and Worship,[15] the music of Marcos Witt,[16] and the propagation of independent-charismatic groups played a big role in it. Cheerful praise songs had made their entrance during the 1980s, but a decade later they became the norm in churches everywhere. While old-time hymns were replaced by chants of all kinds, and the traditional preaching of the Word was relegated to a second or even lower level, people rapidly embraced this style of worship, which began to be called celebration. In a sense, the order of the service — or liturgy in some traditions — had given way to a loose and informal two- or three-hour lively gathering that for many resembled popular rock concerts or big par-

14. Rolando Pérez, "La cultura de los medios en la ritualidad evangélica," *Signos de Vida* (Quito: CLAI), no. 2, November 1996.

15. The Peruvian Bible scholar Moisés Chávez analyzes this movement in his *La Danza y los Movimientos de Renovación y El Meneíto del Rey David* (Lima: Centro de Estudios Bíblicos Casiodoro de Reina, 1995).

16. Regarded by many as the greatest innovator of evangelical music in Latin America.

ties. Believers made worship comparable to celebration, and therefore the sense of quiet intimacy with God, which had been an essential part of traditional worship, was lost. This phenomenon may well be called one of the most significant liturgical renewal movements the Latin American evangelical church has experienced in the last century, but we can also say that it has raised many theological questions pertaining to what worshiping God ought to be.

Worship Today

Interpreting worship in Latin America today is not an easy task. It took a century and a half for evangelical and Pentecostal churches to challenge the religious hegemony held by the Roman Catholic Church for over 500 years,[17] but the neo-Pentecostal churches are already reshaping the evangelical landscape of the region as well. Moving within the general frame of globalization, and thanks to their ability to use media that saturates the market with videos, cassettes, and radio and TV programs, the form of *culto* these new churches practice is showing its ability to redesign the evangelical and Pentecostal worship style throughout Latin America. Forecasting the future of the traditional *culto* might be more difficult than just observing the way it is now. A deeper look at the core practices and emphases of these new churches is necessary in order to understand whether or not this new model is here to stay.

Though worship leaders like to communicate with the congregation in a language seasoned with Pentecostal vocabulary, the message they convey would not seem to deliver the traditional Pentecostal beliefs but rather a new agenda comprised of praise and worship restoration, signs and wonders, spiritual warfare, and the prosperity gospel. With these elements, church services characterized by the new worship style have indeed challenged conventional patterns evangelicals have followed for decades. Traces of the old-time *culto* are still visible in the new model, but are clothed with new meaning. The question before us then is, "To what extent will this new way of worship be legitimized by traditional denomina-

17. Jean-Pierre Bastian, *La Mutación Religiosa de América Latina: Para Una Sociología del Cambio Social en la Modernidad Periférica* (México City: Fondo de Cultura Económica, 1997).

tions?" This is a difficult question to answer, but in the meantime the songs, prayers, preaching, and collection remain part of the service, though they are performed in ways rarely seen before. Collection, for instance, now takes the form of a business deal. Believers give expecting to receive from God healing, new jobs, or simply more money in return. The latter is known as the "Law of Sowing and Reaping."

This transformation is better understood within the setting of a postmodern cultural atmosphere favorable to the style of independent neo-Pentecostal groups. There is a dialectical relationship between these religious expressions that bring changes and the surrounding culture that at the same time is receptive to them and helps to shape them. These churches, where the visual is preferred over the word, are by far the fastest growing communities in Latin America. That is why the sermon, in the past the "most important part" of the service, has been replaced by music and miraculous signs performed right on the platform. Many believe this is the direction Latin American churches ought to go because we live in times when people are spiritual seekers. But we could also argue that the satisfaction that attendants to these meetings get from them may be due to an emotional catharsis they could also get from a rock concert or a soccer game. The specific reference to God and Jesus Christ in Christian spirituality leads people to a deeper personal relationship with God that is transforming towards holiness, a way of life in obedience to God, which may or may not include a strong emotional dimension. Latin culture is known to be emotional, and Latin worship includes that dimension. However, in the face of religious spectacle, where we can be touched by the songs and so forth, it is nonetheless too easy to go home not really having worshiped God at all.

Looking for Legitimacy through the *Culto*

The acts of worship that express the attitude of believers in relation to God are central to the Christian *culto*. The underlying principle of the worship service is that the Holy Spirit will pour out blessings upon the people in an explicit manner. The fact that neo-Pentecostals come to the *culto* expecting God to provide supernatural manifestations makes their worship service different from more traditional evangelical ones, where, generally speaking, attendees would not expect such a manifestation to occur. We need to understand that surprise is an important ingredient in their *culto,* which helps to explain why their services are so unpredictable and full of expectations. This may also explain why so many people from different social strata are attracted to these churches.

In a sense, the renewed *culto* resembles to some degree the classic Pentecostal one, but incorporates new components in order to make it even more emotional and appreciated by its listeners. The chart on p. 119 illustrates some of the differences between these two liturgical practices. For comparative purposes we have included a column for the traditional Protestant worship service in order to note the changes the evangelical *culto* has undergone in the last few years.

Since the *culto* is the most visible expression of collective worship, we intend to analyze it in order to comprehend the dynamic that takes place when leaders and worshipers meet together. Generally speaking, the *culto* involves three main actors whose participation is key to understanding not only the evolution of the evangelical worship service, but also the way this gathering might look in the future. These players include the song leader, the preacher, and the prayer warriors.[18]

The Song Leader

Music plays an important role in the new *culto,* and it is the song leader, with his praise band, who calls people to worship. A wide variety of tunes and rhythms are used, the soft ones being played to set the mood for praising the Lord during a period in which people claim God's presence is manifest.

The song leader follows a basic program structure to ensure the smooth flow of the *culto.* Several upbeat songs that proclaim what God has done or is doing among his people are used to open the service. Believers sing freely, raising their hands and clapping along with the music. Then the leader brings the songs down, moving toward quiet love songs to Jesus that allow worshipers to come into a moment of intimacy with God. This leads into the preaching, which finds a highly motivated audience eager to listen

---

18. I will follow the scheme used by Margaret Paloma from the University of Akron, Ohio, who studied the "Toronto Blessing" movement from a liturgical standpoint in "Charisma and Institutions: A Sociological Account of the 'Toronto Blessing'" (unpublished paper, 1999).

to the message. Musicians also play during the altar call at the end of the worship service. Songs chosen for this period are soft and calm, for they expect the Spirit will minister to those who come forward as well as those who remain seated in their chairs after the sermon has finished.

Differences in Liturgical Practices

Traditional Evangelicals	Classic Pentecostals	Neopentecostals
Conventional prayers	Faith prayers	Spiritual warfare prayers
Few, if any, testimonies	Testimony of personal conversion	Testimony of healing and economic prosperity
Hymns	Contemporary songs and hymns	Contemporary, well prepared music with instrumental and vocal bands
Sitting and standing occasionally	Clapping and raising of hands	Clapping, raising of hands, and liturgical dance
	"Baptized in the Spirit": expressed with seizures and glossolalia	"Slain in the Spirit": evidenced by falling backward, laughing, or imitating animal groans
Expository preaching	Narrative and allegoric preaching	Admonitory preaching urging to seek God's blessings
Tithes and offerings for the local church and denomination	Offerings to support the local pastor and church programs	Tithes and donations to support the different ministries and pastors involved in radio, TV, publications, and so forth
Religious symbols: cross and Bible	Religious symbols: cross, Bible, and pulpit	Religious symbols: cross, Bible, banners, blessed objects, etc.

Depending on the particular circumstances of some churches, the song leaders will play a more dominant role during the service. This is how pastor José Castrillón, the music minister in a Colombian church, describes his function:

It has been the norm for song leaders to lead the *culto* with verbal songs. But now we are seeing that God is speaking through the instruments, revealing things from the heart, and leading us to personal sanctification. This is very astonishing indeed, to the point that it is already 11:00 a.m. and the pastor has to say, "You should stop singing to give time for the Word." But then the drummer would begin to play, releasing times of freedom and spiritual warfare, and one says: "What should I do now?" Nothing but submerge ourselves in the "wave" of the Spirit. We do not need to create the wave of praise. God is raising it up and we are to ride it. I believe the outpouring of the Spirit is more evident every time. What we see now in the Ibero-American Church is something totally different to what we saw in the past. It is as though God were prophesying a new outpouring that we have never seen before. What we have seen until now is just a preparation for something bigger. God has been leading us to break old patterns. But He now wants to take us to a style of life that resembles a mature life in the Spirit. In former years God used liturgical dance to lead His people as a body towards a spontaneous response to the moving of the Lord. Thus, when some speak of it, they basically refer to marching in a symbolic attitude of war. But liturgical dance in itself is a response to the prophetic move of God. For instance, if we are praying for the ministers, the Lord may guide us to dance by using a war dance. We had an unusual experience the day worshipers were kidnapped from *La María* Catholic Church here in Cali.[19] We were in the service and the pastor was just about to preach, when God led us to a moment of silence and worship. Suddenly the drummer began playing his drums like we had never heard him before. The drum sound was urging people to march. People then stood up and marched around the sanctuary. It was an electrifying moment because it was a cry, a war call, and we took banners to surround the church.[20] The Lord

19. This incident took place in the parish *Santa María,* Cali, on 30 May 1999. It was 10:40 a.m., and the Mass was coming to an end, when members of *Ejército de Liberación Nacional* (National Liberation Army) burst into the church and took ninety-nine parishioners hostage. See "En Misa, Secuestrados 99," Colombian newspaper *El Heraldo,* 31 May 1999.

20. In the Spiritual Warfare movement banners play a very important role. The symbolism is taken from the people of Israel who used flags as a sign of authority and showed them off to the enemies during wartime. For Restorationists to raise banners in "spiritual places" is to lift God's name and declare war against spiritual beings. Colored banners have prophetic symbolism. For example, red flags are a symbol of Jesus' blood, and may be used when proclaiming that God is surrounding a country and bringing salvation to that nation. It

then led us to pray for pastors and ministers of our city, and to rebuke the spirit of kidnapping and death. We were still praying when somebody came to the pastor to tell him a woman was on the phone. She had been in *La María* where people had just been kidnapped. She wanted to talk to her sister who worshiped in our congregation. We had not heard anything about the kidnapping, but the Lord had put us to march and declare protection for His people.[21]

The Preacher

The preacher or speaker is the pivotal actor in the renewed *culto*. He or she is expected to address a biblical topic encouraging people to remain faithful to God. In general, these preachers tend to be social communicators in the sense that they use Scripture to uplift people's hearts, rather than oldtime preachers who would deliver solid theological treatises every Sunday. In part this is due to the constituency of the new churches, whose members seem to prefer light discourses, but it is also a function of these pastors' lack of formal theological training.

It is worth noting that preachers not only deliver the Word but also perform signs and wonders in the service as part of their role as pastors and leaders. Believers understand the preacher has the anointing and power of God to heal the sick and drive out evil spirits, and they come to him or her seeking relief for their physical pains and spiritual troubles.

A good example of this dynamic taking place is the *Yo Soy* church in Peru. Pastor Juana Hoyos comes to the pulpit and, after greeting the congregation, rebukes all negative influence present in the sanctuary. Then she turns in her Bible to Exodus 3 and says: "This is the Scripture for this morning."[22]

---

is also used to surround a country's flag to symbolize protection for the land. Blue flags symbolize celestial spheres and the Holy Spirit. A white flag means holiness. The crimson one speaks of redemption. As flag colors have a symbolic meaning, so do flag shapes. Thus spearhead-like flags are used as symbols of destruction and defeat of the enemy.

21. Extracts from an interview by Miguel Angel Palomino of the music minister of the *Comunidad de Fe y Amor* in Colombia, June 1999.

22. Miguel Angel Palomino attended the Sunday morning service in October 1999. The following are extracts of the pastor's sermon that show her hermeneutics within the context of spiritual warfare.

"Facing the Pharaoh" is our topic. Pharaoh is a prototype of Satan. Egypt is a prototype of the world. Israel is a prototype of God's people. And Moses is a prototype of God's servant (Ex. 11:25). God's call is to the 12 tribes of Israel. Remember: the higher the call, the stronger the test. When Pharaoh saw that the Hebrews were multiplying in his land, he said: "let us kill all male children." Here you have the spirit of Pharaoh, the spirit that wants to destroy God's people.

In chapter 5 we see Satan's strategies to separate us from God. Verse 15 is the beginning of the war with Pharaoh. The "spirit of Pharaoh" is the spirit that is in command of your family to prevent your service for the Lord. Pharaoh is not just any demon. He is a "principality." In spiritual warfare, I begin to claim territories that Satan has taken away from me, for example, my family, work, health, and so forth.

Chapter 8:25 teaches us that Satan does not want you to consecrate yourself to the Lord. So Pharaoh tells Moses: "You all may go, but leave your finances with me: cows, oxen, etc." Moses then replies: "We all will go, and leave not even a hoof for you." Everyone say it: *"We'll leave not even a hoof!"* Louder, *"We'll leave not even a hoof!"* I can't hear you: *"We'll leave not even a hoof!"* Your family belongs to the Lord. Your children belong to the Lord. Your house belongs to the Lord. Your grandparents are His. Your friends are His. Your neighbourhood is His. Not even a hoof will we leave for Satan. We should not leave anything for Pharaoh. We need to make this decision ours.

In 14:13 we read that Moses says, "No more." Say it: *"No more"* [the congregation repeats it three times]. The Lord will fight for us. Once you leave Egypt, Pharaoh will not look for you to enslave you but to destroy you. Just remember this — he now wants to wipe you out.

Pastor Juana ends her sermon casting out the spirit of Pharaoh and requesting God's protection for the families of the congregation. Then, she fixes her eyes on her congregation and says, "Pharaoh is defeated! Tell him now: *'Satan, you are defeated'!*" People quickly repeat the phrase clapping frenetically. Immediately the band begins playing a song whose lyrics are full of Old Testament symbolism:

Cantaré al Señor por siempre	I will always sing to the Lord
Su diestra es todo poder	His right hand is all powerful
Ha echado a la mar a quien	He threw our enemies into
nos perseguía	the sea

Jinete y caballo, ha echado a la mar	Horse and rider have been thrown into the sea
Echó a la mar los carros del Faraón	He threw Pharaoh's chariots into the sea
A campo enemigo yo fui	I went to the enemy's field
Y yo tomé lo que me robó	And I took back what the enemy had robbed me of
Tomé lo que me robó	I took back what the enemy had robbed me of
Bajo mis pies	Under my feet
Bajo mis pies	Under my feet
Satanás está bajo mis pies	Satan is under my feet

People sing the song enthusiastically, showing how well they accept Juana's preaching. Everyone, following the rhythm of the music, moves forward in a synchronized manner, pretending they are raiding enemy territory. They then stop and get down as if they were snatching something with their hands, and finally they smash Satan's head with their feet. As they sing the song over and over again, each time it seems that the people sing with greater conviction, knowing that in fact Satan has been defeated indeed. In a sense, this victorious mood is perceptible in the atmosphere of the service and on the followers' faces as well.

Many stand in the front waiting for Pastor Juana to minister to them. She lays hands on some and they fall backwards. She then prays for a sick woman. Pastor Juana seems to be almost screaming at God, reminding him of his promises and asking him to be merciful to the sick woman. The sick woman is crying when she suddenly stops, raises her hands, and claims to be cured. Everybody shouts, "Hallelujah!," while hugging each other, many with tears rolling down their faces. The crowd begins singing again, this time jumping and dancing, with Pastor Juana doing the same. They are celebrating victory over Satan. Certainly believers will come back next Sunday to see more of the same.

The "Prayer Warriors"

The so called "prayer warriors" are men and women with four main tasks. First, they intercede all the time for their leaders and the church programs. Second, they are alert during the service for any disturbance that may come from evil spirits. If anything like this happens, they quickly gather together to rebuke the spirits and make sure the place is clean of demonic influence, ensuring that the *culto* will continue running smoothly. Third, they get involved with the time of "ministration" that usually takes place at the end of the service. Here they counsel those in crisis, help the needy, pray for the heartbroken, and give the first instructions to those who want to follow the new faith. Fourth, in churches where supernatural manifestations happen, they would also serve as "attendants" or "catchers" placing themselves behind those individuals who may get "slain in the Spirit." In this practice, people fall to the floor allegedly under the influence of the Holy Spirit. Since there is the potential for serious injury, the "catcher" stands behind the person being prayed for so he or she does not land on top of another stricken person or on the bare floor. The intent of the "catcher" is not to ritualize the fall but rather to balance the safety factor with the freedom of the Spirit to move so that the individual may have a genuine experience.

In the *Centro Cristiano* of Costa Rica, the prayer warriors play an especially important role in the worship service.[23] The glass façade of the meeting hall gives it the appearance of a commercial building and not of a church. The architectural design helps diminish people's prejudices against evangelical church buildings, as their see-through walls do not hide anything from bystanders. The building seats about 800 people. The front platform resembles a theater stage with backdrops and colored lights, which seems to anticipate the beginning of a theater drama or musical show.

The worship service begins with songs of praise and spiritual warfare. After a few minutes, the song leader requests people to come forward to pray. While the congregation bows, the musicians continue playing and a group of young dancers, boys and girls, join them on the platform to accompany the songs with choreographic movements and banners. The use of colored lights makes the service more vibrant, especially during the time of "spiritual songs," that is to say, singing unto God "in the Spirit." The choreographic group then brings in a gigantic tulle canopy that is extended entirely over the platform at head level to be used in a liturgical dance. As they swing to the rhythm and musical beats, they also wave the

23. Personal notes of Miguel Angel Palomino, taken in a Sunday service, September 1999.

tulle each time the leader shouts, "Higher! Lower!" while the drummer creates an expectant atmosphere with his gong.

After thirty minutes or so, the pastor comes to the platform. He is dressed informally, wearing a striped colored shirt with no tie. Everybody becomes excited, clapping and whistling and shouting. While he greets the people and explains the meaning of praise, some among the congregation begin to laugh and others start falling to the floor. It is at this time that the prayer warriors run to assist those lying on the ground. The pastor then says: "I do not need to touch people for them to fall under God's power, do I? Do you believe it?" The people shout "Amen!" Then, the pastor starts calling names out loud: "José, María" and others, and all the Josés and Marías fall down in their seats. At this point there are not enough prayer warriors to keep the situation under control. People hysterically applaud this demonstration of power, while the pastor continues calling out more names. Many people remain on the floor in a state of unconsciousness, and others cannot stop laughing because they are "filled with the Spirit." On the platform, some of the dancers are falling too, including the song leader who is frantically spinning with her open arms. After some minutes, she finally collapses and two prayer warriors go to help raise her and the other girls who look dazed and can hardly stand on their feet.

An American preacher comes to the platform afterwards. His translator says he is here because he wants the pastor to anoint him. The pastor then asks the congregation to pray with him, and people at once raise their hands, pointing to the visiting pastor. Two prayer warriors stand behind the visitor to hold him in case he is "slain in the Spirit." The pastor starts praying, almost shouting, and claiming God's promises for this man while touching his forehead. He stumbles but does not fall. The pastor tries again, but nothing happens. The pastor insists no more and says to him, "In the name of Jesus, I grant you the creative anointing, so that you will regenerate missing organs in those who come to you for prayer." Everybody says "Amen!" The American pastor gives him a big hug, thanks him, and stays at the pulpit to preach.

Undoubtedly, this service has kept the prayer warriors busy. To common observers the work of the prayer warriors seems to be an exhausting task both emotionally and physically, but for these men and women it is just another *culto* where they did what they were supposed to do.

A Revision of the Theology of *Culto*

Arturo Piedra, professor at the Universidad Bíblica Latinoamericana in Costa Rica, states that what is now happening in Latin American churches has fatal consequences for theology.[24] First, it trivializes the sacred in the sense that it makes worship a mere religiosity full of emotions but with little impact or influence on daily life. And second, it upholds a puerile concept of the demonic, which is seen in acts like blowing off the evil spirits, cornering demons, scaring Satan with war song praises, and so forth. This perception of the demonic ultimately will diminish the foundation of the evangelical tradition, for it ignores the seriousness of evil expressed mainly in idolatry, corruption, and other social ills affecting Latin American society today.

Consequently, the theology of the *culto* needs to be revised. Churches are endorsing new models of worship without giving them much thought. "In practice," a church leader in Brazil told Miguel Angel Palomino, "worship is more something that 'happens' than something thought about down here." Many observers are not surprised at this, for the statement may reveal the way evangelicals were brought up in the old days, when they were taught to experience their faith, but not to reflect on it. This might explain the great emphasis on evangelism and church growth, but at the same time the lack of motivation leaders have to engage themselves in theology because of fear of becoming critics of their own beliefs.

Worship speaks of the intimate and personal relationship that exists between the believer and his or her Creator. The Greek New Testament term for worship *(proskuneo)* describes the act of falling to the ground before an important person, and kissing the soil, his feet, or robes in recognition of his greatness. When the magi went to see Jesus in the manger, they fell down and worshiped him (Matthew 2:11). When the women saw the empty tomb and heard a man talking to them, they recognized it was the Master and held him by his feet and worshiped him (Matthew 28:9). When John saw the vision of the glorified Christ, he fell at his feet as dead (Revelation 1:17). Worshiping God, then, is to surrender everything, with no conditions. It is to put our rights, will, and possessions at God's feet in recognition of God's authority and sovereignty. In this sense, worship is essential to the *culto* because our lives reach fulfillment in it.

24. See Arturo Piedra, *El Rostro Posmoderno del Protestantismo*, Documentos ocasionales, No. 13 (San José, Costa Rica: Visión Mundial Internacional, n/d).

The worship service, therefore, is the voluntary act of adoration and intelligence, which we render to God in response to God's initiative of reaching out to the human race through Jesus Christ. It is the external expression of tribute and worship as God's people gather together before his presence. Yet believers and song leaders struggle sometimes trying to figure out what cultural ingredients should be infused into the worship service in order to keep the *culto* theologically focused. Naturally, there is no single formula simply because there is no single type of church. Nevertheless, there are some elements that can serve as guidelines to develop a theology of *culto*.

Latino authors have rightly pointed out some of the main objectives of the worship service.[25] We will review them and add other points of particular interest for the Latin American context. First there is communion, understood not only as a fellowship between peers but as a spiritual union with God as well. It is in the *culto* that these two dimensions become evident. The physical presence of the people who come to church to partake of the bread and wine at the Lord's Table expresses the intimacy and unity believers share with their Creator. Furthermore, this communion goes beyond the Sunday service to the extent it touches people's daily lives in practical ways. For this reason Luke says that as a result of their relationship with God (Acts 2:42-43), the early Christians had all things in common and took care of the needy among them (Acts 2:44-45; 4:32-35).

Instruction is another objective. Acquiring new information is not enough if knowledge does not affect our life. Writing to Timothy, the Apostle Paul says that all Scripture is profitable "for instruction in righteousness, so the man of God may be perfect, totally well equipped for all good work" (2 Timothy 3:16, 17). Certainly, instruction here has to do with edification. In terms of Christian life, growth, and spiritual maturity, Paul reminds the Corinthian Christians what is expected of them (1 Corinthians 14:26). The *culto*, therefore, must provide worshipers with sound doctrine and teaching that will edify the local church.

A third objective is proclamation, understood as the missionary enterprise. Apparently, the church in Antioch was gathered when the Holy

25. See João Leonel, "A Igreja e a Liturgia," in *Revista Teológica* (Seminário Presbiteriano do Sul, Brazil) 60, no. 51 (Jan.-Apr. 1999): 35-51, Nelson Kirst, *Culto Cristiano: Historia, Teología y Formas* (Quito: CLAI, 2000), and Miguel Angel Darino, *La Adoración* (California: Distribuidora Internacional de Materiales Evangélicos, 1992).

Spirit called Barnabas and Paul for missionary work (Acts 13:1, 2). The Greek *leiturgeo* (v. 2) indicates an act of performing a work, whether by prayer or by instructing others, concerning the way of salvation. In this case, church leaders were praying and fasting when God spoke to them and they responded by sending out the two men (13:3). No doubt, any true experience with God will ignite believers' hearts to the point that they will rise up and go to tell others about their faith.

A fourth objective would be diversity in worship. The place where a church is located will shape its *culto,* and this may vary depending on the region and culture of the congregants. Inhabitants of the coast are not the same as those who live in the highlands; and Africans have different tastes and traditions than those of Asians. Within a given city there are also different types of cultural expressions that will affect the kind of worship at a particular church. The expectation of professionals is not the same as those of the poor. It is vital then to get to know the people we are working with, so the worship service will meet their needs. Transferring worship patterns from the Caribbean to an Andean village would be as strange as trying to impose the liturgy of the Russian Orthodox Church on the Pentecostal churches of the region. For Latin Americans this is a big challenge, in spite of the fact that there are only two main languages and great similarity of culture, as well as an evangelical tradition of more than a hundred years in certain countries. Despite this long tradition some *cultos* would seem to marginalize, for example, those who come from the countryside or indigenous communities.

At a time when well-publicized church growth is taking place in Latin America, it is worth observing that the formation of a deep spiritual life in the believers is as important as numerical success. Moreover, the harmony and unity of the local body of Christ must be reflected when believers worship God. For this reason, we need to be sensitive to the cultural context of the people and flexible to diverse worship styles, which suggests that we should not be theologically negligent. Rigidity about forms is not a sign of spirituality. In a continent as diverse as Latin America, we cannot expect any kind of uniformity when we speak about worship.

The fifth objective deals with the validation of the important role of emotions in worship. The current tendency to encourage emotional services may be a reaction to the time when churches would only pay attention to intellectual sermons, and any sign of emotionalism was perceived with suspicion. As a result the *culto* became ritualistic, and it discouraged believers from expressing their feelings to God. In trying to rescue the fact that people are not only intellectual but emotional and physical beings as well, the renewed *culto* is providing a theological perspective on the whole person as a worshiping being. As Chilean sociologist Cristián Parker argues, individuals are to be seen as mind and heart in one unity, and spirit and body holistically. Regrettably, Western rationalism "made us believe for a long time that we were nothing else but reason, nothing else but thinking beings," where symbolism and religion had no place in life.[26] The challenge then is to reassess the different worship styles now widely present in affective and emotional *cultos,* for they are legitimate forms of spirituality, bringing with them a new worldview that helps to understand worship from new perspectives. For example, the categories of "salvation" and "healing," which are rooted in Pentecostalism and other healing movements,[27] serve us better than the sacred-profane dualism that has been "for almost a century the foundation category for the sociology of religion."[28] Without doubt, these innovative worship styles require new theoretical categories in order to further explore them. But as Parker notes, "It is never too late to remember that it is possible and desirable to think about our own reality in our own terms, because for so long we have been dependent on conceptual theories elaborated in other cultures."[29]

The last point we wish to make has to do with practices involving supernatural phenomena as part of worship services. Changes that have occurred in the *culto* are forcing traditional evangelical church leaders and believers alike to rethink their understanding of spirituality. But solid theological foundations need then to be defined and taught to sustain whatever we do in the *culto.* Subjects such as liturgical dance and choreographies, falling backwards in prayer, and the legitimacy of signs and wonders, all demand an elaboration of a theology of liturgy. Of equal or greater

26. See Cristián Parker, *Popular Religion and Modernization in Latin America: A Different Logic* (Maryknoll, N.Y.: Orbis, 1996).

27. Observers say one of the factors that lead the faithful to make a pilgrimage through various religious groups is their search for salvation. Eventually, many find salvation in Pentecostal churches because these churches offer inner healing as well as physical healing. See Verónica Giménez Béliveau and Juan Cruz Esquivel, "Rastreo de las Identidades Religiosas en los Sectores Populares Urbanos de Buenos Aires," *Caminos* 57 (Octubre 1997): 38.

28. Parker, *Popular Religion and Modernization,* p. 36.

29. Parker, *Popular Religion and Modernization,* p. 33.

importance is the debate concerning the active participation of women in the *culto*. Certainly, renewed churches have tackled this issue in practice by allowing female members to preach, lead in worship, and run ministries. This is causing the *machista* hegemonic structure, which was legitimized for so many years in Latin America, to collapse before the evidence that women can also lead worship services, perform signs, and preach as well as male pastors. For women this is a clear indication that church business is not the monopoly of men, since females are recipients of God's gifts as well.

Evangelical and Pentecostal worship services in Latin America are certainly experiencing a paradigmatic change. Old patterns are giving way to a renewed style of *culto* that believers seem to find appropriate. It is too early yet to tell whether or not mainstream denominations will adopt this kind of *culto*. Many church leaders welcome it, but it is worth mentioning that although new forms and styles are attractive and important, the contents of the worship service are even more important, since form without substance is just intense religiosity but not Christian *culto*. Latin American evangelical churches need to develop a theologically sound *culto*, because popular religiosity is what has subsisted far too long among the people of this continent.

Worship in the Amazon:
The Case of the Aguaruna Evangelical Church

ROBERT J. PRIEST

Editor's Introduction

Robert Priest articulates the fundamental challenge that faces us throughout this volume: "to disentangle the culturally contingent from the universally normative within worship." Priest's extensive fieldwork with the Aguaruna in the northern Peruvian rainforest affords an opportunity to look at how young Christianity takes root in a tribe with centuries of established spiritual mythology.

Priest arrived after the Aguaruna church rejected the hierarchy of its Nazarene founders and affirmed its autonomy and ethnic identity. He describes the visceral ritual of the consumption and regurgitation of *wais*, at the call of the thunderous *tuntui*, with its symbolism of physical and spiritual cleansing. Priest then examines how the Aguaruna conception of God is influenced by the mythology of Apajui, and how worship is integrally linked with proclamation and mission.

•   •

Most writings on Christian worship emerge from social contexts in which church and Bible have long been present. This presence has helped to shape the wider culture, even as the wider culture has influenced the church and its practices. In the case of Europe and North America, the history of this dialectical relationship stretches over centuries. Efforts to analyze the relationship of Christian worship practices with culture, or to disentangle the culturally contingent from the universally normative within worship, face daunting challenges — not least because of the way the two

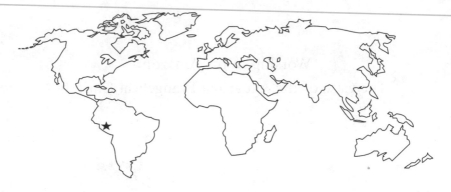

have been fused over time. If one is interested in analyzing the relationship of worship and culture, there are certain advantages to examining a worshiping community in a social context in which Christianity has only recently been introduced. Some of the cultural dynamics are more clearly observable in a context where the culture has not been shaped through interaction with Christianity, and a relatively new church is attempting to find its way towards meaningful worship.

This chapter focuses on such a worshiping community in the northern rainforest of Peru, and is based on nearly two years of anthropological fieldwork carried out between 1987 and 1989 among the 40,000 Aguaruna, a sub-group of the Jivaro. With a strong warrior tradition, the Jivaro soundly repulsed Spanish invaders at the end of the sixteenth century, just as they had repulsed the Incas before them. Aided by mountainous terrain, treacherous rivers, and dense forest, the Aguaruna and other Jivaro are unique in the Americas for having retained control of ancestral territory into the twentieth century, only entering into sustained relations with outsiders in the early twentieth century. Prior to the twentieth century, efforts by Roman Catholic missionaries to initiate a mission to the Aguaruna were met with violence and death, discouraging further attempts. In 1923, under the patronage of Samajein, the last great Aguaruna war chief, Roger Wynans, a Nazarene missionary, commenced a ministry among the Aguaruna. Although he seems to have gained wide personal esteem, and worked hard to learn their language, linguistic barriers hampered communication. Nazarene missionaries who replaced him failed to learn the language, and meaningful communication on religious matters was limited. In the late 1940s both the Jesuits and the Summer Institute of Linguistics

Aguaruna Church Building   from the author's personal collection

(SIL) began work with the Aguaruna. Linguists of the Summer Institute of Linguistics translated the New Testament into Aguaruna, and were able to articulate ideas clearly in Aguaruna that Nazarene missionaries had tried to communicate only in Spanish — a language that few understood even at the most elementary levels. By the 1960s and 1970s there was a major movement in which, in a majority of Aguaruna villages, a large proportion of each village converted to evangelical Christianity. While many subsequently dropped out, a stable core of between 10 percent and 25 percent of adults in most communities continued as faithful worshipers.

Originally all evangelical churches were Nazarene. However, the Nazarene hierarchical structure, which placed the missionary at the top, led to a widespread perception that churches were subservient to the foreign missionary. Missionary insistence that Nazarene churches carry a large sign announcing the Nazarene affiliation was bitterly resented by non Nazarenes as an intrusive imposition of foreign identity within their communities. Disaffected Aguaruna church leaders organized another church in the 1970s, the *Iglesia Evangelica Aguaruna,* emphasizing auton-

**Two Aguaruna
Men**
from the author's
personal collection

omy and ethnic identity. At the time of my fieldwork (1987-1989) this church represented nearly half of all Aguaruna evangelical Christians. It was this church that hosted me during my fieldwork.

On my first night in Tundusa, I stayed up late getting acquainted with Anquash, my nearest neighbor, a church deacon. Anxious to begin collecting data, I asked about the various clay pots I saw lining the walls. He responded:

That is a *yukun*. It is used to prepare *wais*. Our Aguaruna tradition was to rise early in the morning, at 3:00 A.M., drink *wais* and vomit it. In this manner we washed our mouths and stomachs and so kept healthy, energetic, and disciplined, not lazy and sleepy. A father would wake his children up at this time and teach them how to live. But when civilization and education arrived, everyone stopped this practice. We stopped using *wais* years ago, and now there is moral corruption everywhere in our communities. Young people now have no respect for their elders' authority. They are lazy and think only of having lovers. So we, of the church, have made a *yukun,* and have planted *wais*. In our Bible school we are going to revive this practice. Instead of sleeping late and getting up thinking about women, we'll take *wais* and vomit out all our filth. We'll wake up alert, dynamic, and strong to seek God in prayer. You, too, will use *wais*. But first we must wait until the *wais* we've planted has matured.

Eighteen months later, the *wais* was grown. One hundred and twenty male delegates, with faces painted and feather headdresses donned (the better-dressed also wearing blue jeans, tennis shoes, sunglasses, and watches), gathered in Tundusa for the annual church conference. They came from 60 churches representing an announced 2,511 church members. For one week reports were delivered, elections conducted, hymns sung, prayers given, and sermons preached, late into each evening. But in terms of interest, early morning activities held center stage. At 3:00 A.M. each morning we were roused by the sonorous beating of the *tuntui,* a drum made from a hollowed-out log which, I was told, could be heard ten kilometers away. Pots of hot *wais* were waiting. Bowls of *wais* were drunk, and after brief interludes evacuated. Subsequently everyone gathered in church for a period of loud and vigorous prayer to God. Later, men commented on how awake, energetic, and healthy they felt (due in part, no doubt, to the extremely high caffeine content of *Ilex guayusa,* the plant which they had imbibed).[1] They discussed the value of this old custom and attributed

1. The leaves of *Ilex guayusa* are anywhere from 1.5 percent to 7.5 percent caffeine, with the highest caffeine content of any plant. For a full description of the use of this plant

Bowl Used for Early Morning Purgative   from the author's personal collection

laziness, illness, and the lack of moral discipline in the contemporary setting to the abandonment of such practices. How much better to cleanse one's stomach every morning, they argued, and seek God in prayer.

My initial conversation with deacon Anquash about the use of *wais* in worship immediately signaled to me that I was entering another world. In subsequent observations of Aguaruna worship, such as at this church conference, I observed much that was familiar: blue jeans, sunglasses, the Bible, seating arrangements in church, the importance of Jesus to salvation, and the presence of the sermon, singing, and prayer. But much was different, and not just feathers and face paint. Artifacts associated with worship, temporal rhythms of worship, musical forms, practices of prayer,

---

in traditional Jivaroan cultures, see W. H. Lewis, E. J. Kennelly, G. N. Bass, H. J. Wedner, M. P. Elvin-Lewis, D. Fast, "Ritualistic Use of the Holly *Ilex guayusa* by Amazonian Jivaro Indians," *Journal of Ethnopharmacology* 33 (1991): 25-30, 293.

volume, and worship rhetoric all presented me with unfamiliar worship elements. In this chapter I attempt to tease out some of the ways in which Aguaruna Christian worship, as I observed it in the *Iglesia Evangelica Aguaruna* in the late 1980s, does the following: (1) draws on prior cultural patterns; (2) breaks with other cultural patterns; (3) adopts new cultural patterns; and (4) orients itself towards worship of a transcultural God presented in the Christian Scriptures.

"Worship?" and Aguaruna Traditional Religion

The term "worship" points to the sphere of religion. And if one defines religion in terms of interaction with beings which are "other-than-human," then the Aguaruna have long been very religious. Traditional discourses are filled with references to beings that are "other-than-human," as well as to spirits of the human dead. Among the more prominent of these beings are the *Nugkui* "people," which live under the soil and help the garden grow; the *Tsugki* "people" under the river, which, among other things, are powerful sources of love magic; *Pasuk* spirits that assist shamans and possess young women; and *Etsa*, the sun, who helped create the original charters for polygynous marriage, work, and cultural artifacts. Also included are various permutations of spirits of the dead: the *wakan*, souls of the dead that joyfully drink and party; the *iwanch*, demonic or trickster spirits of the dead that sexually molest women or children and beat up men who are drunk; and the *ajutap*, spirits of deceased warrior ancestors that give visions conferring blessing and power. These are but the more prominent among a whole host of beings with which Aguaruna historically interacted.

And yet it is probably a mistake to apply the term "worship" to this interaction. While *anen*, magical songs invoking these spirits, bear a surface resemblance to prayer, *anen* are believed to work through an impersonal logic of power that manipulates spirit power unrelated to any intentionality on the part of the beings invoked in magical song. The *anen* are thought to accomplish their ends quite apart from whether spirit beings hear the songs and quite apart from any intentionality on the part of such beings. Even when young men on a vision quest sing songs appealing to warrior ancestors to visit them with a vision of power, the instant the terrifying apparition appears and has delivered a sentence or two of blessing, the young man must overcome his terror and strike the apparition with a ritual staff, saying, "Bah, you're a nobody, a nothing. Be gone!" Only by aggressively cutting short the visit is the young man able coercively to capture the blessing and not be cursed. The blessing comes to reside in his throat as a physical non-sentient power protecting and empowering.

Furthermore, while Christians think of "other-than-human beings" within a binary opposition between good and evil, with all such beings categorized either as one or the other, Aguaruna beings are not categorized in terms of such an opposition, and human interactions with such beings are not structured by such an opposition. That is not what the spirits are about. The dominant thrust of such interaction is coercive, not submissive, and is centered in one's own material well-being, not organized with reference to a transcendent center of value that one must serve and submit to.

Does this mean that contemporary Aguaruna Christian worship is totally discontinuous with the past? Not at all.

Traditional Knowledge of God

One of the first questions missionaries faced was what word to use for God. The Aguaruna told two stories about a mythic being, Apajui, who some said was the creator, and who occasionally let his presence be felt by sending earthquakes. The first story featured Apajui and a man named Kumpanam, who lived on opposite cliffs where the Maranon river cuts through the last ridge of mountains into the Amazon basin. Kumpanam routinely visited in the home of Apajui. When Apajui noticed that Kumpanam was attracted to his daughter, he forbade Kumpanam to visit his home again and even to look at his daughter. But Kumpanam regularly gazed lustfully across the river at Apajui's daughter, and this gaze mystically caused her to become pregnant. Furious, Apajui left earth for the sky and such visits ceased permanently.

In a second myth, Apajui comes to the earth, dirty and hungry, seeking lodging. He is mocked and turned away. In anger he announces a flood. But to the one family that extended hospitality, he told them how to build a balsa raft, put dirt on it, plant crops, and build a house. Any who had committed incest or killed "without justification" were to be banned from the raft. Any who had committed adultery would have their flesh turn to liquid as soon as the rain touched them. Adults were not to look up

**Aguaruna Man
in Traditional
Regalia**
from the author's
personal collection

at the sky, lest they die. As the water rose, threatening to crush them against the sky, children who were sexually innocent were told to put a staff through the roof and tap three times on the sky, at which point Apajui caused the waters to recede.

The first of these myths corresponds to myths reported around the world of a high god who withdraws from humankind after some transgression. The second corresponds to similar flood myths reported in traditional societies around the world. While Apajui existed in discourse, no regular ritual practices were associated with Apajui. Apajui was thought of as withdrawn, distant, and not normally concerned with the details of individual lives. The single way his presence was sometimes felt was through earthquakes.

But there was one dramatic historical occasion in which Aguaruna re-

**Aguaruna
Husband with
Co-Wives**
from the author's
personal collection

sponded ritually to Apajui. Shortly after the arrival of the missionary Roger Wynans, a series of severe earthquakes and aftershocks hit this region stretching over several months, from May 7 into December of 1928, and measuring up to 7.3 on the Richter scale (a May 14 quake measured 7.3; a July 18 quake measured 7.0).[2] I recorded numerous Aguaruna accounts of these earthquakes, and of Aguaruna responses to them, including eight eye-

2. Lengthy accounts of these quakes are provided by letters written by Nazarene missionaries. The May 14 and July 18 quakes are listed as 7.3 and 7.0 by the United States Department of the Interior Geological Survey *Earthquake Catalog of Peru* (Open-File Report 85-286, 1985).

witness accounts, from communities on four different rivers. Aguaruna accounts describe landslides, salt springs pouring into rivers and killing the fish, and crevices splitting houses in half. Night animals called out in daytime, and day animals at night. Children were warned not to "mock" them. People gathered in larger homes. They spoke in whispers. It was said that Apajui was angry and would destroy people for being *tsuwat* — dirty. Rumors spread that women who had killed their infants would be eaten by worms. No one should have sex, lest Apajui be angry. The incestuous and those who had killed unjustifiably were to be socially excluded lest everyone be destroyed. The flesh of the incestuous would dissolve into liquid. Some said a flood would destroy the world. Apajui, it was said, would send his chicken as a test. Narrators report that animals (including an opossum, ant eater, armadillo, cat, and turkey) entered homes and acted tame. These were said to be the "animals of Apajui" that should be cared for, fed, and released, lest Apajui be angry. People danced and sang to Apajui asking why he created them, if he was now destroying them: "For what sin/crime *(tudau)* do you now destroy us?" They asked for pity, and called attention to their crying children or whimpering dogs. Later the consensus emerged that this dancing must be done nude. Men and women undressed and danced, facing away from each other, holding up babies or puppies as they looked to the sky and asked for pity: "Apajui, you see all of me, as I was born. Have pity. Have pity on my crying baby." As they danced, narrators claimed, the earthquake calmed. Men and women were not to look at each other, but some "bad men" reportedly "did not fear" and looked at women, or reached out to touch them. Each time this happened the earthquake reportedly started again. Adults eventually tired. The children now sang and danced, with puppies held up to Apajui. In some versions, the earthquake stopped only when the children danced. Missionary letters confirm the description of the earthquakes, and confirm elements of these accounts, although the Wynans were clearly unaware of what people were thinking and doing in the communities. This series of events seems to have created a strong desire on the part of some to try to understand the missionaries' message, but no lasting religious changes resulted from this series of events.

Indeed missionaries rejected the name *Apajui* as an appropriate term for God. The idea of Apajui having a daughter and of having lived on the side of a nearby mountain led them to reject this term. Instead they borrowed from Spanish and preached about Dios (pronounced *Yus* by Aguaruna) or *Tatayus*, a hybrid of Quechua and Spanish. For roughly forty years missionaries rejected *Apajui* as an appropriate term for God, and spoke only of *Tatayus* or *Yus*. Knowledge of God was thus marked linguistically as discontinuous from prior cultural knowledge. Worship of God, as initially presented by missionaries, was worship of a foreign God.

And yet, many Aguaruna already equated Apajui with Yus or Tatayus. Magical singing *(anen)* was one place within traditional culture where secret and occult words were employed, and it was common for such songs to employ words from other languages. One genre of *anen* make frequent reference to Apajui.[3] But, as is common in these *anen,* repetition is employed, along with synonyms. In these songs it is clear that *Apajui* and *Yus* and *Tatayus* are used interchangeably. The Spanish *Yus* and Quechua/Spanish *Tatayus* were treated as secret or occult words for the more common Aguaruna *Apajui*. That is, magical songs provided evidence that the Aguaruna themselves understood Apajui as being the same as Tatayus or Yus.[4] While early converts up into the 1960s faithfully used *Tatayus* as the preferred term, and SIL linguists commenced translation of the New Testament using the word *Tatayus,* missionaries were occasionally disconcerted to find devout Christians directing prayers to Apajui, and using *Apajui* interchangeably with *Tatayus* or *Yus*. SIL linguists and Aguaruna Christian leaders commenced a long conversation about this, and eventually concluded that *Apajui* was the appropriate Aguaruna word for God, with the New Testament translation reflecting this assessment. Life histories of Christians collected in the early 1960s make reference exclusively to *Tatayus,* while the more than thirty life histories I collected in the late 1980s make exclusive reference to *Apajui*. *Tatayus* has been eclipsed by *Apajui* as the word for God. When Aguaruna Christians worship *Apajui,* they worship one their ancestors already spoke about.

God and Moral Discourse

While traditional Aguaruna culture was filled with moral discourse, most such moral discourse made no explicit mention of Apajui. When Apajui

---

3. On songs used to avoid being caught and punished for adultery, see Robert Priest, "Defilement, Moral Purity, and Transgressive Power: The Symbolism of Filth in Aguaruna Jivaro Culture" (Ph.D. dissertation, University of California, Berkeley, 1993), pp. 446-64.

4. Priest, "Defilement, Moral Purity, and Transgressive Power," pp. 446-64.

was mentioned, as in the flood myth, there was clear indication Apajui was thought of as a moral being. But he was normally thought of as distant, removed. While dozens of stories were told of Etsa, a male culture hero, and stories and songs celebrating the female Nugkui were central to everyday discourse, stories about Apajui were few, and only occasionally referred to. Apajui existed within traditional Aguaruna discourse, but on the margins of that discourse, not at the center. With the arrival of the missionary, Apajui, for many Aguaruna, began to move from the margins of discourse to the center. Moral and religious discourses became increasingly theocentric.

When Roger Wynans arrived in 1923, he lived on the edge of Aguaruna territory, and was able to communicate only at a rudimentary level. By 1928, few Aguaruna would have personally met or heard him, but everyone would have heard about him, and doubtless understood at some level that he spoke of a righteous deity who would judge sin. This was compatible, in certain respects, with what was known of Apajui from the well-known flood myth. When a series of earthquakes and aftershocks arrived on a magnitude never before experienced, earthquakes that were traditionally thought of as coming from Apajui, this seems to have triggered a mass movement to respond to Apajui in the way outlined above. When asked why Aguaruna in 1928 responded as they did, informants differed in their answers. Some said that a very old man remembered being told this is how one should respond to Apajui if this magnitude earthquake happened. Others said that a message came from the Incas prescribing this way of responding to Apajui. Still others claimed that the Nazarene missionary taught them to dance nude before Apajui in this way. What all could agree on was that, as far as anyone knew, this was a unique one-time pattern of human response to an earthquake and to Apajui.

Fear of God

Contemporary Aguaruna Christians consistently refused to characterize those who danced and sang to Apajui as worshiping. The 1928 respondents, according to contemporary Aguaruna Christians, were terrified by the quakes, but were primarily responding to Apajui in order to fend off judgment, and made no lasting changes in terms of a sustained relationship to Apajui. And yet most Aguaruna Christians would point to a parallel fear of judgment as one component in their own initial response to Apajui. Whatever is involved in worship, clearly fear is one emotion Scripture itself frequently points to: Fear God.

Wynans and later missionaries warned of a "place of fire" where sinners are punished. Fear of judgment by Apajui has clearly contributed to many conversions in recent decades. One Aguaruna evangelist described visiting a village at a time when a small earthquake occurred: "I told them, don't be afraid of the earthquake. It is Apajui you should fear. He is fearsome *(ishamainuk)*. When I said this, everyone from Putjuk contracted themselves (to Apajui)." In many of the life histories which I taped, converts mention fear of Apajui as one motive in conversion. Wishu said,

> I lived in vain, killing people, getting drunk, fighting, and talking in vain. Antonio announced the word of Apajui, that those not contracted to Apajui will not go to heaven *(nayainpinmak)* but to the place of fire. And so I said, "better that I contract myself to Apajui."

Chijiap provides a similar account and concludes, "because I saw the danger, I followed Apajui." In the context of having her sin pointed out, Ducitak told herself, "truly I am going to the place of fire. Thinking of this, I wept much." Chamik heard the "word of Apajui," but rejected it. Later, as he returned from participating in a homicide, he reports becoming overwhelmed with fear, "thinking what would happen to me if I did not deliver myself to Apajui." A year later, he did so. Anquash, a self-described womanizer and killer, reports having been warned by Aguaruna Christians, "if you don't leave your sin *(tudau)*, you will suffer very much."

Both in responses to the 1928 earthquakes and to subsequent preaching of Aguaruna evangelists, fear of God is a central element. Fear is a relational response defined in terms of two poles: the divine other and the human self. Fear was a response to the power of Apajui, evident in the awesome quakes, and repeatedly stressed in contemporary Aguaruna Christian discourse. "Apajui is *muun* (big/great/powerful)!" is a constant refrain. And this power is not morally neutral. That is, the power of Apajui is feared because it is perceived to be the power of a morally concerned being. This moral element was acknowledged tangentially prior to the 1920s, was evident in the 1928 earthquakes, and became increasingly central under the influence of Christianity, and especially the translation of the Bible. Apajui is increasingly understood to be a righteous and holy, as well as all-powerful, being.

Fear reflects not only understandings of God, but understandings of self. One fears a powerful morally concerned being if one senses oneself to be morally delinquent. But while orthodox Christian doctrine insists on our common sinful condition, as an empirical matter of fact many people deny that they sense themselves to be "sinners," and thus presumably lack a key condition for "fearing God." Indeed many anthropologists have stressed that indigenous peoples lack any such "sense of sin," and thus are unlikely to respond to the Christian message.[5] Interestingly, Aguaruna Christians themselves often stress that they lacked a sense of sin prior to "hearing the word of Apajui." Puanchig, a man in his fifties, says, "In the times before following Apajui . . . I did not sense myself to be a sinner *(tudau)* and did not feel that what I did was bad *(pegkegchau)*." Typically converts describe their sense of self as sinner as emergent at the point at which the "word of Apajui" was being preached to them by other Aguaruna evangelists. Ducitak, a grandmother, stated, "When I heard the word of Apajui, I discovered *(dekawamiajai)* my sin *(tudau)*, what I am." Old man Wampagkit said that upon hearing "the word of Apajui . . . I saw/discovered *(wainmamkamiajai)* my sin *(pegkegchaujun)*." Nuwakuk, in her forties, said, "[When] they announced the word of Apajui, I discovered about myself *(dekagmamawamiajai)* that I was a sinner."

Elsewhere I have explored this emergent sense of sin in greater depth, but a few brief observations are in order here.[6] First, when Aguaruna Christians characterize themselves as sinners, they do so through an Aguaruna vocabulary as rich and diverse as that of the ancient Hebrews. Numerous terms speaking of moral failure *(pegkegchau, tudau, katsek, yajau, antuchu, tsuwat, detse)* are applied to the self. Aguaruna Christians needed and employed no new vocabulary by which to speak of themselves as sinners. Second, this emergent sense of sin is not primarily dependent on having learned new and different moral ideas that recode formerly innocent behaviors as sinful. While there was some shift that

5. For example, see Alfred Kroeber, *Anthropology* (New York: Harcourt, Brace and World, 1948), p. 612; Margaret Mead, *Coming of Age in Samoa* (New York: New American Library, 1949), pp. 126, 164, 277; Marshall Sahlins, "The Sadness of Sweetness: The Native Anthropology of Western Cosmology," *Current Anthropology* 37 (1996): 425.

6. Robert J. Priest, "'I Discovered My Sin!': Aguaruna Evangelical Conversion Narratives," in A. Buckser and S. Glazier, eds., *The Anthropology of Religious Conversion* (Lanham, Md.: Rowman and Littlefield, 2003), pp. 95-108.

took place in the behaviors judged as morally wrong,[7] most contemporary Aguaruna Christian discourse about moral failings speaks of failure in areas that had always been assessed by the Aguaruna to be morally problematic (theft, adultery, incest, stinginess, slander, etc.). Third, in traditional Aguaruna discourse nearly all moral accusation is directed toward someone else, not toward the self. While some cultures and religious systems encourage the individual to moral self-examination and confession, traditional Aguaruna culture did not. But in the context of a new theocentric emphasis, with Apajui as the moral accuser, a heightened moral self-examination was introduced. Prior fears of retaliation by an enemy shifts into fear of punishment by an all-seeing and righteous God. Aguaruna increasingly come to experience fear and trembling in the presence of this "ultimate other."

The Beauty of Following God's Path

But while those who danced in the 1928 earthquakes were responding fearfully to danger, contemporary Christians claim to have responded to a positive and attractive message as well. As Aguaruna evangelists preached the "word of Apajui," they stressed a vision of alternative paths, one good and one bad. Puanchig said, "Dati preached the word of Apajui and the good path. . . . From there I became a true follower of Apajui." Repeatedly "the good path" and "good words" and "the word of Apajui" are linked in Aguaruna Christian discourse. "Truly the word of Apajui is good." "Now I live following good words." "I have heard good words about Apajui." "I also want the good path." "How beautiful it is to follow God's path!" Perhaps the most common phrase describing conversion is simply, "I followed (nemagkamiajai) Apajui." Through the constantly articulated metaphor of alternate paths, Christians constantly affirm the attractiveness and beauty of following God's path.

Preconversion lives are frequently presented as lives of personal disorder, as in the following account by Ujukam: "I drank much, sometimes well, sometimes badly. Many times I fought. Village leaders put me in jail. This did not stop me. I drank much, killed someone, and attacked others (verbally). Those who followed Apajui I criticized. I beat my wife, and in-

7. Most notably with revenge killings, polygyny, and drinking manioc beer.

jured her, so that her brothers beat me up." Drinking, retaliatory violence, slander, marital fights, and breakups are typically featured as paradigmatic elements in a way of life subsequently renounced in conversion. Both testimonies and sermons construct a model of the good life characterized by peace, forgiveness, love, sobriety, and fidelity. This good life is to be found by following *Apajui* and his word. That is, in responding to *Apajui,* converts are responding as much to the positive vision of the good life as they are to a message of judgment. "With the word of Apajui, we live in peace," says Chamik, a former killer.

Aguaruna evangelists invariably speak of sin in the context of repentance and forgiveness through the work of *Apu Jesu, apu* being a traditional word for a village leader. Dawai ended his lengthy life story with a two sentence summary: "Before, I was a drunkard, a fighter *(maanin)* and was bad *(pegkegchau)*. . . . Now I know what sin is, but I also know who Jesus Christ is." Esach, after months of inner turmoil over his spiritual state triggered by the death of his son, describes going to the pastor's house: "I wept when I spoke with him. He told me that it was for my sin that Jesus died. And so I confessed my life before Apajui." "Jesus is able to 'throw out' sin," Tiwi affirms. Anquash explains, "I asked Apajui to forgive me *(tsagkugtaugta),* to erase *(esakatujugta)* my sin." Conversion narratives maintain a clear focus on two eschatological alternatives, heaven *(nayainpinmak)* and hell *(jinum)*. As sinners, people deserve hell. However, for those who renounce sin, seek forgiveness based on the death of Jesus, and "contract themselves to Apajui," there is forgiveness.

Personal Relationship with God

While the theme of escape from punishment is clearly one component of Aguaruna response to Apajui, a more central theme of many narratives is that of entering into a personal relationship with Apajui. Entsakua reports, "I contracted myself to Jesus. I came to know that Apajui loves us. I began to obey Apajui. Before I knew Apajui I could not travel alone. After I contracted myself to Jesus, when I traveled I felt as if there were two of us traveling together. Now, praying to Apajui, I travel at night to hunt, without fear." Wishu describes a dream he had at conversion: "Apajui put fragrant medicine in my hair and bathed me. He said, 'I will never leave you. You are my son.' Upon awakening, my body had a fragrant smell. And I prayed to Apajui with deep desire." Mamai said, "When I contracted myself [to Apajui], I felt very contented, light, and good. I prayed all day to Apajui, asking what I should do. Every day I prayed." Again and again when narrators describe sufferings undergone they stress the companionship of Apajui. Fifty-year-old Mamai describes her travails: "Although I suffer much, I am with Apajui. . . . When I get sick, no one cares for me . . . but I have Apajui. I have suffered much . . . , but whatever the sorrow, it passes. In the new life there are other thoughts. We receive joy from Apajui." Again and again Wishu intersperses his life-story and the account of his afflictions with, "Even if I walk alone, I am with Apajui," or "Although I suffer, I go on with Apajui. Apajui is always with me." Puanchig says,

> Having contracted myself [to Apajui], I felt good. It seemed the spirit [*wakani*] lived in my heart, that it taught me and strengthened me. I went into the forest to pray. In this manner I lived, happily. And because I have tried it, I say it is good to pray. . . . It seems the spirit speaks in my heart, this way I feel what I should do in my heart. "Don't do this, truly you cannot do this, those who work the work of Apajui do not go about transgressing!" And I fear. While others commit faults, and I have the thought of eating someone else's fruit, whether papaya or peanuts, into my heart comes the thought that followers of Apajui do not eat the produce of others, and this thought enters my heart. And so it is true what they say, that when the spirit dwells in us, it teaches us.

Worship as Mission

In the late 1980s Aguaruna Christians of the *Iglesia Evangelica Aguaruna* rather consistently generated theocentric discourses. Such discourses were not merely produced within explicitly religious ritual spaces nor sustained only by religious specialists. That is, people of all ages and genders, both literate and illiterate, announced themselves to have "contracted themselves to Apajui," to "follow Apajui," and to obey "the word of Apajui." They routinely describe themselves as "proclaiming" various truths about Apajui to others. When I asked such individuals to tell me their life stories, they responded with alacrity, creating seamless stories with self and Apajui as key characters. It was clear that they had told such stories many times before to family and friends, and that such tales were being explicitly used to proclaim a religious message to others, to commend God and his ways to others. Praise of God was in the service of mission. Stories of spousal abuse, of suicide attempts, of sickness, of witchcraft, of healings, of shamanism all became the occasion for announcing to others that "Apajui is great/big *(muun),*" that "one does not play games with Apajui," that the "way of Apajui is good," that "Apajui is the one who holds us in his hand" (sustaining our lives) and that "with the word of Apajui, we live in peace." The stories of suffering that women tell, frequently as a result of the men in their lives, are poignant. Some describe the companionship and joy brought into their lives by Apajui, despite their expectation that their suffering will continue "in this life." Others describe the benefits of marital life lived in accord with the word of Apajui. As Unug describes her own conversion, following that of her husband, she tells how, at his initiative, they made a promise never to leave each other. "Very beautiful it is, to follow Apajui's path," she concludes.

When western scholars focus on praise and worship within the religious space of a church service, they are reflecting, in part, a western social reality in which God-talk occurs almost exclusively in such social space, directed only towards those already within the community of faith. But if worship involves ascribing worth to God, then many Aguaruna Christians do this routinely in non-church settings. They do this before a community-wide audience, not simply a church audience. They weave discourses about Apajui and his word into all different social settings and discussions that North American or European Christians have learned to keep separate. Furthermore, such discourses are produced by nearly all adults who "follow Apajui," and are not thought of as the special preserve of religious specialists.

Worship: Solitary and Communal

Some worship scholars follow the thinking of Emile Durkheim, who taught us to think of religion as a necessarily group activity.[8] According to this model, worship occurs only within a social gathering. Of course oth-

---

8. Emile Durkheim, *The Elementary Forms of Religious Life* (London: Allen and Unwin Ltd., 1915).

ers, such as William James, believed religious experience emerged out of "solitude."[9] Depending on where one looks, one can find support for either Durkheim or James. In traditional Aguaruna culture, individuals went to the forest alone for days of fasting, taking hallucinogens, and solitary singing designed to elicit visitations and blessings by ancestral spirits. And clearly, for many Aguaruna Christians, Apajui is sought in solitary ways. On repeated occasions I heard references to individuals going "into the forest to pray." Various individuals described crises in their lives where they went away into the forest or mountains for days of fasting and prayer. For example, one pastor's narrative includes the following: "Then I lusted greatly for many women. When this happened I went into the mountain to pray to Apajui. [After days of fasting and prayer] I felt like a child, without sexual desire." Another narrator, after committing adultery, describes his decision to spend time praying to Apajui: "I wept and went into the forest alone. [Based on prior experience] I said to myself, 'when I do this, I will feel good and joyful.' But I felt only empty. I noted that Apajui did not speak to me, and that I was completely abandoned." A couple of older men described themselves as abstaining from sexual relations with their wives in order to have more meaningful times of solitary prayer in the forest. Clearly a prior cultural template stressing solitude, fasting, and sexual abstinence as the appropriate way in which to pursue spiritual relationships continues to underpin and motivate much of the worship behavior of contemporary Aguaruna Christians, even as such practices are also justified in terms of biblical texts.

But Apajui is approached in social and not just solitary settings. Prayer is both private and communal. Within church services there are pastoral prayers, but also periods when everyone prays simultaneously, fervently, and loudly. Any sickness may become the occasion for prayer, with the sick person sometimes brought to the church for prayer — or more commonly with believers gathering in the home of the sick to pray and give other kinds of help. Following the rhythms of traditional life, many Aguaruna men awake at 3:00 or 4:00 A.M. and commence to sing Christian songs, quote Bible verses, and pray, both for their own benefit and for that of the larger family. In Tundusa the drum *(tuntui)*, which historically called people together to commence various ritual activities, is now located in the church, and calls people to Sunday worship, or to gather daily before dawn

9. William James, *The Varieties of Religious Experience* (London: Longman), p. 31.

Taking Communion   from the author's personal collection

for a period of joint prayer prior to heading off for work. Prior to special Sunday services, church leaders sometimes beat the drum periodically all throughout Saturday night — calling the community together for Sunday worship. Church songs include a mix of musical genres, drawing both from imported songs and from traditional musical genres (especially that of *nampet* — a genre of improvisational songs sung on social and festive occasions). Historically, Aguaruna music was not sung in unison. Furthermore, when one learned a song from another, one sang along a word or two behind the teacher, rather than striving to sing in unison. Outsiders are easily distracted then, when congregational singing involves some individuals vigorously leading out and others trailing along several notes behind. But only the outsider finds this problematic.

Worship and Culture

Aguaruna Christian worship, as I observed it in the *Iglesia Evangelica Aguaruna* in the late 1980s, draws on prior cultural patterns. Vocabulary

Drum Used for Calling People to Worship   from the author's personal collection

for God, sin, baptism, and preaching all utilize traditional Aguaruna vocabulary. Other than proper names from the Bible (adjusted phonetically), including that of Jesus, Aguaruna learn no new vocabulary upon becoming Christians. Artifacts of worship are long familiar. Rather than a church bell calling people to worship, the drum, which historically called to commence a vision quest, is employed. The Eucharist is celebrated, not with a special chalice containing wine, but with a traditional bowl used for communal drinking containing a traditional drink made from plantains. Rather than bread, the Aguaruna use manioc, a staple of their lives. Musical patterns, temporal rhythms, architectural patterns, all reflect Aguaruna culture.

But Aguaruna Christian worship also broke with many traditional cultural patterns. Conversion for all Christians was understood as involving a renunciation of all interactions with traditional spirits and all use of the shaman. While individual Christians occasionally resorted to the shaman, just as some occasionally committed adultery or participated in a revenge killing, other Christians immediately sanctioned them. That is, the church itself sustained a consistent ethic insisting on a systematic break with any involvements with the spirits. While the 1928 movement employed dance in worship, under the influence of missionaries, dance has no place in contemporary worship. And while historically manioc beer was the drink of choice for virtually all occasions, most Christians mark their renunciation of manioc beer as a core element in their own conversion. Aguaruna Christian worship also adopted new cultural patterns. An emphasis on a personal relationship with Apajui, on prayer to Apajui, on forgiveness of sins through Jesus Christ, on the importance of obedience to Apajui, on an eschatology of judgment, and on "the word of Apajui" represent major shifts.

Despite many elements of Aguaruna Christian worship that are distinctively Aguaruna, their reliance on the Bible, trust in Christ, and love for and obedience to God aligns them with Christians around the world. While they have a strong desire to be distinctively Aguaruna Christians, they clearly acknowledge their ties to a wider body of believers. Not only did they call me *yatsuju* ("brother"), but they spoke of us having shared "ancestors": Peter and Paul and the other apostles.

Conclusion

Insofar as both worship and mission include the activity of praising and commending God to others, and of inviting others to embrace God as the valued center of life, then worship and mission clearly accompany each other. Certainly they accompany each other among the Aguaruna Christians that I came to know. It is through praise discourses and through personal testimonies of the greatness of God and his ways, aimed continually at audiences of those who have not yet "contracted themselves" to Apajui, that much of the energy, vitality, and life of the church is sustained. As Emil Brunner has argued, "the Church exists by mission as fire exists by burning." We might equally say, "the Church exists by worship." For the Aguaruna, at least, both would appear to be equally true — mutually reinforcing one another. It is in part through the activity of generating discourses commending God to others that Aguaruna Christians stoke the fires of religious faith and sustain a vigorous church.

While members of the *Iglesia Evangelica Aguaruna* did not speak in tongues, they shared several traits with Pentecostal and Charismatic churches, which are growing rapidly in much of the world. Lacking a marked split between clergy and laity, virtually all believers routinely generate religious narratives affirming the greatness of God and the beauty of a life lived with God. Personal testimony is the preferred form of communication, fusing together Christian symbols and personal experience — distinctively Aguaruna experience. Such narratives create vivid images constructing Aguaruna models of the Christian life, modeling the route into a coherent and contextual Christian life for those not yet Christian. Dreams, visions, near-death experiences, and healings are frequent elements within such personal narratives. God is experienced as close, and involved in the daily affairs of life.

All people have been culturally shaped, with culturally contingent musical sensibilities, patterns of emotional and bodily expressivity, temporal rhythms, aesthetic tastes, and valued cultural artifacts. Even as Christians strive to be faithful to the Bible, they nonetheless do so in ways informed by such culturally contingent patterns. Western Christians have grown so accustomed to certain culturally shaped worship patterns that they find it difficult to disentangle the biblically normative from the culturally shaped. As a result, when we encounter those of radically different cultures, like the "Judaizers" Paul contended against, we judge others defective and may well attempt to impose culturally inappropriate worship patterns on others. In a world where migration brings cultural diversity to our doorsteps, it becomes critical that we apply the Pauline principle "nothing is unclean of itself" (Romans 14:14) to many of the worship elements employed by other Christians. When Aguaruna Christians take their own vocabulary, their own temporal rhythms, their own musical sensibilities, their own use of drum, or even their own early morning use of *wais,* and direct these in the service of the worship of God, the natural culturally shaped sensibilities of most westerners fail to resonate positively. And yet it is precisely such contextual worship which calls forth a positive response of worship from other Aguaruna. The historic strength of western forms of Christianity, and the contemporary economic dominance of western Christians, means that culturally shaped worship prejudices of western Christians are likely to have a disproportionate and even hegemonic influence on what are thought to be acceptable worship practices by others. And yet, for the Aguaruna, at least, the very vitality of their faith was underpinned by their ability to worship God in a way which did not subordinate them to alien aesthetic sensibilities. They exulted in the fact that they were both Christian and Aguaruna.

Our ability to understand the worship of others requires that we not simply attend to their rituals or actions, but that we attend to their discourses directed to God, and about God, and about the self in relation to God. In this chapter I have attempted to provide direct quotes from Aguaruna believers — quotes that both guide us into a culturally distinctive world, but also into the inner heart of people's response to God. Mission history has all too frequently provided only the voice of the missionary, and not the voice of indigenous believers. Much more research should be done to "listen" to Christians (old and young, male and female, clergy and laity) from very different cultural backgrounds, non-western backgrounds, as they speak of a great and good God who meets them in the nitty-gritty of everyday life. An adequate worldwide Christian theology of worship must reflect deep understandings of culturally contextual worship in diverse settings worldwide, and must be pursued by Christian scholars who themselves reflect this worldwide diversity.

Celebrating Pentecost in Leauva'a:
Worship, Symbols, and Dance in Samoa

Thomas A. Kane

Editor's Introduction

Samoan worshipers sing and sway, seemingly floating, "in a slight shuffle without lifting their feet from the ground," Thomas Kane writes. Kane's documentaries on "The Dancing Church" have shown us worship that happens, in his words, "with the full body — reverent, holy, and festive."

In this richly detailed portrait of the worshiping church in Oceania, Kane examines the role of liturgical dance and portrays the Samoan penitential rite of kneeling on a fine mat to seek forgiveness for the community. Kane's layout of a Samoan Mass illustrates plainly the intersection between tradition and contextual elements of worship.

•   •

Pentecost in Leauva'a, Samoa[1]

A young man blows the conch shell with its deep resonant tone to call the assembly together and mark the beginning of the celebration. The proces-

---

1. The parish of St. Michael, Leauva'a is halfway between Apia, the capital city, and the Faleolo airport. The people came from the village of Lealetele where the first Catholic missionaries were received. They abandoned their homes and lands because of the volcanic eruptions of Mt. Matavanu from 1905 to 1911. The people resettled at Leauva'a. The foundation of the present church was blessed on September 29, 1917, but the poverty of the war years and consequent epidemic delayed the work. The church was finally blessed on September 29, 1932. The Salesian order took over the care of this parish in April 1992.

sion begins with a group of royal guardsmen of honor in traditional Samoan ceremonial costumes — shirtless with oiled bodies, wearing a tapa cloth lavalava (wraparound skirt) and a necklace of large dark brown round beads. The various ranks of chiefs are also in ceremonial clothing. Then come the acolytes, catechists, concelebrating priests, and finally the main presider, Cardinal Pio Taofinu'u. In the opening song to the Holy Spirit, the community performs an "action song," with the community gesturing their prayer.

For the penitential rite, the paramount chief and his wife kneel and are covered with a fine mat. They represent the community, kneeling before God and asking for reconciliation. This rite follows traditional Samoan village custom for the seeking of forgiveness. The couple remains under the mat during the singing of the *Kyrie.* The presider then greets them with the sign of peace and blesses them with the paschal candle, which is then carried throughout the church.

During the singing of the *Gloria,* symbols of unity and peace are placed inside the sanctuary, in front of the altar table. The *tanoa* bowl with coconut shell cups is presented. This bowl symbolizes community, and it is from this bowl that the community participates in the *kava* ceremony in homes, in villages, and for community gatherings. Kava, a mild narcotic ceremonial drink, is served from the tanoa bowl. Both the kava and the bowl are significant symbols of community throughout much of Polynesia.[2]

---

2. Throughout most of Polynesia, kava is the universal medium of hospitality. The drink is processed from kava, a pepper root, which is dried, crushed, and soaked in water. Kava, the liquid residue of this mixture, is mildly intoxicating, and consumed as a ritual

The solemn entry of the Word involves the talking chiefs and their wives dancing with the gospel book. As the main talking chief holds the book aloft in front of the sanctuary, the community sings an action song with words like these: "The Word of God is very important. It is through the Word that God teaches the people. Come up, come up, listen to the Word, feel the power of God. We pay our respects to God's Word." During the song, the community extends their hands in rhythm with the music, pointing to the Book of the Gospels and then patting their heads, symbolizing their welcoming of God's Word.

During the liturgy of the Word, the paramount talking chief, present on the altar through the entire liturgy, speaks to the people and introduces the theme of the Word. In the response to the first reading, the male dancers circle the sanctuary space and face out as the congregation sings: "Holy Spirit, come, enlighten us!" The hand gestures move gently out from the center of the body with a soft swaying of the torso, as the feet remain in place. Before the proclamation of the gospel, the talking chief presents the talking stick, symbol of God's authority, and the flywhisk, the symbol of the chief's office, to the cardinal. The cardinal receives the symbols, and with them in hand advances to the lectern for the reading of the gospel and the homily.

During the gifts procession, the chiefly couples in full royal attire, with tapa cloth wraparound skirts, mirrored feathered headdresses, beads and feathers around their waist, enter the sanctuary space and dance in the unique style of Samoa, with swaying hand gestures and shifting feet movement. They act as honor guards to the sanctuary. Flowers, fruits, vegetables, and a roasted pig along with the bread and wine are danced down the main aisle. After the presentation, the pig is brought into the courtyard for the feast after the worship, while the fruits and flowers are placed in front of the altar in the sanctuary. Flower leis are also presented to the ministers.

After the Institution narrative, the women's dance-choir gathers around the altar, and, while kneeling, sings and gestures in its direction. During the Lord's Prayer, the entire congregation holds hands as men and women in the sanctuary form a large circle around the altar and the entire congregation sings the Lord's Prayer with accompanying gestures.

After communion, men and women flank the sides of the sanctuary

drink. Kava is served from this round wooden bowl, with four legs and a woven suspension cord attached with shells.

space in a staggered design and sing and dance an *Alleluia* as a communion meditation. There are specific gestures and movement patterns for the men and the women. As they sing, they move sidewise in a slight shuffle without lifting their feet from the ground.

The closing song reinforces the theme of the Spirit, and then everyone proceeds to the courtyard to continue the feasting with yams and roasted pig.

The Journey

Through the generous support of my academic institution, Weston Jesuit School of Theology, my sabbatical projects have allowed me to travel the globe, searching for the intersection of liturgy and culture in Africa, the South Pacific, part of Europe, the American Southwest, and San Antonio, Texas. I have been fortunate to discover the Dancing Church, and more importantly, to survive the trips to tell the story.[3]

In 1995, I began a sabbatical that became a voyage of discovery. My task was to document on videotape various liturgies and rituals of the South Pacific. If you look at a map, Oceania comprises not only small bits of land (islands and archipelagos), but the ocean itself. Rarely does an atlas ever show this area intact. Rarely do we get a complete view of Polynesia and Melanesia, which hold a wealth of cultural, aesthetic, and religious treasures.

The islands do not really seem to matter to the powers that be. The United States used many atolls for testing, polluting the seas and destroying massive amounts of sea life. In addition, the government basically enslaved the native Hawaiians, destroying much of their culture, and forbidding the use of their own language. Investors took away much of the people's lands so their people could eat exotic fruits or sleep in five-star hotels. Even today the native Hawaiians are struggling for land rights and recognition. In Aotearoa (New Zealand), similar struggles continue among the indigenous people, the Maoris, where once they were warriors.

---

3. My documentary work includes: *The Dancing Church of Africa*, *The Dancing Church of the South Pacific*, and *Fiesta! Celebrations at San Fernando Cathedral*. The tapes are available from Paulist Press, Mahwah, New Jersey. My journey to the South Pacific took place in 1995-96.

As I traveled the deep blue waters of the Pacific, I was making two journeys. The outer one covered the itinerary — thousands of air miles and many flight segments. It entailed flying in small planes through the perilous mountain passes, and navigating canoes to avoid crocodiles. There were moments of sheer terror and of total delight. More challenging, the inner journey revealed the landscape of my soul.

Travel broadens one's worldview and raises questions about what one holds dear. Even one's theological stance can be challenged! When I imagine *church*, I no longer see baroque palaces, Renaissance paintings, or the flurry of clerical entourages in scarlet and ermine. I see a community that liberates and nourishes people with a living Word — with painted faces and feathered heads, praying in languages I will never know, dancing, singing and celebrating God's presence in so many different cultural ways.

The "mission church" seems more open to liturgical creativity than the church back home. The concern shifts from getting the liturgy "right" to letting the liturgy speak freely in the local language through words, symbols, and dance. The church dares to celebrate with the full body — reverent, holy, and festive.

It is especially noteworthy to recognize the connection of evangelization with worship. So often both are seen as separate works, independent of each other. Spreading the gospel through celebrating the Eucharist is the work of the church, and careful attention is paid to the quality of the celebration. Reminiscent of the early church, this local church has a feeling of openness and deep affection among the ministers — bishop, priest, sister, catechist, and lay volunteer.

The Pacific is a place rich in cultural diversity and alive with religious faith. Many Pacific islanders, including the Samoans of this case study, are developing a Pacific theology by exploring the integration of their island ways of life and the age-old traditions of Christianity. It is a lively and exciting time to be the church in Oceania.

Inculturation and Worship

Today, not only the world dances, but the church dances. While this may seem shocking to some, liturgical dance is a reality around the globe, especially in cultures where dance is such a vibrant life principle. The use of dance and other cultural forms in worship is part of the process known as inculturation, the blending of culture and faith, which is a hallmark of the Roman Catholic Church after the Second Vatican Council.

Inculturation has become more obvious in recent years because of attention to the world church and the developing world consciousness among church ministers and missionaries. Inculturation, however, has been a part of the church from its foundations as it adapted to the variety of cultures around it.

> History offers a convincing argument in favor of liturgical adaptation. It assures the Church that adaptation to various cultures has been a constant feature of Christian liturgy. Indeed it is part and parcel of her tradition. The apostles did it, and so did the Fathers of the Church and her pastors far into the Middle Ages. Adaptation of the liturgy to various native genius and tradition is not a novelty but fidelity to tradition. Liturgical adaptation is as old as the Church, but it has been brought to the limelight in modern times because of Vatican II's renewed sense of pluralism within the Church and respect for people's cultures.[4]

In today's church, inculturation involves new ways of studying and doing theology. It influences the way local people pray, worship, and understand what it means to be the church. Inculturation is the dynamic dialogue of faith and culture. Pedro Arrupe, the late superior general of the Jesuits, provides us with a good working definition:

> Inculturation is the incarnation of Christian life and of the Christian message in a particular cultural context, in such a way that this experience not only finds expression through elements proper to the culture in question, but becomes a principle that animates, directs and unifies the culture, transforming and remaking it so as to bring about "a new creation."[5]

Inculturation may be taken for granted, or it may not be as evident in certain countries, but the process is very much in evidence in mission lands and has come to the forefront of our awareness with the rise of global consciousness and the reports of returning missionaries. Incultura-

---

4. Anscar Chupungco, *Cultural Adaptation of the Liturgy* (Mahwah, N.J.: Paulist Press, 1982), p. 3.

5. Pedro Arrupe, "Letter to the Whole Society on Inculturation," *Studies in the International Apostolate of Jesuits* 7 (June 1978): 9.

tion relates to proclaiming and living the gospel of Jesus Christ. Inculturation fosters embodied worship, and the very act of worship has a transforming power.

> Inculturation is not only about what happens to the message any more than it is only about what happens to the recipients. It is also, and very much, about what happens to the messengers as they transmit and interpret, model and embody the good news of salvation.[6]

This case study dramatically presents an inculturated worship that brings together the cultural elements of Samoa and the symbols of the Christian faith. Inculturation is no longer a theoretical concept, or what one reads in a theology manual. Inculturation is happening and taking shape in specific ecclesial communities, where the church leadership has begun integrating the Christian symbols with the local culture. This process uses the experience and history of a particular tribe or community as the starting place to express the deepest Christian mysteries.

In particular, the church in Samoa embraces its rich cultural heritage, and fuses that culture with its faith. The feast of Pentecost, as celebrated in St. Michael's Church, Leauva'a, is an example of the creative liturgical work of Pio Taofinu'u, presently the Archbishop Emeritus of Samoa-Apia. The cardinal, born in Samoa, recognizes that the future of the church in Samoa and possibly the world depends on an evangelization that speaks the language and culture of the people.[7] To this end, he has

6. Anthony J Gittins, *Gifts and Strangers: Meeting the Challenges of Inculturation* (Ramsey, N.J.: Paulist Press, 1989), p. x.

7. The first Samoan to become a cardinal of the Roman Catholic Church in 1973, Cardinal Pio Taofinu'u is one of the most prominent spiritual leaders in the Pacific Islands. Born December 8, 1923, at Falealupo, Savaii, Cardinal Pio Taofinu'u studied at the Moamoa Theological College. After attending a seminary in Wallis and Futuna, he entered the Society of Mary and did his novitiate in New York. On his return to Western Samoa he was nominated apostolic vicar of Samoa and Tokelau, and when in 1966 the diocese of Apia was erected he was nominated vicar general. On January 11, 1968, he was named Bishop of Apia, thus becoming the first Polynesian bishop in the history of the Church. His pastoral activity has been non-stop, creating numerous secondary schools and institutions of professional formation, demonstrating dedication to the apostolate and in serving the poor and elderly. He founded a theology institute for the formation of deacons and catechists. He was made a cardinal in 1975 by Pope Paul VI. Cardinal Pio has been leading the reforms of the Catholic Church in Samoa in which aspects of Samoan culture have been blended with the old traditional church practices. He was named archbishop emeritus in 2002.

been designing a Eucharistic liturgy that expresses itself with the rich symbols and folkways of Samoa. The work also requires the creative collaboration of chiefs, catechists, poets, musicians, and dancers.[8]

Outline of Sunday Worship

In order to understand the context of this worship, I will begin with a brief outline of a regular Sunday mass in the Roman Catholic tradition. The mass is divided into two sections: the liturgy of the Word and the liturgy of the Eucharist. I have noted in italic those elements from the case study that include a uniquely Samoan element.[9]

The opening rites:

- *Opening song with procession,* which gathers the assembly
- Greeting, which recognizes the presence of Christ in the assembly
- *Penitential rite* or Kyrie, which highlights our dependence on God
- *Gloria,* which offers praise to the Trinity
- Opening prayer, which gathers the community in prayer and connects to the word that follows.

The liturgy of the Word:

- First reading taken from the Old Testament or Acts of the Apostles
- *Responsorial psalm,* the community's sung response to the first reading

8. Traditional Samoan society is based on a chieftain system of hereditary rank, known as the "Samoan Way" or *fa'a Samoa* way of life. Despite the inroads of Western civilization, local cultural institutions remain the strongest single influence. The *fa'a Samoa* way of life stems from the extended family, with a common allegiance to the *matai,* the family chief who regulates the family's activities. Religious institutions are also very influential in the community, and the village minister or priest is accorded a privileged position, equal in status to a chief or matai. *Fa'a Samoa* is an all-encompassing concept that regulates behavior. It may refer to the obligations that a Samoan owes family, community, and church, and the individual's sense of Samoan identity. One must always respect those older, matais, ministers, politicians, doctors, and teachers

9. For a more detailed description of the Roman rite, consult the Introduction to the *General Instruction of the Roman Missal* (Washington, D.C.: United States Conference of Catholic Bishops, 2003).

- Second reading, usually from St. Paul
- Alleluia, a joyful acclamation to accompany the Gospel procession
- *Gospel proclamation*
- Homily
- Creed
- Prayer of the faithful

The liturgy of the Eucharist begins with the *preparation of gifts and altar,* as the focus shifts from the ambo to the altar table with the gifts of bread and wine brought forth from the community.

The Eucharistic prayer offers God thanks and praise:

- Preface and *Sanctus* (Holy)
- Institution narrative, the Last Supper text
- Prayers of remembering (anamnesis) — the memorial of the death, resurrection, and ascension of Jesus
- Prayers of intercession
- Great Amen — the community's acclamation of the entire prayer
- *Lord's Prayer*
- Lamb of God — breaking of the bread
- Communion
- *Prayer after Communion*

The closing rites include:

- Benediction and dismissal
- *Closing procession*

There are five elements in this Pentecost liturgy that should be especially noted: the various types of liturgical dance, the penitential rite and the fine mat, the use of flowers, the role of the talking chief, and action songs.

Liturgical Dance

Liturgical dance is a religious or sacred dance, employing movement, attitude, and shaping that may be used in Christian services. It may involve an individual dancer, a group of dancers, or the entire assembly. The liturgy of the church has a rich tradition of ritual movement and gestures. As ritual activity, liturgy has always employed different qualities of movement in its ceremonies, such as processing, bowing, kneeling, and standing. Liturgical dance is not performance. It connects to the prayer of the assembly, enriching and deepening the prayer by creating a prayerful environment.

Liturgical dance serves the worship by drawing the community into the mysteries of God, by revealing new dimensions of the scriptures, by witnessing to the beauty of God, and by eliciting a faith response from the community. At the service of the assembly, liturgical dance bridges the visible and the invisible world of the spirit. By its unique, nonverbal interaction of spirit and body, liturgical dance captures the nonverbal movements of the Holy Spirit, as the assembly enters into the mysteries of the liturgy.

The style and shape of liturgical movement of this case study derives from a specific Samoan dance tradition. On the surface, the dance style may not be what we might consider proper liturgical dance; that is, gestures or movement designed specifically for the liturgy. Rather, the movements are traditional and natural, flowing from island dance styles known to everyone, learned in childhood. The particular stylistic elements in the performance identify the dance movements as clearly and uniquely Samoan. While Polynesian dances all share common movement styles, such as the swaying of the torso and gentle undulating hand movements, the costuming and the specific styling differentiate each island style. By placement within the liturgy and adaptation to the sanctuary space, the island dances are transformed into true, prayerful liturgical dance.

Liturgical movement and dance aim to express in a genuine way the faith of the assembly because the dance presupposes a prayer life and a faith commitment on the part of those involved. Even simple gestures can enhance the community prayer when the entire assembly embodies the prayer. Because liturgical dance takes place within the structure of the worship service, dance types are determined according to placement and function within the liturgy. Three types of liturgical dance are used in this case study: procession dance, prayer dance, and meditation dance.

Procession dance is the purest form of religious dance. A procession moves from one place to another with a sense of purpose. Procession dance is primarily functional movement, which accomplishes a particular task. All processions, whether danced or not, possess a dance-like quality. Within this liturgy, there are four occasions that involve procession-like movement:

The entrance procession gathers all those assembled, sets the Pentecostal theme of the celebration, and accompanies the ministers to the celebration space. This procession is most colorful: many of those involved wear the traditional dress of Samoa, tapa cloth skirts, and brown bead necklaces. The men and women have oiled bodies; some wear chiefly attire, with feathered and mirrored headdresses, and the chiefs carry their symbols of authority. In contrast, the liturgical ministers are dressed in traditional church vesture.

The entry of the Word and Gospel procession highlights the proclamation of the good news of salvation from the Bible. The movement involves subtle hand gestures that reflect a Polynesian dance style, with a tilting of the head. The *Alleluia* acclamation accompanies the procession to the ambo where the scripture is proclaimed. The Book of Scriptures is ordinarily held high with sustained, graceful movement.

The gifts procession highlights the preparation of the table and the bringing forth the elements of bread and wine from the community along with other symbols. Fruits and vegetables in baskets are carried down the main aisle and received by the presider and placed around the front of the altar. Four men carry a roasted pig on a large wooden stretcher. The pig is brought into the courtyard of the church for the feast after the worship. An abundance of flower leis are also presented to the ministers.

The closing procession completes the liturgy and accompanies the ministers from the celebration space to the courtyard, where the celebration continues with the roasted pig dinner.

Acclamation and invocation form two kinds of prayer dance. Acclamations are shouts of joy arising from the assembly affirming God's word and action. In the case study, these include the *Sanctus*, the memorial acclamation, and the great Amen. During the memorial acclamation, the dance choir performs a reverential gestural dance while inclined forward on the floor of the sanctuary, facing the altar table. Simultaneously, an honor guard brings in a large flower lei to encircle the gifts of bread and wine on the table.

Invocations are prayers of praise and thanksgiving, including the *Gloria* and the Lord's Prayer. During the singing of the Lord's Prayer, the entire community joins hands as the dance choir and honor guards join hands with the presider and form a large circle around the altar in the sanctuary space. This action symbolizes the unity of the assembly as they offer prayers together.

Meditation dance is reflective by nature, a response to a reading, a commentary on a group of thematic readings, or a thanksgiving. This dance may inspire, challenge, or proclaim the message of salvation in a special way. The dance draws the assembly into reflecting on the impact of the message in their daily lives. The meditation dance of the case study takes place after communion. The young and men and women form a double line on each side of the sanctuary with the women in the front, offering a meditation on the Holy Spirit. As the ritual draws to a close, this contemplative time reinforces the theme of the celebration, the gift of the Spirit, and draws the community together in a spirit of thanksgiving.

Because liturgical dance operates within the ritual structure of the liturgy, it is clearly prayer and not performance, involving all the participants in the ritual action. Liturgical dance is communal, drawing the assembly together; inspirational, uplifting the spirit to God; evangelical, witnessing to the message of salvation; and prophetic, challenging the participants to live the gospel message. This study opens new possibilities for worshiping God and celebrating the Spirit.

The Penitential Rite and the Fine Mat

The penitential rite is the most unique element in the case study because it combines a traditional Samoan ceremony with a liturgical rite. The village ceremony is found only in Samoa. At the beginning of the liturgy, the elderly chiefly couple approaches the sanctuary and kneels in the center of the space, representing the entire community. As they kneel, a very large fine mat is placed over them as the community sings, "Lord, have mercy," which is the traditional chant for the rite. The couple seeks reconciliation from God on behalf of all present. This ceremony mirrors a forgiveness rite that happens in the village, during which the chief acts on behalf of the entire community. After the chant is completed, the presider greets the couple with a sign of peace.

The fine mat is used in the penitential rite, covering the chiefly couple, and another mat is presented during the presentation of the gifts. Fine mats are woven from *pandanus* leaves and have been used for centuries in Samoa. They hold a very special place in the Samoan way of life. Many would say a fine mat is the most valued treasure and symbol in the culture. When you present a fine mat, you are presenting the culture.

The Use of Flowers

Throughout Polynesia, flowers play an important part in celebration. It is very common to weave flowers into leis that are worn around the neck or on the head. The flowers are festive, sensual, and provide a sweet aroma for the whole day. In western culture, flowers tend to be placed in vases and are stationary. In Samoa and elsewhere, giving and receiving flowers is an interactive ritual. In presenting the flower lei, one is greeted usually by the maker. The lei is placed around the neck with some ceremony and afterwards one is usually kissed on one or both cheeks, or given a warm hug. The leis are a gift of love and time, because it is an arduous task to make a lei, since some leis are quite intricate, involving the interweaving of many different kinds of flowers and greens. The lei is also a symbol of unity — from the garden a variety of flowers are woven into one strand.

The Role of the Talking Chief

Samoan culture is rich in hierarchy and there are various rankings of chief. The "talking chief" is gifted with oratory. In this uniquely Samoan ritual, the presider approaches the chief and receives the symbols of the talking chief, the staff and fly whisk, also religious symbols of God's authority. In recognizing the value of culture and the *fa'a Samoa,* the presider embodies this respect by approaching the talking chief to receive the symbols of authority before reading the gospel and preaching. The transfer of symbols to the cardinal reinforces the charism of both teaching and preaching.

Action Songs

Action songs are similar to what many young people do at summer or church camp when they enact songs with gestures. It is quite common throughout Samoa that young people act out the texts with full body gestures. On Pentecost, the Our Father and the responsorial psalm invoking the Holy Spirit are both sung and accompanied with full body gestures. This is full, active, conscious liturgical participation, which was encouraged in Vatican II.

Implications

From this case study we can see how worship and mission are interconnected. The mission of preaching the good news of Jesus Christ is rooted in the liturgical celebrations of the local community. These celebrations reflect the ancient traditions of the church in the language and symbols of a local people. The means of communication is the cultural medium of symbols, dance, and the folkways of Samoa. The liturgy is specific to Samoa and the Samoan people. By celebrating the liturgy in this Samoan way they are expressing themselves as members of Christ's body. We also celebrate according to our received tradition and continue to look for ways to enhance and deepen our prayer and celebration.

Celebration describes the community activity on a Sunday morning. Celebration is a defiant act. We dare to gather on Sunday to remember, to hear again the stories of faith, and to be nourished by word and sacrament. The theologian Harvey Cox reminds us that celebration should: (1) be a joyful affirmation to life — a glorious Yes; (2) be juxtaposed to the everyday; and (3) be consciously excessive.[10]

So our gathering on Sunday is more than a mere gathering. It is a coming together as a faith community to encounter Christ through remembering, sharing, and eating together, engaging in the transformation brought about by his life, death, and rising. Renewing our Sunday worship requires courage and energy. It also requires our working with our own cultural forms and traditions, struggling to uncover new ways to express the age-old truths in new ways that reflect who we are as members of Christ's living body.

Art and ritual can elevate and expand our spiritual horizons. Symbols can express what the heart feels but the tongue cannot articulate. Let this case study invite you to a ritual world of symbols, art, and dance. Just as poetry transcends the use of everyday language, even though the words employed are the same, so too does ritual transcend ordinary body move-

---

10. Harvey Cox, *Feast of Fools* (New York: Harper and Row, 1969).

ment to elevate and uplift the spirit. Together, let us dare to raise new questions and open new possibilities for worshiping God and celebrating God's spirit who frees us. As technology shrinks the world and we are more aware of a worldwide community, the practices and customs of the world will touch us in new ways. Now is the time to receive from the world church, to learn from Christians very different from ourselves, to receive a new spirit of Pentecost. May that same Spirit challenge and transform us, bringing fire and light to our lives, our faith, and our community worship.

Worship as Mission: The Personal and Social Ends of Papuan Worship in the Glory Hut

CHARLES E. FARHADIAN

Editor's Introduction

Under the corrugated metal roof that envelops Papuan Christians as they worship, dancers in white wave colorful streamers, performing a dance that originated as a native ritual practice but has been given new resonance in Christian worship. Charles Farhadian introduces us to the *Pondok Kemuliaan,* the Glory Hut, where vibrant dancing, fervent preaching, moving confession, and robust singing punctuates worship in the Pentecostal tradition and the Papuan culture.

Among the most striking features of Papuan worship is the way it spills out into society. What Farhadian calls the "structural openness" of the hut in the open field physically blurs the line between sacred space and societal space. Worship is given public continuity in weekday evening meetings in parks and other public places. What Farhadian calls "the portability of worship" stands, as he says, in both "continuity and discontinuity with highland culture."

Farhadian highlights the themes of rehabilitation and peace that worshipers experience in the midst of personal destruction and social tension. He notes how the practice of confession is jarringly countercultural. Farhadian also observes, importantly, how the music of Papuan worship fulfills a subtle teaching function about the truths of the gospel. This chapter probes the theology of

The author would like to thank Jim Yost for his insightful comments on the church in Papua. International research for this chapter was supported in part by a Calvin Research Fellowship grant.

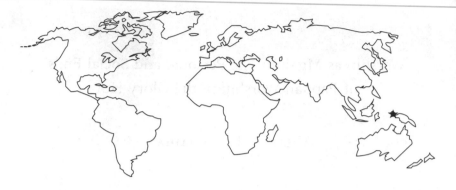

the practice of Papuan worship and ends with questions for discussion and re-flection on the purpose of worship and its relationship to culture.

•   •

Visiting the Glory Hut

On any given Sunday morning off the main street in Hawai, Papua (Indo-nesia), on the island of New Guinea, one can hear energetic praise music played by enthusiastic Papuan youth inside the Glory Hut (*Pondok Kemuliaan*), a Pentecostal fellowship of over 600 mostly young people.[1] The sounds of beating drums and tambourines, strumming guitars, and plunking bass rattle through the air, spilling out into the neighborhood in-habited by a mixture of Melanesians and Austronesians, who dwell in tradi-tional thatched-roof huts and modern cinder-block homes, in the largest Muslim country in the world.[2] The drums are not traditional Papuan *tifa* drums; they are similar to those used by Euro-North American rock bands.

1. Images and sound data of *Pondok Kemuliaan* can be found on the Internet at http://www.calvin.edu/worship/think/photo/pondok_kemul.htm

2. I employ the term "Austronesian" to refer to all Malay-Indonesians. Given the so-cial and political history of Papua it is useful to distinguish between Papuans (Melanesians) and non-Papuans (Austronesians). Since the region of Papua is located in the Republic of Indonesia, I use the terms "Austronesian" to refer to non-indigenous persons living in Papua and "Papuan" to refer to indigenes, rather than to use the politically inaccurate distinction "Indonesian" versus "Papuan."

Glory Hut   Photo by Stephan Babuljak

Drumming in the Glory Hut   Photo by Stephan Babuljak

Worship Band   Photo by Stephan Babuljak

Brilliant tropical flora and fauna surround the Glory Hut. Below one sees rocks worn smooth from decades of foot traffic, and a dirt path that leads to the entrance of the Glory Hut, with banana trees graced by wild parrots overhead. One inhales hot, humid air redolent with both exhaust fumes and sweet-smelling local plant life. Above it all, in this region just a few degrees south of the equator, is the blazing sun from which one cannot escape, much like the vibrant music streaming out over the landscape.

Today's worship service is like most at the Glory Hut. Hundreds of neatly dressed men and women — young and old, boys and girls, Papuan and Austronesian, educated and uneducated — gather together under the corrugated metal roof for more than two hours. Preaching, community announcements, and music are amplified through a modern sound system, with large speakers, multi-track soundboard, and microphones. An old overhead projector launches words of the songs onto a screen in front of the worshipers, as they jump and dance, and wave their arms up and down and side to side. Songs are sung in one of three languages: Indonesian, English, or Dani, in music ranging from tribal to modern, tranquil to fast-paced.

At the front are two young highland Papuan women in white dresses dancing with colorful streamers. The dancers' grandparents performed these same dances on the occasion of an important appeasement ceremony in which pigs were sacrificed in traditional highland ritual practice. Today these dance steps have been revalorized within this community of common faith.

A leader of the Glory Hut invites those needing healing from sin to come forward to be delivered from their burden. Almost immediately, three young highland Papuan men quickly come forward, tearfully confessing that they have fallen back into the sinful life from which they have been saved. They confess to drinking alcohol heavily. Their bodies are shaking, their voices low and trembling. The confessions are extraordinarily intimate and emotionally transparent. Others, from various ethnic groups from throughout Indonesia — including Javanese, Moluccans, Ambonese, and coastal and highland Papuans — come forward and place their hands on the shoulders and backs of the confessors. They pray fervently and empathetically, as though they were taking on the burden themselves. As the music continues and the prayers of the entire congregation are verbalized, the confessors and supporters are moved to tears, overwhelmed with the knowledge of God's mercy and tender love. Supporters pray for forgiveness and grace. Confessors are released from their sense of guilt.

A Subjugated Environment

This chapter highlights Christian worship practices at the Glory Hut, a church in Papua, Indonesia.[3] Public confession and healing at the Glory Hut resemble those in Pentecostal worship services throughout the world, and in countless smaller fellowships emerging in almost every corner of the globe. What makes worship unique at the Glory Hut is, in part, the social and ethnic backgrounds of the worshipers, and the history of the region.

Papua occupies the border region between one of the most Christianized areas of the world, the Pacific, and one of the least, Southeast

3. In the past several decades Papua has been referred to as "Nederland Nieuw Guinea," under Dutch sovereignty, and "Irian Barat," or "Irian Jaya," under Indonesian sovereignty.

Asia. It is the easternmost province of Indonesia. Since the late 1960s, when the Republic of Indonesia annexed Papua after two decades of conflict between Indonesia and the Netherlands, Papuans have fought hard for political independence from Indonesia.[4] Complicating the matter is the province's rich natural resources, which include some of the world's largest gold and copper deposits.[5] Environmental degradation and marginalization of local Papuan groups due to the influx of multinational companies has given rise to increased conflict between social forces intent on gaining political independence and government powers that aim to keep Papua within the national boundaries of the Republic of Indonesia.[6] Moreover, flames of social and ethnic tension have been fanned by the harsh treatment of Papuans by the Indonesian armed forces, including ongoing extra-judicial killing, intimidation, and a host of other horrendous actions to dissuade Papuans from pursuing political independence.[7]

4. See Charles E. Farhadian, *Christianity, Islam, and Nationalism in Indonesia* (London: Routledge, 2005), and Carmel Budiardjo, *West Papua: The Obliteration of a People* (Surrey, U.K.: Thornton Heath, 1988).

5. The Grasberg site, operated by Freeport-McMoRan Gold & Copper, based in Louisiana, is an engineering monstrosity, with 1,333 men "moving half a million tons a day"; see George Mealey, *Grasberg: Mining the Richest and Most Remote Deposit of Copper and Gold in the World* (New Orleans, La.: Freeport-McMoRan Copper & Gold Inc., 1996), p. 185. Using the world's largest trucks, Caterpillar 793Bs, with a load rating of 218 tons, the Grasberg mine extracts massive amounts of copper and gold, and guarantees investors many more years of profit; see Mealey, *Grasberg*, p. 196. Furthermore, in 1995 Freeport-McMoRan was Indonesia's fourth-largest taxpayer; see John McBeth, "Treasure Island," in *Far Eastern Economic Review* 157 (10), 48 (1994a): 49. Today the mine continues to be one of the highest taxpayers to the central government of Jakarta. In the words of Mealey, the president and chief operating officer of Freeport-McMoRan Copper & Gold, "[t]he average *daily* revenue being generated by our Irian Jaya mines is more than $5 million" (p. 186), with estimates that the copper-gold porphyry contains a deposit worth almost $80 billion. Conflicts between the local Amungme tribe and the American-based company have drawn international attention, pitting tribal land rights against an extremely lucrative international extractive industry; see John McBeth, "The Lost Mountain: Plunged into the 20th Century, Tribes Struggle to Cope," in *Far Eastern Economic Review* 157 (12), 31 (1994b): 1.

6. See R. W. Baker, "The Deforesting of Irian Jaya," in *The Nation* 258, no. 5 (1994): 162-63.

7. See Amnesty International, USA, *Indonesia: Continuing Human Rights Violations in Irian Jaya* (New York: Amnesty International, USA, 1991), Dale Gietzelt, "The Indonesianization of West Papua," *Oceania* 59 (1989): 201-21, and Benny Giay, *Menuju Papua Baru: Beberapa Pokok Pikiran Sikatar Emanisipasi Orang Papua* (Jayapura/Port Numbay, West Papua: Deiyai Press).

One strategy to Indonesianize and Islamize the province of Papua involves implementing a government-sponsored transmigration program. Since the late 1960s, this program has moved tens of thousands of families from overcrowded islands in the archipelago, such as Java and Sumatra, to less densely populated islands, such as Papua and Kalimantan. Visitors to Papua feel they have entered a militarily occupied territory (unlike the well-known European tourist destination of Bali, where the military remain fairly inconspicuous). While the overwhelming majority of Papuans crave political independence, a massive military presence dominates social space, fiercely controlling any attempt to raise the Papuan independence flag.[8]

The governmental policy of providing transmigrants with free land, housing, education, and healthcare — while forcing Papuans from the land they have inhabited for thousands of years — exacerbates social tensions between Papuans and off-island transmigrants. Since the 1980s, the urban centers of Papua have become increasingly dominated by Austronesian peoples and cultures, leaving many Papuans socially and economically sidelined. As young highland Papuans move to the urban regency of Jayapura on the north coast of the island, having left their villages and extended families far behind, they soon realize they lack the skills, education, and financial means to compete with any degree of success with Austronesian newcomers, and the government has done little to provide assistance to Papuans.

Brief History of the Glory Hut

The Glory Hut *(Pondok Kemuliaan)* began in March of 2000 as an offshoot of the Restoration Hut *(Pondok Pemulihan)*, which was started in early 1998 by a Javanese man, Sumiran, and an American, Jim Yost. Both churches began in response to the spiritual needs of younger generations, who desired churches with greater relevance to their urban lives. Today, members of the Glory Hut consist primarily of young Papuans, whereas the Restoration Hut attracts mostly off-islanders (i.e., Austronesians). However, both churches are multi-ethnic, with representatives of Austronesian and Papuan groups.

8. See Charles Farhadian, "Raising the Morning Star: A Social and Ethnographic History of Urban Dani Christians in New Order Indonesia" (Ph.D. dissertation, Boston University, 2001).

The Restoration Hut began as a rehabilitation outreach geared toward helping young highland Papuans whose lives were broken and wounded from alcoholism, huffing (sniffing glue), and other self-destructive behaviors. Today the Glory Hut continues its ministry of rehabilitation, focusing on young people whose self-image has been destroyed. The Glory Hut states that it envisions a church as a center where people from many tribes and backgrounds can come together and break down the social prejudices of Papuan society. The Glory Hut sees itself as having the dual function of elevating the strengths of Papuans as well as being an avenue for evangelism.

According to its mission statement, the members of the Glory Hut seek to create a space "where broken people are restored and then become leaders with influence who can be sent out to impact the education system, the political system, the military, the social system, the arts, communication, and the economy until every segment of society is penetrated with the love of Christ." Leaders of the Glory Hut have adopted a cell-group model, where small groups meet weekly for accountability, prayer, and teaching. Many members of the Glory Hut were raised in either mainline Protestant or Evangelical churches, and some come from the families of pastors. These young people have found mainline and evangelical churches irrelevant to their daily lives. In addition, more and more Euro-North American missionaries have found their spiritual home at the Glory Hut, adding to the complexity of ethnic plurality of the weekly assembly.

Whereas most Papuan churches are led by one "big-man" pastor, leadership at the Glory Hut consists eventually of nearly anyone who desires to lead; in fact, all persons are encouraged at some point to lead some aspect of worship. As such, one person does not alone have leadership over the entire congregation. Rather, individuals are encouraged to utilize their natural gifts. The church is youth-oriented, and it is evangelistic, with about ten more people professing faith in Christ each week. The church also emphasizes creative thinking of its leaders and lay members, rather than rote memory — the typical catechismal practice in Papuan churches.

Contours of Continuity and Discontinuity

In the following section I would like to highlight some of the characteristics that make worship at the Glory Hut unique compared to the vast majority of churches in urban Papua.[9] It is important to keep in mind that the Glory Hut represents one of the fastest growing Christian movements in Papua. As such, the present paucity of Pentecostal fellowships in the province belies their present and future influence in Papuan society.

Worship Space

Pondok Kemuliaan (the Glory Hut) lies on an open field adjacent to the home of a leader of the fellowship. Nearby are a full-size basketball court and two large chicken coops, suspended over a large pond with alligators for guards. Members of the Glory Hut sell the eggs the chickens produce — just one way the fellowship provides work and income for its people.

Pondok Kemuliaan can be translated as either "Hut of Glory" or "House of Glory." The term *pondok* means temporary dwelling place, shack, lodge, or cabin. The emphasis is on the temporariness of the structure. Patterned after the surrounding indigenous Sentani huts made of thatched roofs and walls that consist of dried palm leaves, the worship space differs only in size from those in the neighborhood. The Glory Hut is a Sentani hut writ large, a structurally continuous building, able to cover more than 600 people. Early each Sunday morning, before the worship service, volunteers set up hundreds of red folding chairs. The roof consists of corrugated metal, with the sides of the structure open except for palm leaves that extend to about five feet from the ground. There are no windows in the Glory Hut. Worship happens on a dirt floor.

The worship space inside the Glory Hut is conspicuously plain and simple. Absent are images of Jesus or of any biblical personage. Absent too are crucifixes, crosses, or any other religiously potent Christian symbols. The only signage may be a banner announcing boldly the vision of the fellowship — "Papua Blesses the Nations." The church explicitly focuses on transforming individual lives, with the belief that remade lives

9. In significant ways mainline Protestant and evangelical churches in urban Papua reflect the architectural structure, theological commitments, and polity of their Euro-North American and Australian mission forbears. For instance, many mainline Protestant pastors still wear a black gown and clerical collar. In both mainline and evangelical churches it is not uncommon for hymnals to consist almost entirely of translated Euro-North American hymns, such as "Amazing Grace," "Holy, Holy, Holy," and "How Great Thou Art"; see Farhadian, "Raising the Morning Star," p. 278.

Exterior of the Glory Hut   Photo by Charles E. Farhadian

will transform the world, and the banners publicize that change can indeed happen.

What is most striking about the Glory Hut's worship space is its structural openness to the surrounding community. Worship, through music, testimony, preaching, and praying, pours out into the wider neighborhood. As such, the entire worshiping community functions as a witnessing community to inhabitants in the local area. The open architecture is innocuous to curious passersby, who are free to stay outside or enter the fellowship space without feeling intimidated. And many do in fact stroll in and join the assembly inconspicuously.

Music and Bodily Participation

Music makes up the central part of the worship experience at the Glory Hut, played by a mixed Austronesian and Papuan band through the entire service. The music is usually, but not always, fast-paced, upbeat, and energetic. Frequently the music is punctuated by ecstatic voices praising God

Dancing in the Glory Hut   Photo by Stephan Babuljak

and exhilarated bodies jumping in place and running around. Slower-paced music encourages quietness before God during times when reflection is encouraged.

While most songs are in *Bahasa Indonesia* (Indonesian language), written outside of Papua, several songs each Sunday are in English and others in a vernacular tribal language, most often the Dani tribal language. The rhythms and harmonies of Indonesian and English language songs are patterned on popular Euro-North American music, particularly rock, blues, and increasingly, West Indies reggae. For instance, Christian lyrics are put to the melodies of songs by the popular Irish rock band U2 as well as the American (Latino) band Los Lobos.

It is important to note that although their degree of physicality is toned down, even the evangelical churches in areas that have electric generators have adopted a "contemporary style" worship service, accompanied by electronic instruments, drums, and hand clapping. Within Pentecostal worship services, physical boundaries become blurred as congregational members feel free to dance, shout, raise their hands in praise, and clap vigorously. The Pentecostal style of worship is distinguished from the mainline worship pattern in Papua, which is more physically subdued, and is marked by hymnal-based singing, a higher degree of ritual liturgical formality, overall conservative bodily participation, and the presence of rigid boundaries among worshipers and between laypersons and clergy.

Village churches, on the other hand, show little evidence of "contemporary" styles of worship replete with electric instruments and praises choruses, which in large part is due to the absence of electricity in most hinterland villages, the inconceivable expense of purchasing Western instruments, and sometimes a reluctance to adopt new religious patterns, coupled with an overall conservativeness of Papuan culture in remote regions. It is not implausible, however, to suppose that contemporary styles of worship will accompany the expansion of electricity throughout the highlands in the near future, particularly with the introduction of generators and other forms of electricity to those areas.

Frequently at the Glory Hut a group of Dani young people provides special music — an indigenous Dani Christian song using Dani language, traditional harmonies, and rhythms. Songs, whether in a Dani language or Bahasa Indonesia, serve a teaching function in the church, highlighting important themes within Christianity. The song below comes from the language of the Grand Valley Dani. It is sung in the Glory Hut as well as in evangelical congregations consisting of a majority of Dani. The melody is traditional Dani:

O Jesus, You Are Great

O Yesus kanyat meke	O Jesus, you are great
Nenalok nen at wagaike	Why did you come?
Nenalok nen at watuka	Why did you die?
O Yesus kanyat meke (2x)	O Jesus, you are great
Weakma lasak meke	When we didn't have the power
Yesus nen at telninapike	Jesus redeemed us
Hat heki owa'ne owa	His hand is powerful
Hat hane owa'ne owa	Let's receive his Word
Nit hano telninapigin	We all have been saved.

It is important to note the didactic function of songs sung in the Glory Hut. Since many worshipers are illiterate, songs recount biblical stories, and serve as a powerful means of communicating the gospel message. Music functions the same way among traditional highland gatherings, where, in the pre-Christian period, congregational singing retold significant tribal stories of origin and myth.

Portable Worship

It is one thing to worship in an enormous open hut near the main road of a popular town, but it is quite another to take the entire fellowship to the street to publicly worship outdoors, becoming a roaming worshiping community. On weekday evenings, members of the Glory Hut worship en masse in public places such as parks, dirt lots, and open fields. Although not all worshipers from the Glory Hut attend the evening public worship services, often hundreds are present, along with a band playing amplified electric instruments and tambourines, singing the same praise choruses they sang during the Sunday morning gathering. Worship is portable. It can go anywhere. And it includes the majority of the Glory Hut congregation rather than one or two evangelists, which would more closely typify street evangelism in the Euro-North American context.[10]

Prior to their conversion to Christianity, when worship practices became privatized, practiced within the four walls of Euro-North American mission-established churches, highland Papuan religion was, in significant ways, public.[11] For instance, a taboo violation of the spirit world would require a ceremony of reconciliation, in which ancestral spirits were appeased through blood offering from a sacrificed pig in a ceremony that was performed, as it were, in the village square — publicly.[12] No one was ex-

---

10. In small groups the Glory Hut also holds outreaches to a local prostitution house and prison. The church has started a motorcycle repair shop and coffee house to employ their members and provide hospitality to the local community.

11. See Charles Farhadian, "Comparing Conversions Among the Dani of Irian Jaya," in Andrew Bucker and Stephen Glazier, eds., *The Anthropology of Religious Conversion* (New York: Rowman & Littlefield Publishers, Inc., 2003).

12. For example, see Karl Heider, "The Grand Valley Dani Pig Feast: A Ritual of Passage and Intensification," *Oceania* 42, no. 3 (1972): 169-97; Gordon Larson, "The Structure and Demography of the Cycle of Warfare Among the Ilaga Dani of Irian Jaya" (Ph.D. dissertation, University of Michigan, 1987), pp. 246f.; James Sunda, *Church Growth in the Central Highlands of Western New Guinea* (Lucknow: Lucknow Publishing House, 1963), pp. 40-43.

cluded from participating, or at least observing the ceremony. The public nature of highland Papuan religion was delimited in part through contact with early Euro-North American missionaries, whose own cultures valorized church buildings as "houses of worship." An additional force of privatization was modernity. Highlanders returning from coastal cities, having been educated in a modern educational system replete with school buildings, wanted modern buildings in their villages. Church buildings gave visible evidence of the growth of Christianity, which further encouraged prayer and financial support.

Furthermore, the access to religious knowledge distinguishes highland traditional religious practice from urban Christian worship at the Glory Hut. Whereas religious knowledge in the highlands was held privately by the big-men of the village, who closely guarded the secret wisdom of the tribe, in the Glory Hut the truth of the gospel is proclaimed to all who will listen.[13] No one is excluded from access to the knowledge of salvation; men, women, young and old have an opportunity to hear the message. The goal of the Glory Hut is to share the gospel with the world, beginning with its own neighborhood and city.[14] Of course, mission is a common and necessary feature of Christian churches worldwide. Yet, when the public nature of verbal proclamation is combined with the public and portable possibility of worship, the Glory Hut deeply resonates with Papuan lifeways.

Given the social context of religion in the traditional environs, where worship practice was public and religious knowledge was private, the portability of worship at the Glory Hut displays elements of continuity and discontinuity with highland culture. Just as traditional highland religious practices were not limited to one or two locations within the village (i.e., Papuans could sacrifice a pig nearly anywhere), so too worshipers at the Glory Hut do not feel compelled to remain confined within the "walls" of

13. In the traditional highland context the "big-man" designation denotes a person who possesses social and economic influence in village life. Although rare, "big-women" are extant. This pattern is to be distinguished from the chiefdom designation in Polynesia, where heredity determined political ascendancy. See Marshall Sahlins, "Poor Man, Rich Man, Big Man, Chief: Political Types in Melanesia and Polynesia," *Comparative Studies in Society and History* 5 (1963): 285-303.

14. The mission of the Glory Hut not only involves verbal proclamation but also includes behaviors and actions. For instance, large teams of church members have cleaned the grounds of the local mosque and refurbished the structure of the local taxi stand. The Glory Hut also trains its members in motorcycle repair, computers, and literacy.

their ecclesial worship space. Instead, they naturally feel confident that worship ought to be made public. In fact, Christian worship, when combined with Papuan cultures, cannot exist as an isolated enclave cut off from the rest of society. In this sense, the portability of worship at the Glory Hut mirrors the public nature of religion in the pre-Christian environment. Yet it expands traditional Papuan notions of religion by democratizing truth, rather than assuming it to be secret knowledge of a select few, and publicizing that truth with universal intent.

Public Confessions

Perhaps the most salient feature of worship at the Glory Hut is the role played by public testimony and confession. By "confessions" I am referring not to formal creeds and confessional documents summarized in such statements as the Apostles' Creed, Nicene Creed, Augsburg Confession, or Westminster Confession, read aloud in many churches worldwide. Confessions at the Glory Hut refer to moments in which worshipers extemporaneously admit to such wrongdoing or wrong thinking as to impair the believer's relationship with God. During times of confession worshipers recount how they once were estranged from God but now have been reconciled, giving the details of their spiritual journey. Confessional narratives tend to be either open-ended, from those still needing reconciliation, or closed-ended, from those who already sense healing from God and the community. The confession time is deeply moving for most worshipers and lasts several minutes, and sometimes confessions can spontaneously erupt to take over the entire worship service.

What happens during the time of confession? Autobiographical statements and biblical passages are woven together into a nearly seamless narrative that communicates the worshiper's desire for forgiveness or healing. Personal testimonies of worshipers at the Glory Hut exhibit biographical continuity with biblical stories. Sunday sermons and mid-week small-group discussions often employ stories of biblical personages as models of living, against which worshipers can measure their own struggles and victories. Outsiders may be startled by the transparency and honest humility of confessors, who display immense courage in the public assembly. Tears often accompany the sharing of one's story. Those who openly admit their sin have the attention of the entire gathering.

Most notably, the dominant theme that emerges during confession is the struggle with sin, and the confession of such personal sin serves as the central component to the oral narratives. In fact, one reason for the popularity of the Glory Hut is the free space provided through the personal openness during worship that encourages public confession of sin. The confession of sin has become perhaps the most significant and consistent element of both large-scale public and small-group (known as cell-group) worship. Confessors know they are not alone in their admission of guilt. Instead, they are keenly aware of the full support they receive from fellow worshipers. Public confession of wrongdoing, or "wrong being," runs counter to the logic of Papuan culture. According to a leader of the Glory Hut, "Confession of sin goes against the grain here. . . . Sin in [Papua] is defined socially. Sin is wrongdoing, what I do against somebody else that they find out about. If I do it, and nobody finds out about it, it's not sin."[15]

What is the meaning of public confession for Papuans? Public confession of sin is both like and unlike traditional Papuan culture. During traditional warfare, it was assumed that the losing side had not confessed all its sins against the community, spirits, or the natural world. Therefore, it was common that the losing side would break away from ritual warfare to sacrifice a pig and confess the sin preventing the warring party from success. Usually confession was given only in dire circumstances, only after all efforts on a human level were exhausted. According to missionary reports, early highland Papuan converts to Christianity proclaimed their acceptance of Christ in the following terms: "I have confessed all my sins and Jesus has cleansed my heart with his blood" and *Ninago dleko — Jetu ninago* ("We have no sacrifice pigs. Jesus is our sacrifice").[16] This phrase became the earliest credo of the highland Papuan Christian community. Although it was a final solution, confession was no less important. Rather, in the pre-Christian period the act of confession represented an extreme performance of contrition to save the life of the clan. In the context of war, Papuan confessional practices affirmed the clan identity of the warring party as well as corrected the broken relationship between confessor and either community, spirits, or land. As such, admission of guilt played a profound role in the identity maintenance and overall well-being of the tribe.

15. Interview of Jim Yost, 1998.
16. Sunda, *Church Growth in the Central Highlands of Western New Guinea*, pp. 40-43.

Yet within the context of urban Christianity, where clan identities no longer provide a canopy of shared meaning, Papuan confession functions as a potent symbol at once representing the desire for spiritual and material success as well as the recognition that those within the multiethnic Christian community are among the confessor's closest companions. That is to say, those gathered each Sunday in worship, namely Austronesians and Papuans, form a new clan, a distinct volunteer association cemented together by a radically different social and religious glue than what bound and maintained clan identities in the traditional highlands — religious ties have replaced blood ties.[17] Ethnicities enjoy little opportunity to be held as ultimate when relativized under the banner of Christian fellowship and charity. In his own words, a young Papuan compares the new sense of community he experiences at the Glory Hut with the relationship he has with his own family:

> If I meet one of the congregational members [in the street], I truly feel that they are members of my family. Whether he's white, black, or brown, I feel they are my family. If I walk down the street and see a church member I feel in my heart, "Hey, that's my family." But, if I meet my [biological] family, I don't feel the same way — I don't feel anything special. My church family feels closer to me than my [biological] family. . . . My church family knows one another heart to heart, not just skin to skin, superficially. So, I look inside one's heart to know whether the other person is really part of my family. So, it is possible to change our attitude and knowledge of each other. We feel closer to each other than we do to our own families that we never speak to, or share our problems with. Here, in this church family, our relationships are more special. I feel that I can tell anyone here anything that's in my heart, and they can tell me anything that's in their heart as well. That makes us more close and open with one another.

17. Ernest Gellner asserts that "It is the high religions [e.g., Christianity], those which are fortified by a script and sustained by specialized personnel, which sometimes, but by no means always, become the basis of a new collective identity in the industrial world." Gellner, however, does not account for the ways in which social carriers of knowledge and religious insight may in fact be illiterate or lack the education required of specialized scriptural interpreters. Furthermore, his perspective does not account for the ways in which diverse ethnic congeries might be sustained in a new collectivity. See Ernest Gellner, *Nations and Nationalism* (Ithaca, N.Y.: Cornell University Press, 1983).

Prayer in the Glory Hut   Photo by Stephan Babuljak

Public confession in the multiethnic Glory Hut signifies a radical statement of personal and social reorientation, away from putative tribal identities to a broader identity encompassing Papuan and Austronesian, educated and uneducated, old and young, and men and women. No longer are sacrificial pigs required to win the war. The new war is a spiritual one, fought on an individual level, with the help of the community of fellow believers. Drinking, fornication, and thievery no longer rule an individual heart, but are subjugated to the power of the Holy Spirit. The cold estrangement that most Papuans felt when entering the urban center dissipates quickly in the warm fellowship of believers.

Cell Groups

The social structural organization of the Glory Hut also serves to attract people and intensifies the confessional component of worship. The church is organized on a small group or "cell group" model where nearly each person who attends the church commits to a small group of six to twelve people that meet weekly for an intimate time of sharing prayer concerns, reflecting on the previous Sunday's sermon, and intentionally being devoted to each other. According to a leader at the Glory Hut, "Rather than waiting until Sunday celebration service, we now encourage daily confession. So our cell groups are divided [into] even smaller groups of two or three people who will see each other often during the week." Intensive small group worship entails "three things — exhale (confess sin), inhale (take in the Word together) and open your eyes (pray for your unsaved friends and neighbors)." Furthermore, suggests a leader, "the only way for lives to be restored is to confess what really needs restoring." Confession for restoration occurs in cell groups, intensive small groups, and the larger weekly assembly, encouraging the profession of sin to happen almost daily in a structured environment of supportive friendship.

Dance

Euro-North American missionary notions of worship behavior introduced to churches throughout Papua the belief that worshipers should display decorum appropriate for presence in the "house of God." Good churchly behavior entailed worshiping in a bodily posture that was constrained, uptight, and — in the eyes of Papuan young people — rigid. The highlight of traditional Papuan celebratory performance always focused on dance and bodily movement. Traditional Papuan festivities were marked by a high degree of plasticity, rather than the physical fixity so common in Euro-North American congregations. That is to say, some Euro-North American missionaries unwittingly suppressed Papuan bodily expression in worship, believing bodily movement dishonored the living God. A young Papuan explains the importance of bodily movement in worship:

> Especially for [highland Papuan] people, worshiping God involves dancing, much like the experience of King David. But Western missionaries came and said, "Dancing is not good. In front of God you have to be polite." So the people followed the tradition of worship set out by the Western missionaries. That pattern became a church rule. Church leaders today tell Christians to worship that way, even though [highland Papuans] always gave bodily expression to worship in their traditional religion. When the missionaries entered and said, "You

can't. Don't. In front of God you have to be polite," people believed them.

But here, at the Glory Hut, the spirit of Papuaness is alive . . . we don't feel like foreigners, because this is our culture, this way of worship. . . . In the past, when [the Papuans] sang a song to praise the Lord, they did it by dancing and forming a circle. And when the pastor would begin to preach, the pastor would say, "Stop dancing, I will preach now." So the local people followed the missionaries' model.

It is Papuan to be expressive, active in worship, rather than passively observant. Papuans at the Glory Hut argue that they feel greater freedom to worship than in either mainline or evangelical churches. Beyond the traditional Papuan dance styles performed by liturgical dancers, break-dance teams and interpretive worship dance teams also perform in front of the congregation. Break-dancing holds the attention of young Papuans because they are influenced by the music and dance styles presented on MTV. Interpretive dance appeals to worshipers because it accentuates the Papuan strength for communicating truth via dance. Besides these teams, the entire congregation dances during worship. To worshipers at the Glory Hut, the freedom to dance enables them to feel at home, providing the familiar in an unfamiliar urban milieu.

Preaching

Following the pattern of group meetings in hinterland Papua, the preaching style at the Glory Hut is interactive, permitting members of the congregation freedom to address the preacher directly. The leader of the conversation may be "pastor" or "big-man," but the community has the right and responsibility to remain engaged with the topic at hand through active discourse with the one delivering the sermon. In remote villages, such gatherings serve as arenas for the communication of the most important issues of the clan or tribe, such as whether or not to go to war or political decisions that may impact the entire community.

In village life, male members of the clan have the freedom to inquire of leaders and challenge ideas. On several occasions I have been to remote village churches where members of the congregation directly engage the pastor during the delivery of the sermon. A hand may go up to signal the need for clarification on a part of the message. Or an impromptu comment may challenge the ideas presented by the pastor. Needless to say, often these sermons-turned-pastoral-conversations follow trajectories beyond the scope of the sermon topic, but the dialogues reveal what is important in the hearts and minds of the congregation.

The verbal fluidity between preacher and congregation is encouraged in the worship service at the Glory Hut. In fact, during preaching, a worship leader in the middle of the sermon may invite some young people to the front to act out a point spontaneously. And the worshipers will do it. Worshipers may also inquire of the preacher to clarify a point or may relate a story of how the topic impacts their life.

In important ways the communicative patterns engendered in the Glory Hut differ from those followed in the highlands. The content of communication no longer consists of tribal warfare or appeasing the spirits of ancestors, with the attending fear of failure. Rather, discussions center on topics such as God's love for people, recognizing oneself as bearing the image of God, being the temple of the Holy Spirit, and forgiveness — that is, learning how to be close to God and others without the fear of retribution. Furthermore, whereas highland meetings permit only male members of the clan to counter remarks made by other "big-men" leaders, in the assembly of the Glory Hut both men and women are encouraged to communicate publicly. Women have recognized gifts and insights necessary for the community of believers. Communicative fluidity between congregation and leader is a natural trajectory from verbal to performative discourse, translated and expanded through the inclusion of women, to the urban center.

Initial Questions

Worship practices at the Glory Hut raise important questions for Christian worship worldwide today. Worship is never an isolated experience; it is embedded in social, historical, and political circumstances that give it meaning. Since they are subjugated people, the fact that Papuans worship alongside Austronesians, and consistently refer in intimate terms to the relationship they share together, represents a radical social reorientation. Young Papuans are attracted to the Glory Hut because the worship services combine modern and traditional ways. That is to say, Papuans can go to church without leaving their cultural particularities at the door. Wor-

Worship Technology — Projection
Photo by Charles E. Farhadian

shipers sense an affirmation of things present, yet at the same time they get a glimpse of a more expansive world through the employment of modern instruments and technology.[18] The best of Papuan culture is given new

18. What is significant about the use of modern technologies such as amplified sound equipment and microphones is not merely the particular message that is announced, but rather the idea that is transmitted — that the social conditions have changed. The medium matters because it ennobles a particular language and style and represents a new "centralized, standardized, one to many communication" (Gellner, *Nations and Nationalism*, p. 127).

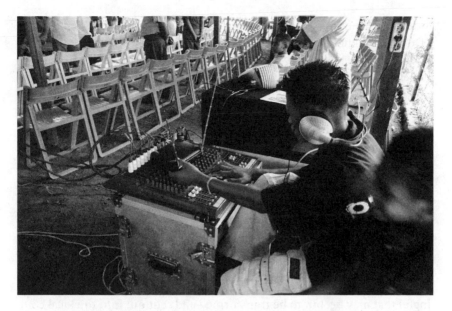

Worship Technology — Sound Board   Photo by Charles E. Farhadian

worth as some of those elements shunned by mainline and evangelical churches in the past are esteemed within the worshiping community at the Glory Hut. How might particular cultural elements be incorporated into worship? What are the constraints of doing so?

In addition, the architecture of the Glory Hut raises important questions for Christian worship. How should we understand worship space? Can space be inherently sacred? If so, what makes a worship space sacred? If not, then should worship space be perceived as merely continuous with the secular space that surrounds it? The case of the Glory Hut challenges an overly close identification between particular spaces and authentic worship. For worshipers at the Glory Hut, genuine worship occurs when believers are gathered together, giving honor, praise, and reverence to the living God who transforms individual and social lives. Naturally, worship also includes listening to the Word of God, through preaching, performance, and singing. Any notion of sacred space among worshipers at the Glory Hut relies on the conviction that sacredness applies to one's individual body and the body of believers rather than to the physical space enclosed by the architectural structure exclusively. The biblical statement in 1 Corinthians 6:19 provides an apt summary of the perspectives of worshipers at the Glory Hut: "Do you not know that your body is a temple of the Holy Spirit, who is in you, whom you have received from God? You are not your own." The meaning of worship for those at the Glory Hut has more to do with the community's faithful relationship with God rather than its presence in a particular space. How might worship be portable in other locations? What are the possibilities and pitfalls? What social and cultural conditions might constrain or encourage the portability of the assembly?

What is the purpose of worship in the Glory Hut? All elements of worship are geared toward one end — *metanoia,* a turning toward God by being reconciled to the Creator and a turning toward the world animated by a missional identity. Worshipers desire to be remade in the image of God — their personal and corporate lives are rejuvenated and they become new creations embedded in a community that affirms their human frailty and yet celebrates the forgiveness and grace offered by God. Yet the end *(telos)* of worship is not to be gathered together, no matter how meaningful that may be, but to be transformed and sent out into the local community, the nation, and the world.

The movement into and out of the worshiping community reflects the robust missional movement of the Glory Hut, the intentional focus of worship in the gathered community. The missional identity of the worshiping community gives it purpose and resolve. Worshipers expect God to meet them during worship in ways that are deeply personal, yet they cannot predict how the Spirit of God will move them toward personal reflection and mission. In this sense, what happens during worship at the Glory Hut should not be understood as sensual abandon, but rather a thoughtful and embodied expression of submission to God, with the hope of being personally and corporately transformed. Mission begins with *metanoia,* and it is within the space of worship that change begins. Why does the church around the world exist? What is the purpose of worship? How might churches throughout the world today be missionally relevant and purposeful?

Conclusion

In the subjugated environment of Papua, where religion is often politicized by the powers that be and tensions between indigenes and immigrants is palpable, the church represents perhaps the only possibility for learning civil behavior in the context of social and religious plurality. Worship builds new communities in urban centers by fostering new creations out of broken individuals and communities. As such, worship at the Glory Hut represents the extremes, combining modern cultural elements with the expressions from a 9,000-year-old tribal tradition to give new meaning to honoring God. Cultural elements once overlooked or even anathematized by some early Euro-North American missionaries find renewed significance in the context of worship.

PART III

Practices

Editor's Introduction

We have seen so far in this book what John Witvliet writes in his series preface: "worship is an occasion when the instinctive beliefs, dispositions, and values of a given community are on full display." The practice of public worship is inseparable from the public profession of faith. As Witvliet writes, "worship expresses through cultural forms of communication both explicit truth claims and basic intuitions of God's presence."

Our observations of the communal expression of worship in its cultural context inevitably lead us to articulate a theology of worship. The form of communal expression of public worship, as we have already seen, can best be considered alongside the meaning and purpose of public worship, especially in a survey of worship worldwide. It is here that sociology meets theology, and each informs the other. Sociological research about worshiping communities reminds us that worship is something that is practiced, not just discussed. Theological explorations call us to realize the more profound proclamation of God's truth that is inherent in the act of worship.

The case studies in the previous section illustrate the immense variety of expressions of Christian worship. Yet certain common features, transcultural and timeless, remain. Worship, throughout a variety of traditions, continents, and centuries, has central underpinnings or characteristics that are constant. Some of them could be articulated this way:

- Vital worship is not something that human ingenuity or creativity can produce or engineer, but is a gift of God's Spirit.

197

- Vital worship mines the riches of scripture and leads worshipers to deeper encounters with the message of the gospel.
- Vital worship arises out of and leads to the full, conscious, and active participation of all worshipers.
- Vital worship leads a community beyond itself, to give itself to ministering to the needs of the local community and the world.
- Vital worship happens best in healthy communities, which are marked by honesty, integrity, unity, and pastoral concern for each worshiper.

In the following chapters that highlight key themes in the history and practice of worship around the world, many of the themes, theories, and principles the authors establish fit naturally under one of these five statements.

As these authors examine the principles behind the practice of worship, consider which of these five statements is at work. How does embodied participation in worship become a gift of the Spirit, and the epitome of active participation in worship? How does liturgy mine the riches of scripture and lead a community beyond itself? How does prayer lead worshipers to deeper encounters with the divine? How can cultural incorporation of worship rites arise out of, and contribute to, healthy community life?

The practice of worship is inextricably linked with the purpose of worship. This section shows how a deeper understanding of each illumines the other.

Participation in Worship — Worship-full Hearts: A Meditation on Luke 7 and Matthew 15

OGBU U. KALU

Editor's Introduction

The motif of the heart is one that transcends different denominations, traditions, and cultures. What can be shared is the common conviction that authentic worship is visceral, uncontainable, and un-confinable. Ogbu Kalu turns a luminous phrase as he invites us to explore "the choreography of the worship-full heart."

In the stories of the woman who washes Jesus' feet with her hair and the insistent mother of the demon-possessed daughter whose pursuit and kneeling compels Jesus to heal the girl, Kalu sees the ultimate act of complete worship — worship that topples barriers and assumptions, worship that is wholly embodied, and worship that surrenders to the all-sufficient love of God. Compellingly, Kalu calls us to form communities that embody these "worship-full hearts," and to reflect: How can worship practice serve as a springboard to new self-understandings and understandings of others? How is Christian worship a boundary-breaking practice that eliminates divisions between social classes that were once marked by mistrust and suspicion? What are the sources of a renewed Christian community?

•   •

Someone observed that by the end of January most New Year resolutions fizzle out as bold, unsustainable endeavors. How is it that we always wish one another that the New Year would be happy, or encourage one another that God would bless us more abundantly in the New Year than in the past year? I am taken aback when people impress persistently that we should, in addition, wish that each one of us give more to God this year than we did last year. Does this mean time, money, or more intensive lecturing? Some may add more hours on the picket lines or in pursuit of social justice causes. I daresay that all these are valuable gifts that God will not reject. But a danger always lurks behind our activities for God: we can be very active without much communication with God, and cover the shallowness with the right words and right actions. We can dine with Christ at the Lord's Table without knowing him. A commentator observed that this happens because people wish to be in control and avoid any spirituality that may indicate otherwise. He says that it may happen because people are afraid of touching base with their real selves. We can pray regularly without ministering to God. This is because most of us lack worshipful hearts.

Last year I taught a course on "African and African American Women in Conversation." One of the challenges of a womanist discourse is to learn to read the Bible from a woman's perspective: to recover voice, to give voice, to re-tell old stories from the eyes of those who have been victims of institutionalized patriarchy. It was a voyage in discovery for two reasons: whenever Jesus encountered a woman (at the well, on the crowded road, in Simon's house, or even in the tomb), the reader learned something deep about the reality of Christ. In their encounters with Jesus, women illustrated the different characteristics of "worship-full hearts." Two cases will suffice.

The first is the woman whose name is omitted (though the names of the men in the saga are documented). She is not only a faceless woman but stigmatized. She is a sinful woman in the city. With our prejudices and moral judgment duly primed, we are treated to a shocking encounter. The occasion was odd. A Pharisee named Simon invited Jesus to a meal. I always think of Bonhoeffer's observation that whenever Jesus encountered the Pharisees, something would be said about true discipleship. In this story, the uninvited, stigmatized outsider breaks all cultural and religious protocols and boundaries to enter the house of the Pharisee and join the company of males. Somebody has observed that the woman appears to know the terrain sufficiently to move about with familiarity; that Simon was being a true Pharisee by being pharisaic. At first I feared to consider the speculation, until it occurred to me that we tend to dodge the fact that the word *prostitution* is not necessarily in the feminine gender. It is gender neutral or colorless, applying to a condition variously described by the psalmist as miry clay and a pit into which men and women sink. A good example is the young man whom we euphemistically refer to as "the prodigal son." He was really a male prostitute just like the stigmatized woman. He and those with whom he wasted his money became united in the same condition and controlled by the same spiritual force. The problem, therefore, is not the gender of the person, but whether there is a power, from an inexplicable source, that could draw one out of the miry clay or pit. It must take resurrection power for the person to stand up and walk away from the swine diet in the pigsty. Many people who have been in similar states testify that only an inexplicable power pulled them out from desperate life conditions, out from the allure of street life and out of drug or alcohol abuse. So, whether Simon threw the first moralistic stone or not, he was implicated in the uncanny background to this story. Her action teaches us the first lesson for a worship-full heart: namely, that the person must break out, break boundaries, to come boldly into God's presence to seek help in time of need. Paul encourages us to come boldly and reverently.

So the narrative takes us to the reverent movement as she stands behind Jesus (meaning that this was not the lap dance that might be expected by the prejudiced). Then, she sinks to his feet as a sign of vulnerability. People from certain southern regions of the world would recognize this cultural facet: people kneel in reverence when they meet superior persons such as a father, mother, an aged person, a priest, chief, or king. In humility, she starts to worship and adore Christ. She weeps and weeps and weeps. As Joel 2:12 would say, "Yet even now, says the Lord, return to me with all your heart, with fasting, with weeping, and with mourning." It was not a loud wailing but groaning in brokenness. Deep worship arises from being broken and contrite. As the psalmist would say, the sacrifice acceptable to God is a broken spirit; a broken and contrite heart, O God, you will not despise (Psalm 51:17). Have you ever worshiped at that depth? Or do you quickly recite your list to God and rush off? Paul said that at such moments, the Spirit takes over and searches the heart of God on our behalf with groans that we cannot understand.

The Bible passage says that she shed many tears, so many that she could wash the feet of the Lord of Lords — he of whom the Bible says that it pleased God that in him the whole Godhead could bodily dwell; that he is the shining glory of the Father and the expressed image of his person. This "sinful" abused woman worshiped Christ at a deep level. Foot washing in ancient Israel had both cultural and religious significance. As a sign of hospitality, the servant of the host would wash clean the feet of the guest who had just walked through a dusty terrain. It was an act of servant-hood. Jesus would later enact it at the Last Supper to underscore this dimension. It could be interpreted as a cleansing ritual, even a spiritual cleansing from the sinful dust gathered in our human interactions. Normally, we would ask Christ to clean us. But this woman was cleaning Jesus as a sign of his humanity, even though he was without sin. She gave Jesus what the ordinary praying saint would ask from Jesus.

The choreography of a worship-full heart went deeper. She touched and kissed the feet of the holy one of Israel. Just as our mouths touch the elements that signify his body, her mouth touched and kissed the body of Christ. As Luther would say, Christ is in the elements as fire is in a hot iron. The Roman Catholic liturgy puts it even more vividly: that Christ is *ac vereliter ac realiter in membrum sensum continetur,* that is, he is truly and really in the elements. True worship is such that the votary touches God; the channel of communication opens.

Then she gave her valued material possession as an ingredient of worship. Her alabaster box freshened and perfumed Christ. Some may read the act as prophetic signification of his death, but Jesus compared the act with anointing one's head with oil. This is the psalmist's daily prayer that asks for the Holy Spirit's enduement, because John 16:14 says that the Holy Spirit's duty is to glorify Jesus. The Holy Spirit joins in the act of worship, oiling and lubricating the contact, aiding it, and carrying the incense of prayer to the nostrils of the Father. Simply put, a worship-full heart gives to God what others expect from God. It places God in a relationship that says God desires our offerings, rejoices over us as the prophet Zephaniah would say, and wants us to rejoice over him. The psalmist could declare that God inhabits the praises of his people. A regular prayer life at this depth ensures a healthy ministry because only a worship-full heart can truly serve as a minister of our God. But stop for a moment and exult with Paul at the riches of both the wisdom and knowledge of God; how unsearchable are his judgments and how inscrutable his ways! Who has known the mind of the Lord? Who has been his counselor? (Romans 11:33-34). Who could have imagined that this core lesson would come from a sinful woman in the city, who had been caught in a vicious circle of a lifestyle that diminished self-respect!

Whenever Jesus encountered a woman, a deep lesson in Christian living would follow, because he used the weak position of the excluded and vulnerable to teach the strong that they should take heed, lest they fall. In this case, he told Simon that it was possible for someone to sit at a meal with Jesus and yet fail to know him, to realize who he is, to worship, or develop a deep relationship with him. We do well to theologize on the fettered access to the table, but we often fail to emphasize that many come to the table but do not meet him. As an African American spiritual puts it, many talk "'bout heaven but ain't going there." Jesus answers prayers: the eyes of the Lord are upon the righteous; the righteous cry and the Lord hears them. He forgave her sins, restored her battered self-image, redeemed her past, and made her an apostle of the gospel. Many songs have been written about her alabaster box!

Another outsider, a Canaanite woman, confirms it. Hers was a life cluttered with barriers and exclusion: gender, class, status, and race. Ethnically, she came from the wrong place, outside the boundaries of Israel and the itinerary of Christ's ministry. Her family was broken with an inexplicable affliction, namely a demonic oppression. It was particularly painful because the key victim was her daughter; one could imagine a mother's guilt when she could do nothing to help her suffering daughter! She responded by doing what pastors teach us to do when we are distressed, vulnerable, and desperate: she went to Jesus. She even called him by his messianic name, son of David. We recall that when the blind Bartimaeus called him by this title in a crowd, Jesus responded. Instead of such sympathetic response, we hear the most stunning verse in the Bible: "But he did not answer her at all" (Matthew 15:23). This is like walking through the dark night of the soul, confronted with spiritual dryness and a silent God. We could hear the psalmist plead that God should not be silent lest he might be like those who go down to the grave. The psalmist cajoles that dead people cannot praise God. The exclusion is worsened by the attitude of the disciples. It is as if the community network became an accomplice in her distress. In spite of the exclusion clause in the divine economy, she worshiped at the master's feet. Jesus used a version of vernacular idiom to explain the situation. This was a proverb about dogs, crumbs from the master's table, and the children's food. Variations of this proverb occur in many African languages. Jesus did not call her a dog and was, in fact, talking to the disciples in response to their suggestion. With a measure of agency that womanist theologians deploy against proverbs that demean women, the Canaanite woman reversed the interpretation of the customary saying, because in the feeding of the multitudes, the quantity of crumbs indicated that God has more than the children could eat. She virtually declared that the proverb could not apply to her situation or to any situation when one comes to Christ for help precisely because of the power of God, who gives in large measure. God declared in the psalms that "the cattle upon the thousand hills are mine!" His crumbs are more than enough; his abounding goodness is more than sufficient for both Jews and Gentiles. Masters, children, and dogs have enough in Christ's "abounding goodness." Jesus recognized that the excluded woman, from the wrong ethnic group, knew the reality of Christ better than the children of the bedchamber. Worship-full hearts enter Christ's presence and touch the depths of his power; they reach out to the reality of Christ and change physical realities through worship. Luke 6:18 explained that when worship-filled hearts touched Christ, life situations changed, because "power came out from him and healed all of them."

It could be that there are hindrances from your busyness, intelligence, self-esteem, enlightened worldview, or fear of losing control or dealing with your real self. It could be that there are cultural barriers to entering into the world of the narrative, feeling the power of the gospel, or accessing the inner power of the words. The world of Jesus resonates with the world of the Southern Hemisphere; the stories come alive when heard in these places, and this explains the charismatic stamp on Southern Christianity. But location is quite important because there are some of us whose lives do not worship Christ sufficiently, do not minister to him, and do not bring our alabaster boxes. We go through prayer regimens without being broken because of the strength of the will and soul force or the regnant worldview. These excluded women teach us about the power of worship-filled hearts as it lifts from the pit and breaks protocols. A worship-filled heart could entail a struggle through the dark night of the soul, but it changes things because it enables us to touch the power that comes out of Christ.

Our challenges as Christians are to be a community of worship-full hearts who cultivate a worship-full community. Being a community of worship-full hearts enables us to be sensitive to the needs of those who are hurt, marginalized, excluded, stigmatized, vulnerable, and need to be led to the Master's feet for worship and healing. An effective engagement with the world must come from first cultivating a worship-full heart. Yet it is so easy and avant-garde to put the cart before the horse.

Praying Globally: Pitfalls and Possibilities
of Cross-cultural Liturgical Appropriation

C. MICHAEL HAWN

Editor's Introduction

Throughout this book, the tension between the contextual and the cross-cultural, transcultural, and counter-cultural have been examined in concrete ways. Now, Michael Hawn, scholar of global music and global worship, provides us with central themes and questions in the theology of worship as we have seen it exhibited. Specifically, he raises this question: How do we distinguish between the contextual and the cross-cultural in worship? What is lost, and what is gained, when a cultural ritual or symbol is incorporated by another culture? What are the limits and uses of this kind of incorporation? As Hawn asks, "Can Western worship incorporate the rites, rituals, and symbolic expressions of other cultures in such a way that neither stereotypes nor denigrates the sending cultures? Do all rituals have cross-cultural potential?"

To help us sort through these questions and their implications, Hawn helpfully lays out six assertions about "liturgical pluralilty," and proceeds to explore other crucial themes regarding identity and community in cross-cultural worship. Mindful of the southern geographical focus of the case studies in this volume, Hawn's chapter reflects on the historic and contemporary expressions of liturgical plurality within the North Atlantic context, noting that liturgical plurality has been the mainstay of Christian worship since its beginning. We are left to consider these questions: How has the Christian church historically adopted liturgical practices from the Bible, from its immediate surroundings, and from cultural areas and historical periods distant from itself? What are some guidelines for authentic multicultural worship?

• •

I recently heard the most powerful rendition of J. S. Bach's *Passion Accord-ing to St. Matthew* that I may ever experience. The choir had virtually memorized the parts and had total command of the original German text; the Evangelist admirably presented the Gospel narrative while other solo-ists provided musical meditation and theological commentary on the bib-lical account; the instrumentalists were a dynamic partner in the music-making, providing color and articulation to the text beautifully enunciated by the choir; and the conductor guided the entire ensemble in a dramatic unfolding of the passion story. The audience was rapt by the artistry, preci-sion, and power of the performance. By any musical standards, this was a world-class presentation of one of the masterpieces of the Western musical tradition.

The evening was even more remarkable because the choir perform-ing this Western masterwork was the Bach Collegium Japan. Except for the Evangelist and one bass soloist from Germany, the role of Jesus sung by a bass from the Netherlands, and a countertenor from Great Britain, all of the remaining vocal soloists, choral and instrumental musicians were from Japan. How does the music of Bach, now over 250 years old, speak so pro-foundly to a contemporary Japanese culture where only one percent of the country professes Christianity? How can a Japanese Christian musician, so knowledgeable about and capable in the presentation of the music of a German master composer, communicate so profoundly to a North Ameri-can audience? This was a night to remember by any artistic criteria, but a night to treasure because the resources of three continents came together to produce a profound evening of worship — a German composer with Japanese musicians, appreciated by a North American audience.

This essay addresses the issue of the appropriation of rites, rituals, symbols, and artistic expressions from one cultural setting into another. In the example cited above, the cross-cultural dimensions are evident. The people of one culture, Japan, had become so proficient in the music of an-other culture — separated from the world of J. S. Bach by thousands of miles in distance and over 250 years in time. Imagine an ensemble from the United States presenting a traditional Japanese *Noh* drama to an audience in Germany at such an artistic level that the German audience was pro-foundly moved by the experience.

Earlier chapters in this book have presented descriptions of Christian rituals from around the world. Witnessing the growth of the gospel seed, planted in various cultures of the world, is enlightening and encouraging. Many congregations around the world have learned songs and rituals from the Western church and these have become integral to the way that they express their corporate spirituality. Should not the church in the West, especially in the wake of the worship reforms of the Second Vatican Council (1962-1965), consider incorporating the rites, rituals, and symbols of other cultures into their corporate worship life even though these expressions are far removed from them in place and cultural perspective? Can Western worship incorporate the rites, rituals, and symbolic expressions of other cultures in such a way that neither stereotypes nor denigrates the sending cultures? Do all rituals have cross-cultural potential? Are local congregations enriched by exposure to liturgical expressions of the universal church? Will congregations increase the diversity of their membership by expanding the range of cultural expressions they employ in worship?

Conversely, other questions raise cautions about such practices even if the intentions are laudable. Are congregations more comfortable using only cultural expressions closest to their experience? Can a congregation primarily from one culture learn to incorporate liturgical expressions from another competently and appropriately without offending the sending culture? Do not people from other cultures prefer to be with those from their own ethnic background? Will not people be confused by too many different or unusual rituals in their worship? Who will teach a congregation the right way to do these new rituals? Is cross-cultural worship another example of a multicultural, politically correct agenda?

All of these questions have merit. The waters of cross-cultural change should be approached with eyes wide open. Some may find these waters exhilarating, while others find them troubling, resulting in feelings ranging from disorientation to anger. This chapter will discuss some of the pitfalls and possibilities of cross-cultural worship. The conclusion offers guidelines for appropriating aspects of liturgy from beyond the normative culture of the congregation — prayers, rituals, music — for use in worship. Cross-cultural liturgical appropriation is not only possible but desirable if carried out in a careful and thoughtful manner.

Choosing Liturgical Plurality rather than
Cultural Uniformity in Liturgy

Paul Bradshaw poses the thesis that primitive Christian worship was not as uniform as might be assumed by some interpretations of early sources. Indeed he suggests that the range of worship practices of the early church throughout the world was quite varied or "pluriform." Pluriformity extended not only to theological variations within different traditions, but to the very structure of rites and rituals.[1] In spite of moves toward uniformity of rite and ritual within major ecclesiastical traditions over the centuries, the church seems to be returning to pluriformity once again. This is, however, a different pluriformity than that of the first centuries of Christianity. During the early days contact between congregations was minimal and often regional at best. The pluriformity of liturgical practice that was, according to Bradshaw, characteristic of the early Christian church in the first millennium C.E. corresponds in many ways to a cultural diversity or liturgical plurality that is increasingly a part of worship in the third millennium.[2] While there is evidence that the liturgical practices of one group may have influenced others, the process was very selective and slow.

Since the Second Vatican Council, several overarching trends have determined liturgical practice. One is the increased dialogue between Roman Catholics and many Protestant groups in areas of lectionary and the rites of Christian initiation and Eucharist. While the results of these discussions do not indicate conformity in theology and liturgical practice, many worship traditions have much more in common in the area of lectionary and the general structure of the sacraments than in the days preceding the Second Vatican Council. Another trend is the process of inculturation that has taken root in many areas of the world, especially in Africa, Latin America, and, to a lesser degree, in parts of Asia. Aylward Shorter defines inculturation as "the on-going dialogue between faith and culture or cultures. More fully, it is the creative and dynamic relationship

1. Paul Bradshaw, *The Search for the Origins of Christian Worship* (New York: Oxford University Press, 1992), p. 54.
2. See Paul Bradshaw, "The Homogenization of Christian Liturgy — Ancient and Modern: Presidential Address," *Studia Liturgica* 26, no. 1 (1996).

between the Christian message and a culture or cultures."[3] Anscar Chupungco enlarges on this definition:

> [Inculturation is a] process of reciprocal assimilation between Christianity and culture and the resulting interior transformation of culture on the one hand and the rooting of Christianity in culture on the other. . . . [This] process of interaction and mutual assimilation brings progress to both [worship and culture]; it does not cause mutual extinction.[4]

Inculturation has encouraged much more diversity in style, especially in the areas of the arts — visual arts, dance, and music. The plurality of liturgical practice found in the late twentieth century differs from the relative isolation found in the centers of early church worship. The liturgical plurality of today reflects the diversity of practice and style that exists in a world that is extremely connected. One of the greatest areas of liturgical cross-pollination is in congregational song. Many denominational hymnals published in the United States after 1980, in the post–Second Vatican Council period, reflect an incipient liturgical plurality by including not only songs and hymns that bear the heritage of a specific faith tradition, but by introducing a cross-section of congregational song from virtually every other major denominational tradition, several intentional ecumenical communities, and some parachurch groups. A few North American English-language hymnals, especially those published since 1987, also reflect global plurality in varying degrees.[5]

3. Aylward Shorter, *Toward a Theology of Inculturation* (Maryknoll, N.Y.: Orbis Books, 1988), p. 11.

4. Anscar Chupungco, *Liturgical Inculturation: Sacramentals, Religiosity, and Catechesis* (Collegeville, Minn.: The Liturgical Press, 1992), p. 29. The term "inculturation" is derived from the Latin *inculturatio* and is currently used almost exclusively when referring to the relationship between liturgy and culture. "Enculturation" is a term reserved by anthropologists for the socialization of individuals.

5. English-language hymnals and hymnal supplements from Canada and the United States with significant numbers of global hymns include *The Psalter Hymnal* (1987), *The United Methodist Hymnal* (1989), *The Presbyterian Hymnal* (1990), *Hymnal: A Worship Book* (1992), *The Chalice Hymnal* (1995), *The New Century Hymnal* (1995), *With One Voice* (1995), a supplement to the *Lutheran Book of Worship*, *Voices United* (1996), *The Book of Praise* (1997), *The Faith We Sing* (2000), a supplement for the *United Methodist Hymnal*, and *Sing! A New Creation* (2001), a supplement for the *Psalter Hymnal*.

What is liturgical inculturation within the United States? Most of the literature and all of the case studies presented in this book focus on how countries and cultures outside of the Euro-North American sphere can enrich their worship traditions in ways that reflect their specific cultural roots. What are the cultural roots of the United States? Clearly, the majority of Christians globally now live outside the Euro-American context, and ethnic and cultural diversity within the United States will continue to increase.[6] Virtually every metropolitan area of the United States is becoming a microcosm of the world's diversity. Cultural diversity is at our doorstep. Is liturgical plurality a way to bring new vitality to our worship?

Defining Liturgical Plurality for the Twenty-first Century

Six general assertions frame my understanding of liturgical plurality as a model for cross-cultural worship rather than uniformity or eclecticism — three assertions about what it *is not,* and three about what it *is.*

1. Liturgical plurality is not "ethno-tourism." Madeleine Forell Marshall, commenting on what she calls "Third World/liberation" hymnody, cautions us against this danger. Congregations should not be allowed to think that showing solidarity with others by singing global songs is the same as "having fun in the sun in Mexico."[7]

2. Liturgical plurality is not denying one's cultural heritage of faith in song, prayer, and ritual. It is a conscious effort to lay one's cultural heritage and perspective alongside another's, critique each, and learn from the experience. Margot Fassler and Peter Jeffery express well the importance of established musical forms within the contemporary context:

> Chant and polyphony will not go away, indeed they are more popular among some of the general public than they have been for centuries. Just as the church, while it must be open to new theological insights from every quarter, can never abandon its biblical and historical Greek and Latin heritage, so the church, while it must penetrate and

---

6. See Philip Jenkins, *The Next Christendom: The Coming of Global Christianity* (New York: Oxford University Press, 2002), pp. 79-105, for a detailed discussion of the growth of Christianity from the South and its influence on the shape of Christianity in the North.

7. Madeleine Forell Marshall, *Common Hymnsense* (Chicago: GIA Publications, 1995), p. 162.

redeem every culture in the modern world, can never forget its musical heritage.[8]

3. Liturgical plurality does not necessarily imply a synthesis of styles into one "universal" form. To the contrary, it is an acknowledgment of and participation in a diversity of voices within a liturgical structure. Inevitably the juxtaposition of styles has an influence on each other.[9] Liturgical plurality implies, however, that we attempt to appreciate *sui generis* the contribution of each perspective to our understanding of God. Rather than a melting pot that synthesizes, the image of a mosaic comes to mind. Each piece of a mosaic has its own shape and hue, yet it fits together to form a larger whole. Analogously, each cultural contribution has its own distinct cultural shape and hue, but all come together as they contribute to the overall shape of the liturgy.

4. Liturgical plurality is a *counter-cultural* expression of faith that calls into question the context of the normative culture in light of the *transcultural* message of the gospel and the historical shape of Christian liturgy. As liturgical materials from Others — persons beyond our cultural worldview also formed in God's image — are placed side-by-side with rites and rituals from our culture(s) of origin, unfamiliar prayers, creeds, ac-

8. "From the Bible to the Renaissance," in *Sacred Sound and Social Change: Liturgical Music in Jewish and Christian Experience,* ed. Lawrence A. Hoffman and Janet R. Walton, (Notre Dame: University of Notre Dame Press, 1992), pp. 115-16.

9. Such cross-stylistic influences are manifest in a variety of ways in music including the combination of text, melody, accompaniment, instrumentation, and movement from two or more cultures in the performance of a single piece of music. Depending on the social dynamics of these combinations, they may be viewed as liberating or imperialistic. I-to Loh explores some of these dynamics in "Contemporary Issues in Inculturation, Arts and Liturgy: Music," *The Hymnology Annual: An International Forum on the Hymn and Worship,* vol. 3, ed. Vernon Wicker (Berrien Springs, Mich.: Vande Vere Publishing Ltd., 1993), pp. 49-56. At what point these combinations become a synthesis of styles is open to question. In "Toward Contextualization of Church Music in Asia," *The Hymnology Annual,* vol. 1, Loh prefers the term "syncretism," which he defines as "new compositions in the native style using traditional or contemporary Western harmonic idiom[s that are] skillfully integrated into a new composition. The melody may be native, but the harmony remains Western, thereby elements of both are syncretized" (p. 95). In other rites, a congregation who uses the Apostles' Creed might include an affirmation of faith or creed from another tradition. The existential reality is that the earlier creed, firmly in the memory banks of the people, is juxtaposed with the more recent creed simultaneously, opening up new meanings for both creeds.

tions, and songs may act as a filter for our normative cultural assumptions, modifying or transforming our perspective and our local liturgical practices.[10] Liturgical plurality — the juxtaposition and integration of cross-cultural rites and rituals in worship — may guard against an inappropriate syncretism between culture and liturgy, avoiding those elements that undermine or contradict the gospel. Liturgy, when under the intense influence of popular, media/market-driven forms of music and art, may be in danger of cultural captivity. Such captivity may lead to the idolatry of culture.[11]

5. Liturgical plurality celebrates the incarnation as a *cross-cultural* manifestation of God among us — all of us. This does not deny the validity of our culture(s) of origin. Participating in the incarnational experience of others much different than ourselves enables us to place in perspective our localized views of the Other who became one of us. Awareness of the universal deepens the experience of the particular.

6. Liturgical plurality raises our consciousness of those who have been invisible to us — listening to, learning from, and sharing in their prayers, and joining with them in common intercessory prayer for the world.[12] The "voice of the voiceless" becomes heard in our worship in the realization of liturgical plurality.[13] In short, liturgical plurality is

10. The concepts of trans-cultural, contextual, counter-cultural, and cross-cultural influences on liturgy are clearly stated in the "Nairobi Statement on Worship and Culture: Contemporary Challenges and Opportunities," *Christian Worship: Unity in Cultural Diversity*, ed. S. Anita Stauffer (Geneva: Lutheran World Federation, 1996), pp. 25-28. In this same volume, Gordon W. Lathrop develops the role of the trans-cultural core or *ordo* and the counter-cultural critique in the process of contextualization or localization of liturgy in "Worship: Local Yet Universal," pp. 47-66. The value of cross-cultural critique, though supported generally in multi-cultural settings, is less explicit in the book.

11. The dangers of syncretism and cultural captivity are discussed by S. Anita Stauffer in "Worship: Ecumenical Core and Cultural Context," *Christian Worship*, on pages 12 and 21 respectively. Stauffer's use of syncretism differs from I-to Loh's stylistic syncretism in note 9 above.

12. Melva Wilson Costen explores invisibility in liturgy in the context of the African American church in the United States in Chapter 3, "Worship in the Invisible Institution," *African American Christian Worship* (Nashville: Abingdon Press, 1993), pp. 36-49. Marjorie Procter-Smith raises this theme in the context of women as invisible throughout liturgical history in her book *In Her Own Rite: Constructing Feminist Liturgical Traditions* (Nashville: Abingdon Press, 1989), pp. 14ff.

13. From Archbishop Oscar Romero's Fourth Pastoral Letter, "The Church's Mission amid the National Crisis," in *Voice of the Voiceless*, trans. Michael J. Walsh (Maryknoll, N.Y.: Orbis Books, 1985), delivered August 6, 1979. Archbishop Romero uses this concept in his

making room at Christ's table for all those who have been formed in God's image.[14]

Identity, Community, and Change: Themes for Cross-cultural Diversity in Worship

The fear that many people feel concerning the increasing degree of cultural diversity in the United States was expressed well in a letter to the editor in *USA Today* that grew out of the Supreme Court's decision in June 2003 to uphold, for the most part, affirmative action in the admission of students to institutions of higher education. The letter writer observed:

> Diversity is not what made America great; it is freedom. If you doubt this, ask yourself a few questions. Why is it that people will do anything to come to America — beg, borrow, steal, escape — and then, once they arrive, do all they can to make America the very country they left by segregating and building little villages, continuing to wear their native garb and refusing to speak English? Why is it that once they have a taste of freedom, they try to impose their former way of life on Americans? If it were diversity they craved, they would leave their old lifestyles behind and blend. The freedom that we enjoy in this America is not the same freedom it once was, I'm sorry to say. As a senior citizen, I recall immigrants coming to my hometown. They were so thrilled to be on this soil they worshiped the very ground they walked on. They worked hard to make America the greatest land. But today's immigrants seem so different. Diversity has been our downfall not our reward. It's time we put behind our diverse ways and become one so that we can continue to be the greatest country in the world.[15]

---

pastoral letter, saying that the "church, then, would betray its own love for God and its fidelity to the gospel if it stopped being 'the voice of the voiceless,' a defender of the rights of the poor, a promoter of every just aspiration for liberation, a guide, an empowerer, a humanizer of every legitimate struggle to achieve a more just society, a society that prepares the way for the true kingdom of God in history" (p. 138).

14. This is the theme that is developed in *Making Room at the Table: An Invitation to Multicultural Worship*, ed. Brian K. Blount and Leonora Tubbs Tisdale (Louisville: Westminster John Knox, 2001).

15. "Diversity is our downfall," *USA Today*, June 26, 2003, 12A.

This letter from Indianapolis articulates the feelings and fears of many.[16] The fear of threat and difference is understandable. The underlying sense of nostalgia for a time that never existed is regrettable. The ignorance of the contribution and plight of today's immigrants is undeniable. Prejudice bred through fear, nostalgia, and ignorance is lamentable. For this person and perhaps many others, immigration equals invasion.

What is a Christian response to those who do not know how to navigate the cross-cultural currents of the future? How might our liturgies foster understanding, offer hope, and build community? That is, how might we help to establish the sense of oneness the letter writer longs for, in an increasingly diverse world?

Loss of identity (national and cultural in this case rather than ecclesiological), fear of a breakdown in community, and an inability to cope with change seem to be at the core of the author of this letter. To examine each of these in detail would require three separate chapters. I will only be able to suggest an initial approach to identity, community, and change in this context.

Identity

Christian identity finds its foundation in the Pentecost church. It was birthed in the confluence of many cultures and languages who, by the power of the Holy Spirit, understood each other. As the church grew during the first four centuries, it took root in myriad cultures and survived not by uniform rites, but by pluriform manifestations of a Spirit-filled gospel. Political and cultural centers in the West have come and gone for the last 2000 years — Greece, Ireland, Rome, Spain, England — and now the United States takes its turn as the preeminent political, military, and economic power. During the last fifty years of the twentieth century, however, Christians from an increasing array of cultural perspectives — especially

---

16. The letter is from a senior citizen. I have noted elsewhere that I have found that, on the whole, senior adults throughout the country are open and engaged by cross-cultural worship because of the fresh energy that it brings to liturgy, involving all generations actively, and the full circle of "reverse missions" that they sense, many having supported world missions all of their lives and now see the fruits of mission efforts coming back to the United States to enrich us. See C. Michael Hawn, *One Bread, One Body: Exploring Cultural Diversity in Worship* (Bethesda, Md.: The Alban Institute, 2003), p. 123.

from the Southern Hemisphere — have emerged from beyond the ecclesial horizon, reflecting the spirit of Pentecost. Their numbers, diversity, and growth are amazing. They are mostly from the South — especially from Africa, Asia, and Latin America — and are holding sway in the North, sometimes through patterns of human migration, but also through the influence of their worldviews on the decision-making bodies of established faith traditions embedded in Western society.[17] *The Future Is Mestizo*, proclaims Mexican American theologian Virgilio Elizondo, in his book by this title. The majority of the church already reflects the Jesus of Galilee who was born of mixed parentage to an unwed mother in an occupied country in a marginalized village outside the gates of economic, political, and military power.[18]

The emergence of independent or indigenous Christian faith traditions — independent from the Western ecclesial bodies — especially from Africa, and their mission efforts to evangelize the North are a further sign of a renewed Pentecost spirit.[19] Moreover, charismatic winds and Pentecostal fires are drawing the Roman Catholic and mainline Protestant faithful away from these long-established traditions. Referring to the Liberation Theology movement birthed by Catholic theologian Gustavo Gutiérrez, Andrew Chestnut notes that "the Catholic Church has chosen the poor, but the poor chose the Pentecostals."[20] Pentecostal winds are still blowing strongly from the South and are obviously oblivious to any notion of hegemony in the northern church.

This news may be alarming to many. The church's complexion is "browning," but some suggest positively that the Good News of centuries is being repackaged in new and unexpected ways.[21] Rather than lament the change, Gordon Lathrop suggests that we reframe the reality in ecclesiological terms when he notes that the primary "mission [of the church as assembly] may well be to maintain strong and healthy communal symbols of the truth about God and to do so for the sake of the well-being of the

17. Philip Jenkins, *The Next Christendom*, notes the political influence of Anglican and Roman Catholic bishops from Africa, Asia, and Latin America in the reshaping of these previously Western ecclesial bodies; see pp. 194-204.

18. Virgilio Elizondo, *The Future Is Mestizo*, rev. ed. (Boulder: University of Colorado Press, 2000), 84. See also Elizondo's *Galilean Journey* (Maryknoll, N.Y.: Orbis, 2000), p. 91.

19. See Jenkins, *The Next Christendom*, pp. 204-9.

20. Quoted in Jenkins, *The Next Christendom*, p. 156.

21. Jenkins, *The Next Christendom*, p. 139.

world."[22] Could it be that the southern church will revitalize the North by providing it with new and vibrant "communal symbols" — rites, rituals, songs — for our liturgies, and in doing so assist northern Christians in praying more fully for the needs of the world? Simultaneously, might our efforts to pray together cross-culturally open up eschatological visions of a time when all faithful will, in the early third-century words of Hippolytus, be "gather[ed] into one"?[23] An identity based on the Pentecost church recognizes the diversity of the church and the movement of the fresh winds of the Spirit. Given the fast-paced change and unpredictable future before us, the Spirit, in this case, may seem less analogous to the placid, serene dove descending from the heavens and more like the peripatetic undomesticated gyrations of the Iona Community's wild goose.[24]

Community

The concept of community also needs to be reconsidered. Anthropologist Robert Redfield identified four qualities of community in 1960: "smallness of social scale; a homogeneity of activities and states of mind of members; a self-sufficiency across a broad range of needs and through time; and a consciousness of distinctiveness."[25] Definitions of community that stress small social scale and homogeneity, such as Redfield's, seem inadequate in African communities, for example, where tribal members have strong connections, though separated by continents because of patterns of migration, and share an intense communal affinity with ancestors. Homogeneity does not describe congregations that are diverse culturally, sociologically, and politically.

22. Gordon Lathrop, *Holy People: A Liturgical Ecclesiology* (Minneapolis: Fortress Press, 1999), p. 13.

23. Paul F. Bradshaw, Maxwell E. Johnson, L. Edward Philips, *The Apostolic Tradition* (Minneapolis: Fortress Press, 2002), p. 40; from the Latin text.

24. On August 13, 2001, I heard Brian Woodcock, Warden of the Iona Community until August 2001, relate a story about the origins of the wild goose as a symbol of the Holy Spirit. Ron Ferguson, leader of the community, was asked by George MacLeod about the Celtic origins of the wild goose symbolism. Ferguson told MacLeod that he had borrowed the idea from MacLeod some years earlier. Ferguson then asked MacLeod if the wild goose was indeed a symbol of the Holy Spirit. MacLeod responded, "It is now."

25. Robert Redfield, *The Little Community, and Peasant Society and Culture* (1960), quoted in Nigel Rapport and Joanna Overing, *Social and Cultural Anthropology: The Key Concepts* (New York: Routledge, 2000), p. 60.

Anthony Cohen, in contrast, focuses less on common behavior and activities, and more on a "common body of symbols, and a shared vocabulary of value."[26] An affinity exists between Cohen's understanding of community and Lathrop's understanding of the church's mission to "maintain strong and healthy communal symbols . . . for the sake of the well-being of the world." Both suggest that a Christian community can encompass a diverse congregation united in oneness of the Spirit around common symbols of faith. A shared vocabulary develops out of a common understanding of the biblical witness and the salvation story. Diversity, in this case, relishes difference that reflects humanity in God's image, and mirrors the variety of creation.

I would not suggest that a Christian community is incomplete without cultural difference. Cultural uniformity within a congregation does not indicate that it cannot worship fully and faithfully. Even when worshiping in cultural isolation or homogeny, however, we worship through the common symbols of the church throughout the last two millennia — water, bread, and wine. Our communion rites invite Christians of *all times and places* to sing "Holy, holy, holy." Christians find community with other faithful throughout the world and, like Africans who sense the daily presence and guidance of ancestors, in communion with the saints. Even culturally uniform congregations cannot avoid worshiping at the table across time and space with Christians of other cultures.

Change

Congregations are notorious for their inability to change. For the purpose of this chapter we can briefly address change in two areas — social change and ritual change. Religious sociologist Nancy Ammerman relates change to vision in her study of hundreds of congregations: "Of those [congregations] currently experiencing serious declines in membership and resources, all have either actively resisted change or have continued with existing patterns, apparently unable to envision how things might be different."[27] An imagination for change combined with a mission to en-

26. Anthony Cohen, *The Symbolic Construction of Community* (1985), quoted in Rapport and Overing, *Social and Cultural Anthropology*, p. 63.

27. Nancy Tatom Ammerman, *Congregation and Community* (New York: Routledge, 1997), pp. 322-23.

gage the diversity of the world and its needs leads a congregation to a broader vision.

The tendency to avoid change is not just a congregational problem; anthropologists have it also. Anthropological functionalists have focused on the ways that society "reproduced and maintained itself" (a conservative approach) rather than "how communities changed over time" (a progressive approach). Up until the beginning of the Second World War, the notion of studying "societies as if they were static" was dominant until "challenged by anthropologists interested in what was termed 'culture contact' in the colonial territories."[28] Perhaps because of the church's lack of understanding about the decreasing numbers of the northern church and the increasing significance of the church in the South, the mainline denominations in North America and Europe have been slow to understand the reality and nature of change.

Ritual change is unavoidable when worship takes cross-cultural confluences into account. Ronald Grimes notes the reluctance of anthropologists to accept emerging rituals as a reality. He remarks that ritual "emerging under the pressures of intercultural conflict is necessarily self-conscious, because ritual construction often occurs within a few years, within a single lifetime rather than across generations or aeons."[29] In taking this approach Grimes challenges those who assume that "ritual [must be] traditional (rather than invented), collective (rather than individual), pre-critical (rather than self-conscious and reflective), and meaningful (that is, referential)."[30] Grimes's appreciation for the possibility of invented or emerging rituals, and self-conscious and reflective rituals is essential. The following guidelines for worship worldwide assume that new rituals in cross-cultural liturgy, though rooted in liturgical tradition, may need to be "invented," and that the process for developing emerging rituals is self-conscious because of

28. Katy Gardner and David Lewis, *Anthropology, Development and the Post-Modern Challenge* (Chicago: Pluto Press, 1996), p. 27. I am grateful to Helen Phalen, University of Limerick, for assistance in locating selected sources in the area of anthropological and ritual change.

29. Ronald Grimes, *Reading, Writing and Ritualizing: Ritual in Fictive, Liturgical, and Public Places* (Washington, D.C.: The Pastoral Press, 2003), p. 6.

30. Grimes, *Reading, Writing and Ritualizing*, p. 7. Grimes does not deny that rituals may be traditional, collective, pre-conscious, and meaningful; she simply means that they may also have broader characteristics as well — invented, individual, self-conscious, and non-referential.

the need to understand the rites and rituals of other ethnic groups and the varying sense of identity that each culture brings to worship. The possibility of sharing rituals across cultures expands our identity as Christians and opens up new ways of worshiping together.

Guidelines for Worship Worldwide

The discussion above has already cautioned us that cross-cultural worship — liturgical plurality — is not to be undertaken lightly. Neither is it easy. Praying with the worldwide church — though doing so may expose our vulnerabilities, threaten our provincial routines, challenge our orthodoxies, and confront our cultural hegemony — offers northern Christians the option of shedding cultural superiority by entering into partnership with other Christians — blending our voices and sharing songs in a reciprocal spirit with Christian brothers and sisters from the South. Appropriating rituals from other cultural contexts — historic or contemporary — requires adaptation of the liturgy or established rites and rituals that constitute the liturgy. Noted anthropologist Roy Rappaport defines adaptation as the "processes through which living systems of all sorts maintain themselves, or persist, in the face of perturbations, originating in their environments or themselves, through reversible changes in their states, less reversible transformations of their structures, or actions eliminating perturbing factors."[31] Cross-cultural ritual appropriations will undoubtedly be greeted by some as "perturbing factors." Yet experiencing the rituals of others often clarifies our own liturgical identity just as studying a second language brings understanding to the uniqueness, beauty, and limitations of our first tongue. The following list provides preliminary criteria for adapting, evaluating, and appropriating rituals from other cultures for use in liturgy.

Is the appropriated rite or ritual integral to the structure and performance of liturgy?

Does imported cross-cultural material call attention to itself or does it support the structural integrity of the liturgy? Is the appropriated rite or ritual a sensational anomaly that stands alone or an integral expression

---

31. Roy A. Rappaport, *Ritual and Religion in the Making of Humanity* (New York: Cambridge University Press, 1999), p. 408.

that enlarges the community's prayer? African music, in all its joy and vitality, may be co-opted by northern congregations to make them "feel good" without understanding the struggles out of which such music usually is born.[32] Is an African refrain being used to make us feel good — a "fun" interjection into worship — or to help us pray more fully? An African song of joy may enlarge our prayers of praise and adoration if it is integral to the progression of the liturgy or it may be ingested like a piece of candy that gives a temporary surge of energy that soon dissipates.

Thematic integration of appropriated material is always fitting. Does the appropriated rite or ritual enlarge the theme or offer insight into the biblical narrative? Integrating cross-cultural materials into the recurring cycles of Christian liturgy is also a possible strategy. Roy Rappaport stresses the importance of "circadian rhythms" or rituals that occur at set periods ("time-dependent regulation") providing "a convenient framework for organizing recurrent activities."[33] Recurring observances or seasons may lend themselves to a greater use of cross-cultural materials, for example: World Communion Sunday; Advent/Christmas — God made visible to all places and cultures; Epiphany — a traditional season of mission; Pentecost — the birthday of a diverse church. Incorporating an appropriated ritual into recurring liturgical observances or structures not only provides an authentic context for the new material, but also helps to ensure the greater likelihood of its acceptance. Each Sunday provides possibilities for reminding a congregation of the dialectic between local congregations and the church universal.

Does the cross-cultural rite or ritual give voice to the voiceless or make visible the invisible persons from the community?

Singing the *estribillo* (refrain) of a Spanish-language hymn in the original language by a majority English-speaking congregation may say more about hospitality to Latinos and Latinas within the community than handshakes by the ushers or words of greeting from the minister. Hearing the gospel in the majority language of the congregation and in Mandarin, for example, may express both a worldwide Christian faith and establish a bond between two very different cultures. Dancing to an African song of

---

32. For an orientation to the cultural context of Christian music in Southern Africa, see C. Michael Hawn, *Gather into One: Praying and Singing Globally* (Grand Rapids: Wm. B. Eerdmans, 2003), chapters 4 and 5.

33. Rappaport, *Ritual and Religion in the Making of Humanity,* p. 412.

joy may not only enliven the entire assembly but also delight any African Christians present. Many in the northern world assume a dualism between the mind and body. Grimes reminds us that "bodies are enculturated [by the values, rituals, and environment of society] and cultures are embodied. . . . Societies have their most persistent root in the human body itself, and the body is always — no matter how closeted or private — socially inscribed."[34] An African Christian might interpret Grimes to say, "When you sing, you dance." Participating in cross-cultural liturgy with Christians from the South will be a more ritually embodied process than many northern congregations are accustomed to.

Ritual competence is a question that often arises when encountering new liturgical materials. Christians from the Northern Hemisphere might be concerned that they do not perform the African dance correctly, for example. Those from the culture receiving a ritual should demonstrate this kind of cultural sensitivity. Yet I would suggest that an obsession with ritual competence might lead to liturgical paralysis — a state of being afraid to try anything new for fear of offending persons from the culture from which the ritual is borrowed. Ritual competence assumes preparation and repetition. It is a skill learned over time. Invite persons who understand the cultural context and can demonstrate the ritual performance of the rite or ritual. When in doubt, presiders and other worship leaders should assume a student posture — listening and watching. Enter into dialogue with the teacher and seek to embody the new rite or ritual. Develop a strategy and reserve some time, often at the beginning of worship, to teach the new rite or ritual to the congregation. Openness and vulnerability toward a new ritual from the receiving culture, rather than perfect execution, is overwhelmingly appreciated by the sending culture. Taking time to develop ritual competence demonstrates an abiding interest in the sending culture rather than an ephemeral experience in liturgical ethno-tourism.[35]

Does the cross-cultural rite or ritual help the assembly pray for the needs of the world?

Each week the media makes us aware of places in the world where human suffering and injustice is overwhelming. These may be places of war, natu-

---

34. Grimes, *Reading, Writing and Ritualizing*, p. 11.

35. C. Michael Hawn, *One Bread, One Body,* offers specific guidance for building congregational competence in cross-cultural liturgy. See Chapter Six, pp. 123-26.

ral disaster, economic collapse, or political instability. The tendency to feel overwhelmed by these manifestations of estrangement between God and humanity may bring about desires for liturgical insulation among worshipers from the crushing needs of the world. Rites have evolved over time that allow for integral expressions of prayer for the world. If the church does not plead before God for the pain of humanity, who will? Our belief in the efficacy of prayer calls us to intercede corporately not only for those who are near and dear but also for those we may never see.

Rappaport refers to the importance of "Ultimate Sacred Postulates" that are self-evident and/or carry the weight of "cosmological axioms"[36] or truths of the highest importance. These postulates ground our rites and rituals. Praying for the needs of the world has been ritualized since the earliest days of Christian worship.[37] Concern for the needs of others was a primary teaching of Jesus in Matthew 25:31-46, when Christ said, "as you did it not to one of the least of these [feed the hungry, welcome the stranger, clothe the naked, visit the prisoners], you did it not to me" (v. 45). Voiced in many forms, the prayers of the people offer the assembly the option of taking the concerns of others more deeply into their hearts through rituals, songs, and stories from a variety of cultures. While theologians might argue about which "sacred postulates" are "ultimate," Luke's gospel tells us that Christ responded to a question concerning the means to achieve eternal life by pointing the inquirer to the law: "You shall love the Lord your God with all your heart . . . and your neighbor as yourself" (Luke 10:27). To a further question, "Who is my neighbor?" Jesus responded with the parable of the Good Samaritan.

Even this limited discussion poses the possibility that the early church took Jesus' words to heart and incorporated the concern and care for others as a central concern of liturgy. Ultimate sacred postulates are axiomatic and not likely to be changed. Worship that includes petitions for the needs of the world, regardless of cultural origin, expresses a Christian

36. Rappaport, *Ritual and Religion in the Making of Humanity*, p. 425.

37. By the middle of the second century C.E., Justin Martyr's *Apologies* record the centrality of the prayers of the people in the liturgy. At the conclusion of the Eucharist, a collection is taken and deposited with the president who "succors the orphans and the widows, and those who, through sickness or any other cause, are in want, and those who are in bonds [prison], and the strangers who are sojourning among us, and in a word takes care of all who are in need." *The Apostolic Tradition* of Hippolytus expresses a similar concern for the widows and poor by the early third century C.E.

tenet so foundational that it can unite persons across cultures. Through the prayers of the people we may offer intercessions for those from regions where the pain is beyond bearing. Through this rite we are sharing the suffering of those who may not be able to sustain the load alone. Solidarity through cross-cultural rites and rituals changes both the prayer and the pray-er. Praying in solidarity with those who are in need by using their own words and songs allows for a deeper liturgical interpathy — cross-cultural understanding.[38] Choose cross-cultural rites and rituals that offer hope to a troubled world.

Does the cross-cultural rite or ritual unify the body of Christ?

Many cross-cultural opportunities may be so distant in experience that they may not be performed well. Their uniqueness is so dependent upon the context of the sending culture that they may serve only to divide rather than unify believers. Furthermore, performing some rites and rituals by groups from another culture may offend the members of the sending culture unless specific permission is given. An analogy might be importing, for example, a Passover Seder into a Christian Holy Week liturgy without giving thought as to how the use of the Seder, a ritual crucial to the identity of the Jewish community, might appear to the sending culture. Ritual theft does not unify diverse groups. Anglo leaders should be cautious when importing songs from Native Americans, for example. Some musical instruments may only be played by specific individuals in a tribe. The integrity of the cross-cultural ritual is strengthened if permission is received and leadership shared.

Essential to this criterion is the idea of sustaining and nurturing the ecclesia — the body of Christ called to witness and work in the world for Christ's sake and to intercede for the needs of the world. Pastoral sensitivity is required to foster discernment that leads to choosing cross-cultural rituals that prevent division and promote a fuller unity among the household of faith.

Does the use of the appropriated rite or ritual anticipate the eschaton?

Much is available on an apocalyptic vision of the future. Many Christians from the Southern Hemisphere find that the book of Revelation articulates

---

38. The term "interpathy" has been coined by David Augsburger in *Pastoral Counseling across Cultures* (Philadelphia: Westminster Press, 1986), p. 41.

an existential reality. As Philip Jenkins notes, the book of Revelation "looks like true prophecy on an epic scale, however unpopular or discredited it may be for most Americans or Europeans. In the South, Revelation simply makes sense, in a description of a world ruled by monstrous demonic powers."[39] Though the perspective of many Christians confirms the validity of this view of Revelation because of the state of world events, one may also find hope in its pages. Consider the eschaton in light of Revelation 7:9-10 (RSV): "all tribes, and peoples, and tongues, [will stand] before the throne, and before the Lamb, clothed with white robes, and with palm branches in their hands, and crying out with a loud voice, 'Salvation to our God who sits upon the throne, and to the Lamb.'"

Throughout the history of Christianity the Eucharist has been the central Christian ritual imbued with eschatological promise of a time when all will be gathered around a single table.[40] Although our efforts to achieve this understanding in the current reality may be penultimate at best, foretastes of the future are available to the assembly now. The Eucharist may offer one of the best ritual contexts for hearing the voice of the church universal, glimpsing the body of Christ more fully, and tasting the fruits and grains of the heavenly banquet. At the table all are equal. The spiritual sustenance received in this ritual may nourish those gathered even though bruised, disenchanted, oppressed, despairing, and even hopeless. The proleptic potential of the table offers many options for cross-cultural rituals and songs. Appropriate cross-cultural ritual performance may engage the assembly in eschatological hope that sustains and unites them. When any congregation gathers at the table, they share the meal with the faithful of all places and times.

The Case Studies in This Book and Liturgical Appropriation

It may be tempting to read the case studies in this book with the intent of finding specific rites or rituals that one could apply directly to the worship of a local congregation. Anyone who reads this book for such a purpose will be

39. Jenkins, *The Next Christendom*, p. 219.
40. Paul Bradshaw, *The Search for the Origins of Christian Worship*, p. 53, reminds us that "there seems to be a general consensus that in the earliest period of the Church's existence it was the eschatological theme which dominated eucharistic practice . . . combined with the remembrance of the death of Christ in the early Palestinian tradition."

sorely disappointed, I believe, and, more importantly, may miss the joy of discovering how broadly and variously the incarnation is embodied in the breadth of humanity. It is highly unlikely, for example, that North American congregations will take up the cleansing practice of the Aguaruna in the Amazon by drinking *wais* before sunrise, followed by a communal purging. A North American congregation might ask, however, how its members prepare for common worship. Does the community prepare for worship by centering on the scriptures of the day? Have they confessed their sins before God and prayed for the church, its members, and its mission in preparation for worship with the gathered community? Many North American congregations may benefit by encouraging rituals of domestic worship — a spiritual purging — that support and prepare their members for common prayer. The general education level of North Americans may deceive us into thinking that sin may be treated as a vestige of "primitive" thinking rather than thoughts, words, and deeds that are painful to God and destructive of relationships with others. Domestic rituals that support a spiritual purging before the gathering of the faithful may enhance the worship of the North American church.

As a practitioner of worship, I am always searching for songs, rituals, dances, confessions, prayers, and biblical reflections from Christians around the world that might have local meaning, especially as outlined in the criteria above. The case studies in this book, however, offer us a broader look at ourselves as particular worshipers within the universal church. How do we differ in our expectations of worship? In what ways are we similar? When placed alongside our liturgical ethos, how do our different ways of communal worship reflect on each other (a process identified as acculturation)? Do these differences suggest any possibilities for changing our practice and enlarging our prayer for the sake of the world?

Connection with Nature

One of the common aspects running through most of the case studies is the direct relationship between the worshiping community and nature. The *Chusok* (harvest festival) discussed by Seung Joong Joo and the harvest festival in the Zion Apostolic Church in southern Africa described by M. L. Daneel and Dana Robert demonstrate an understanding of the relationship between the cycles of the earth and the liturgical life of the people. Furthermore, Joo and Daneel and Robert link thanksgiving with the Great

Thanksgiving of the Eucharist. Linking communion with the more civil observance of Thanksgiving in the United States may be one way to more clearly incorporate the holiday into the liturgical context.

Sacred Space

The space devoted to sacred assembly is an important aspect in the shaping of the community's worship. Charles Farhadian introduces the *Pondok Kemuliaan* (Glory Hut) as a place for Papuan worship. The Glory Hut (formerly the Restoration Hut) is designed for rehabilitation and outreach to those who are suffering in some way, usually because of alcoholism or other substance abuse. Accessible to all in need, the Glory Hut is a place "where people from many tribes and backgrounds can come together and break down social prejudices that dominate Papuan society." This sacred space functions as a gathering place for smaller cell groups as well as common worship. In many ways, the Glory Hut combines the functions of urban rescue mission and local congregation.

The Glory Hut is open on all sides to the surrounding community so that acts of worship are by nature a witness to all. Daneel and Robert also discuss worship that takes place out of doors among the Apostles and Zionists in southern Africa. The worship space of the Roman Catholic Church in Leauva'a, Western Samoa, allows for various kinds of dances.

While it is unlikely that many open-sided churches will be built in North America, the accessibility, flexibility, and openness of worship spaces used by Christians in other parts of the world give us pause. In many cases our buildings are sealed off from the world to which the congregation is to minister. The spaces may be off-putting to those with disabilities or from socioeconomic situations that differ from the majority who attend the worship service. Many North American places of worship are designed for listening and watching the speakers in the front rather than singing and dancing together as one body in Christ. In some cases, North American places of worship seem to be virtually hermetically sealed to all except those who are members of the congregation.

The openness and accessibility of places of worship in many congregations may be seen as a result of climate. North American congregations that worship in more inaccessible and limiting spaces, however, may reflect a theology of exclusiveness to those on the outside. Within the cultural and climatic considerations of North America, it is possible to create places of worship that invite outsiders and integrate the body of Christ with each other rather than exclude some and stifle the interactions of the assembly.

Using the Body in Worship

Worship around the world, especially in the Southern Hemisphere, is physical. Dancing and gestures permeate worship. Among the case studies, Thomas Kane focuses explicitly on this aspect of worship in Western Samoa. Hand gestures, dance, and other ritual movements are common throughout the Pacific. While special ensembles or leaders perform some movements, many are congregational. Daneel and Robert note that the Zionists and Apostles "usually begin the service with singing and dancing." Furthermore, "Singing and dancing play extremely important roles in Spirit-type churches, as through them people work themselves up into higher states. People enjoy the singing and dancing, and it continues throughout the service between the sermons." Farhadian notes that music in the Glory Hut "is punctuated by ecstatic voices praising God and exhilarated bodies jumping and running around."

For many North American congregations, dancing, especially of an ecstatic nature, is difficult. Worship spaces are designed to listen to rather than move to the Word. Cultural sensibilities of many parishioners above forty years of age restrict their appreciation for and participation in congregational movement. Some congregations tolerate movement with songs when children and young people participate. Others may accept the occasional sacred dance presented by an ensemble. More and more, however, churches in various traditions are opening up to congregational movement in varying degrees. Children and young people are much more kinesthetically aware than their parents. What is common in many African American and Pentecostal congregations may become normative throughout churches in the Northern Hemisphere within the next twenty-five years.

Although I encourage movement when singing African songs, for example, I rarely use an "authentic" dance with congregations. Striving for authentic movements from Africa or the Pacific may not unify the body of Christ — one criterion included above. Simple swaying (shifting the weight of the body without lifting the feet) or an uncomplicated back-

and-forth step often invigorate a congregation and offer a kinesthetic and visual experience in becoming the body of Christ. In my experience, congregational movement brings people together. While some resist, young and old are drawn together by singing and swaying as a community on suitable songs and in appropriate places in the liturgy.[41]

More Questions from the Case Studies

Worshiping across cultures requires discernment. While songs, gestures, confessions, and prayers from other cultures may enhance worship, worship leaders should establish clear criteria so that the congregation borrowing from others avoids cultural stereotyping and liturgical ethnotourism. The five criteria above provide a basis for this conversation.

The case studies in this book, however, may tell us more about our liturgical priorities by comparison with other ways of worshiping rather than appropriation of others' rites and rituals. Views of nature, the shape of the worship space, and the use of the body in worship have been discussed above, but other topics remain. Readers may also wish to read the case studies in light of the following questions and then compare their findings to worship in North American congregations.

1. How do the congregations in this study incorporate spontaneity and improvisation within their worship structures?
2. How do clergy and laity interact throughout worship?
3. What is the role of non-verbal activities and materials in worship, such as gesture, ritual, dance, use of artifacts, or clothing?
4. What is the sense of time in the congregations encountered in the case studies?
5. How do the congregations in the case studies balance worship for the faithful and evangelism?
6. How is worship in the case studies culturally specific and culturally universal?

---

41. See C. Michael Hawn, *One Bread, One Body*, Appendix E, "Ten Steps Toward a Dancing Congregation," by Marcia McFee.

The Hard Work of Liturgical Plurality

Many contemporary trends seem to mitigate against cross-cultural diversity in worship. Church growth movements often thrive on cultural uniformity for "growth." The Supreme Court's decision to re-endorse affirmative action has spawned not only angry sentiments like the letter to the editor cited above, but also extreme criticism by academics such as Abigail Thernstrom, a senior fellow at the Manhattan Institute and a commissioner on the U.S. Commission on Civil Rights, who stated within a few days of the decision that the "Supreme Court has told those of us who abhor racial preferences to get lost. Our principles, arguments and evidence about how those preferences work have been dumped in a dead-letter box. The proponents of racial-driven decision-making have won. Big-time."[42] Liturgical plurality should not be considered a kind of affirmative action, however. It is much more a pursuit of oneness in Christ. Liturgical plurality is following through with the assertion of the early church that just as Christ is one with God (John 10:30) therefore "we, who are many, are one body in Christ" (Romans 12:5, NSRV). Jesus prayed repeatedly for the oneness of humanity even as he is one with his Father (John 17:11, 21, 22). Other Epistles confirm this theme: "Because there is one bread, we who are many are one body, for we all partake of the one bread" (1 Corinthians 10:17, NRSV); "There is one body and one Spirit, just as you are called to the one hope of your calling, one Lord, one faith, one baptism, one God and Father of all, who is above all and through all and in all" (Ephesians 4:4-6, NRSV).

The Pentecost paradigm hovers over the church. Acts 4:32 states that "the multitude of them that believed, were of one heart, and one soul; neither said any of them, that aught of the things which he possessed, was his own, but they had all things in common." Though some might see an example of early Christian economic socialism in this passage, could it be that this verse refers also to the sharing of even more valuable resources — our ways of embodying our faith in rites and rituals and expanding our common prayer across cultures?[43]

---

42. Abigail Thernstrom, "College Rulings Add Insult to Injury," *Los Angeles Times,* Sunday, June 29, 2003, M1.

43. I am grateful to Lim Swee Hong, a former student at Perkins School of Theology, Southern Methodist University, and current Ph.D. candidate at Drew University in liturgical studies, for this valuable insight.

Liturgical Theology and Criticism — Things of Heaven and Things of the Earth: Some Reflections on Worship, World Christianity, and Culture

Bryan D. Spinks

Editor's Introduction

Bryan Spinks provides an essential framework for evaluating worship and culture, in the context of the relationship between theology and culture. Spinks discusses "the scandal of particularity" and the first-century controversy over what aspects of Jewish and Christian culture were essential to the faith and missions.

Spinks's treatment of these abstract principles is anchored in case studies, such as the use of oil in baptism, the East Syrian Malk and Hnana, and three eighteenth-century liturgies. As Spinks notes, liturgies have always blended "things of heaven" with "things of earth." Readers may reflect: which are which? What are the marks of a genuine inculturated liturgy? What liturgical elements may be considered unchanging and essential to worship?

•　　　•

The 1947 Roman Catholic Encyclical on liturgy, *Mediator Dei*, contained the following statement: "For in the liturgy there are human elements as well as divine. The latter, obviously, having been established by the divine Redeemer cannot under any circumstances be changed by men; but the human elements may be modified in various ways approved by the hierarchy under the guidance of the Holy Spirit, according as time, circumstances, and the needs of souls may demand." Some fifteen years later, *Sacrosanctum Concilium* similarly stated, "For the liturgy is made up of unchangeable elements divinely instituted, and of elements subject to

230

change." Though both documents recognized that Christian worship consists of what might be termed things of heaven and things of the earth, neither spelled out what might constitute the unchanging elements. However, what both documents noted is that liturgy, even if divinely mandated, is also a human activity, and as such, is influenced by the culture in which it is celebrated and developed.

It is, of course, a problem as to how to define what is meant by culture. Professor David Power described it as "whatever is expressed in traditions, beliefs, customs, institutions, art, artifacts, symbols, myths and rites; its core is the values and the meaning on which human life, individual and collective, is based."[1] Hugh Montifiori described it thus: "It forms the background of the lives of people who live in a country, and it is compounded of its dominant religion (or lack of it), its ethics and ideology, its literature and art, its science and technology, its philosophical and ethical traditions, and its ethos and way of life."[2] And Clifford Geertz described it as "webs of significance."[3]

Of course, the way the word *culture* is used reveals very quickly that we are always talking about *cultures,* and the plural is crucial. First and most obvious, there are differences among European, African, and Asian cultures. But second, there is no single European, African, or Asian culture, or really even one national culture. Furthermore, at least in North Atlantic First World cultures, there is a high culture and popular culture. However, worldwide Christianity, which embraces this wide spectrum of human life that we call cultures, also encounters global culture — based around popular music, films, video and TV, the Internet, and international corporations. Though in theory neutral, this culture is in fact closely tied to capital and profit. It interacts with and impinges upon most cultures of the world, and thus all cultures are in constant flux and change.

A prior question to that of liturgy and culture is that of the relationship of theology to culture. First, all human institutions and societies stand under the judgment of God as Creator and Redeemer. However one wishes to interpret the Fall in Genesis, Paul is clear in Romans that all have gone astray, and there is none righteous. At one level, therefore, all

1. David Power, *Worship, Theology and Culture* (Washington, D.C.: Pastoral Press, 1990), pp. 39-52.

2. Hugh Montifiore, ed., *The Gospel and Contemporary Culture* (London: Mowbray, 1992), p. 2.

3. Clifford Geertz, *The Interpretation of Cultures* (New York: Basic Books, 1973), p. 5.

human cultures are alienated from God. Second, however, whoever accepts Christianity has to accept the scandal of the particularity of Israel. Having indicted all humanity, Paul in Romans 9–11 reminds all gentiles that they are grafted onto the olive tree of God's chosen people. The church does not replace Israel, for salvation is of the Jews, and the gospel can only be the gospel as it stands alongside of the Hebrew Scriptures. Thus this particular Semitic culture is singled out as having special significance. Third, the incarnation intensifies the scandal of particularity, because incarnation means God subjecting himself to the space-time continuum; it means being born from a particular woman in a particular place, at a particular time, and being a particular person. In historical terms, this means late BCE and early CE Palestine, with its mixture of Greco-Roman and Semitic traditions. That point is made forcefully in St. John's Gospel, where the words over the cross, "The King of the Jews," were written in Hebrew, Latin, and Greek. But it also means that the incarnate God, Jesus Christ, is also the way, the truth, and the life; one alone is singled out as savior.

Already in the New Testament we see the problems that this particularity brings to human culture, in terms of what is human and what is divine, or what is negotiable and what is non-negotiable. Thus for example in the Acts of the Apostles, the so-called Council of Jerusalem expected certain Jewish practices of gentile Christians, but no one had to embrace Judaism and all the ritual regulations first. In 1 Corinthians, Paul warned against eating meat that had been associated with pagan rituals. It is possible that the Corinthian dispute over the resurrection of the body was partly colored by the common custom of cremation in the Roman Empire over against burial in Judaism. In the *Didache,* which is usually dated c. 80 C.E., in the region of Antioch we see a Jewish-Christian community salvaging as much of the Torah as possible; but some of the writings that come from Gnostic documents seem to lean to the other direction, with Jewish culture and theology being jettisoned to suit the magic and philosophy of Hellenistic culture. In other words, the question of what is divine and what is human, what is non-negotiable and what is negotiable, what is theological and what is culture, is as old as the gospel itself. In fact, the gospel as it is lived through a community of faith must itself be regarded as a cultural, symbolic world, a social construct with its own interests and concerns, and thus inculturation is not an incarnation of a timeless, unchanging, and acultural reality into a particular culture, but always an intercultural encounter or dialogue between at least two cultures.[4]

Examples from History and the Case Studies

How does this play out in worship? It is more easily illustrated by reference to historic examples. Here I will present four.

The Use of Oil in Baptism

Though the Reformation managed to excise the use of oil from baptismal rites as being a human ceremony without divine mandate, anointing with oil at baptism, in normal conditions, seems to have been common from at least the second century, though allusions in the New Testament might be real rather than metaphorical. According to the reading of the accounts in the *Acts of Thomas,* in the Greek version of that work, it would seem that some Christian communities used only oil for initiation, and not water. The Syriac versions are corrected to include water. However, the debate amongst liturgists has been whether there was a development and reordering of the sequence. The Tübingen liturgical scholar Gabriele Winkler argued that in the *Acts of Thomas* we find on some occasions the head alone being anointed, and in other accounts both the head and the body. In each case the anointing precedes the act of baptism in water. But we find in fourth-century Jerusalem, and in the West, an anointing before and after baptism. The former was with olive oil, and the latter with perfumed oil, or chrism. Winkler argued for a developmental pattern:[5] at first the head only was anointed, with a messianic interpretation that appealed to the anointing of priests in the Old Testament — a sort of ritualizing of 1 Peter, in which Christians become a royal priesthood. Later, Winkler suggested, this was extended to anointing the whole body. Later still it was duplicated and was given a second meaning related to protection from evil, and as prepa-

---

4. I am indebted to Peter C. Phan, "Liturgical Inculturation: Unity in Diversity in the Postmodern Age," in Keith Pecklers, ed., *Liturgy in a Postmodern World* (New York: Continuum, 2003), pp. 5-64; p. 64 for this observation.

5. Gabriele Winkler, "The Original Meaning of the Prebaptismal Anointing and Its Implications," *Worship* 52 (1978): 24-45.

ration for an athletic struggle. At a later date still, in the late fourth century and continuing into the fifth, as a result of a strict reading of the Synoptic accounts of the baptism of Jesus, a post-baptismal anointing developed, using chrism as representing the gift of the Spirit, even imparting that gift. Later still, consecrated oil was poured into the baptismal font.

This developmental pattern has been widely accepted by liturgical scholars, providing a trajectory from simplicity to complexity — and at least from the perspective of the Reformation, one human ceremony on top of another. However, had Winkler looked at Greco-Roman culture, especially the culture of bathing, the evidence might have dictated a different scenario. The first problem for this theory is that second-century Gnostic documents, particularly the *Gospel of Philip,* witness to a pattern of baptism in water and anointing with oil afterwards. Since these documents are contemporary with the *Acts of Thomas* (also "Gnostic"), the evidence would suggest a plurality of ritual patterns, co-existing. In addition, scholars of classical studies have brought to light that bathing customs in the Roman Empire almost always used oil. Oil was used before bathing, and seen as essential for the vigorous exercises that were practiced before bathing, which was regarded as a form of protection and a path to good health.[6] This included the head, and then the whole body, the latter often being anointed by slaves. Furthermore, it was quite common for oil to be poured into the bath. In some places an anointing after the bath followed, and for wealthy patrons this was with perfumed oil, or chrism. In other words, we find quite a variety of secular bathing anointing rituals. There is thus no need to resort to a developmental theory; all we need note is that different Christian communities apparently adopted and adapted a number of the secular bathing etiquettes, which they later synthesized. Oil as protection or for athletic exercise was a widely accepted secular use that Christians seem to have spiritualized. The only special Christian contribution to the cultural practice and understanding was to articulate the obvious biblical messianic association.

6. See Fikret Yegul, *Baths and Bathing in Classical Antiquity* (Cambridge, Mass.: MIT Press, 1992); J. DeLaine and D. E. Johnston, eds., *Roman Baths and Bathing,* Parts 1 and 2 (Portsmouth, Rhode Island: Journal of Roman Archeology, 1999).

The East Syrian Mystery (Sacrament) of the Malka and Hnana

According to the practice of the Church of the East (mistakenly referred to as Nestorian), the *Malka,* the holy leaven, is added to the Eucharistic bread prior to baking. Canon law stipulates that no Eucharistic bread is to be used for consecration without the holy leaven. It has a counterpart in holy oil, which, whenever blessed, is added to from what is called the oil of the horn. This latter is supposed to go back to John the Baptist.

The fourteenth century Church of the East commentator, Yohanan bar Zobi, explained the rite as follows:

> I confess two sacraments in the holy Church — one the sacrament of Baptism, and the other the sacrament of the Body and Blood. The foundation of these two is laid in the flesh of our Lord, and it is fit that I should explain this for the edification of the sons of the Church. Peter the Apostle wrote this account, and I am therefore bound to record it without any alteration. When our Saviour was baptized of John in the river Jordan, John beheld his greatness, i.e., his Divinity and humanity, and understood that he did not submit to be baptized on his own account, but in order to set us an example that we should be baptized even as he was. And the blessed John was graciously inspired to take from Christ's baptism a little leaven for our baptism. So when the Lord went up out of the water whilst the water was yet dripping from his body, John approached our Lord, and collected these drops in a phial; and when the day of his martyrdom arrived he committed it to his disciple, and commanded him to preserve it with great care until the time should come when it would be required. This disciple was John the son of Zebedee, who he knew would become our Lord's steward. Accordingly, after his baptism, our Lord called John, and made him his beloved disciple; and when he was about to close his dispensation, and his passion and death drew nigh, on the evening preceding the Friday he committed his Passover to his disciples in the bread and wine, as it is written, and gave to each a loaf; but to John he gave two loaves, and put it into his heart to eat one and to preserve the other, that it might serve as leaven to be retained in the Church for perpetual commemoration. After this, when our Lord was seized by the Jews, and the disciples through fear hid themselves, John was the only one who remained. And when they crucified the Lord in much ignominy with the thieves, John alone was present, determined to see what would become of him. Then

the chief priests ordered that the crucified ones should be taken down from the cross, and that their legs should be broken, in order that if yet alive they might die outright. The soldiers did this to the thieves, but when they came to our Lord and found that he was dead already, they brake not his legs, but one of them with a spear pierced his side, and straightway there came out blood and water, of which John was witness. Now this blood is a token of the sacrament of the body and blood in the Church, and the water is a token of the new birth in believers. John was the only one who perceived this separateness of the water and the blood, and he bear witness thereof, as he says, that we might believe. He declares that he saw them unmixed, in that he did not take of them together, but of each separately. He took of the blood upon the loaf, which he had reserved from the paschal feast, and he took of the water in that same vessel which had been committed to him by John the Baptist. The very blood of his body, therefore, mixed with the bread, which he had called his body, and the water from his side mingled with the water from his baptism. After he rose from the grave and ascended up in glory to his Father, and sent the grace of his Spirit upon his disciples to endow them with wisdom, he commanded his apostles to ordain in his Church that same leaven which they had taken from his body to be for the sacrament of his body, and also for the sacrament of baptism. And when the disciples went forth to convert the nations, they divided this leaven amongst themselves, and they took oil of unction and mixed it with the water, which was kept in the vessel, and they divided this also amongst themselves to be a leaven for baptism. The loaf which John had, and which was mixed with the blood which flowed from his side, they bruised into powder, then mixed it with flour and salt, and divided it among them, each portion being put into a separate vessel to serve as leaven for the body and blood of Christ in the Church. This is the account which I have read, which bore the sign of Peter, and I have written it as I found it for the benefit of such as may read this our epistle.[7]

To Western ears trained in the methods of modernity, the historicity of this account may be a cause for some skepticism. The actual contents of the holy leaven are wheat, flour, salt, olive oil, and a few drops of water, and then it is dried.

7. Cited in P. G. Badger, *The Nestorians and Their Rituals*, 2 vols., reprint (London: Darf Publishers, 1987), vol. 2, pp. 151-53.

Liturgical scholars speculate that the origin of this rite lies in something similar to the rite called the *fermentum* at Rome. Particles of the bread used at the Papal mass in Rome were carried to the other churches in the city of Rome, and placed in the chalice to symbolize unity, and that technically there is only one Eucharist in a city, presided over by the bishop.[8] It may be that as the Church of the East became a missionary church — into Mongolia, China, and India — the Patriarchate of Seleucia-Ctesiphon instituted this sort of dehydrated, long-life, dried bread — a sort of liturgical Twinkie — to symbolize unity with the Patriarchate.

Yet if this was the ecclesiastical cultural origin, it has been given a theological meaning, as evidenced by Yohanan bar Zobi. Its origin is traced to the Last Supper, to stale bread that John kept, which somehow got the blood of Jesus on it — an interesting extra-canonical tale. But what are the theological motives underlying the narrative? It is in one sense an attempt to distinguish the divine and human elements in the Eucharist, and the belief that it is the divine which validates it. Thus this strange custom is an attempt to link each celebration of the Eucharist, the Lord's Supper, with the Last Supper. Given that the oldest Eucharistic prayer of this tradition, Addai and Mari, has no institution narrative, it could be seen as ritual substitution. If the words of institution are recited as an oral linking with our Eucharist to the Last Supper, this ritual of the *Malka* is a visual and symbolic way of linking each Eucharist with the Last Supper. That of course is also the intention of adding the oil of the horn to the baptismal oil, linking each baptism with the baptism of Jesus himself. Both become the divine legitimizing of the present earthly action.

The second cultural custom in the East Syrian rite is the *Hnana* in the marriage rite. Like several Eastern marriage rites, the East Syrian has a cup from which the bride and groom drink. But into this cup of wine is placed the ring, a small cross, and *Hnana*. What is the *Hnana*? It is dust taken from the tomb of a martyr or saint — and to the Westerner, even more unappetizing than the worm in tequila. However, the symbolism is powerful. The blessing of the ring makes it clear that the ring takes on the symbolism of all rings mentioned in scripture, and is a sign of the covenant of grace. It is *the* holy ring. The cross encapsulates all that is divine.

---

8. For recent thoughts on the Roman fermentum, see the paper given by John Baldovin at NAAL, New York, January 4, 2004, "The Fermentum at Rome in the Fifth Century: A Reconsideration."

The dust is from those who are already in heaven — it is eschatological dust. It is the very opposite of the *adamah* from which Adam was made. This is the *adamah* of heaven. The cup of wine, while certainly recalling the wine at the wedding of Cana in Galilee as well as the eucharistic cup, is a human element, to which is added three divine elements — God's ring, God's cross, and God's dust. The drink becomes an eschatological drink, symbolizing the wedding feast of the Kingdom.

Anglo-Saxon Liturgical Developments

Owing largely to Reformation prejudice and propaganda, the medieval period is frequently portrayed as the dark ages, a monolithic time block. In fact the several centuries covered by the term *medieval* were a time of great changes, many regional differences, and at times great creativity. Anglo-Saxon England is one such locus of creativity. The primary liturgical model was the *Gregorian Sacramentary,* shared by much of the Western Church, but there are important Anglo-Saxon versions such as the *Aethelwold Benedictional,* c. 980, and the *Red Book of Darley,* c. 1060. This period was a time of considerable cultural diversity. The older Celtic Christianity had been overlaid by the Anglo-Saxon conversions by Augustine on behalf of Rome. But Norse settlers brought their own culture and religious ideas, as did the numerous Norman French settlers who came to England prior to the Norman conquest of 1066.

First of importance is *The Red Book of Darley's* baptismal rite. The baptismal rite is quite unremarkable, except for the fact that the rubrics are in Anglo-Saxon — the incorporation of the vernacular some 200 years before the Continent.

Second, it is in the rites for Holy Week that we first find developments towards liturgical drama — where the rememorative becomes representational. Thus monks enact the part of the women visiting the empty tomb. It is disputed whether this spawned the later mystery plays, or was subsumed by them, but it is an Anglo-Saxon development.

Third, it is perhaps no accident that in England the Paschal feast was called Easter after Eostre, the Anglo-Saxon goddess of spring. It is of course difficult for most North Atlantic moderns and postmoderns to begin to envisage the agrarian life of Anglo-Saxon England, where most settlements were of a few hundred people at most, and often far fewer. Anglo-

Saxon deities had been invoked to ensure good weather, harvest, and harmony. Rogationtide processions have an older Christian origin, and were important in Rome. But in England they became inextricably bound up with Ascension. So in Anglo-Saxon England at this time of the liturgical calendar crops were blessed, disaster averted, Christian principles learned and strengthened, and heaven made nearer. One homily exhorted, "We must bless our earthly places, which are the acres and woods and our cattle and all of the things that God has given us to enjoy."[9]

The processions covered a sampling of the locality, stopping at certain sites — other churches and shrines — for prayer. The pre-history of those shrines suggests a christianizing of earlier pagan holy spots. We also find prohibition against riding, hunting, carrying weapons, and gaming — all evidence that in continuity with the pre-Christian culture, this was a wild adventure and leisure time. But as Bradford Bedingfield comments,

> It is more than just a dedication of fruits, trees, and livestock to God. What vernacular descriptions of the procession illustrate is that those walking about with Christ's cross and the holy relics are spreading about the presence of God, marking God's territory by allowing the divinity that has been accorded the cross, the gospel books, and the holy relics to drive out the presence of the devil and to unify the earthly places with God's divinity, which is also the central idea of the Ascension.[10]

The things of heaven and the things of earth are fused; gospel and culture interact. What was good for Anglo-Saxon England may well be good for Korean Christians at *Chusok*.

Three Eighteenth-Century Liturgies

The eighteenth century witnessed the rise and consolidation of that movement categorized as the Enlightenment.[11] In England it gave rise to Newtonian physics and a great interest in natural religion. The impact of this

---

9. Cited in M. Bradford Bedingfield, *The Dramatic Liturgy of Anglo-Saxon England* (Woodbridge: Boydell & Brewer Press, 2002), p. 195.

10. Bedingfield, *The Dramatic Liturgy of Anglo-Saxon England*, p. 200.

11. Jonathan I. Israel, *Radical Enlightenment: Philosophy and the Making of Modernity 1650-1750* (Oxford: Oxford University Press, 2001).

on theological thought can be seen in the neo-Arian treatment of the Trinity in two of Newton's disciples, Samuel Clarke and William Whiston. Both these divines made proposals for the reform of the Anglican *Book of Common Prayer* to bring it in line with the Newtonian scriptural idea of the Trinity.[12] Clarke's suggestions were revived by Theophilus Lindsey in 1774. As might be expected, the Athanasian Creed was omitted, but also the *Benedictus* and *Magnificat*.

This attempt to reform the liturgy in accordance with Newtonian theology was well known in the eighteenth-century English Church. It is no accident, therefore, that three American liturgies were all inspired in some way or other by the proposed revisions. In 1782 the King's Chapel, Boston, thinking itself to be at the cutting edge of American Anglican thinking, published a Prayer Book for use in the chapel that was based on the Clarke/Lindsey proposals. In 1786 the American Episcopal clergy met in Philadelphia and produced a proposed revision of the *Book of Common Prayer* for the American Anglican Church. While not unitarian, it too omitted the Athanasian Creed, and tailored the 1662 rite to suit Enlightenment thought on natural religion. For example, the Psalms were edited to cut out verses that offended eighteenth-century Enlightenment sensitivities. The book that was finally adopted in 1789 was a more conservative revision than that proposed in 1786, but even that book echoes the Newtonian theological climate. In 1784 John Wesley had published his *Sunday Service of the Methodists in North America*. It was in fact used only sparingly in Wesley's lifetime, and dropped from use on his death. However, here too we find, albeit from a more evangelical piety, similar Enlightenment sensitivities, such as omission of the Athanasian Creed, suspicion of magical ideas of "regeneration" in baptism, and a select psalter which omitted elements objectionable to Enlightenment ideas on violence.

History thus illustrates to us the fact of inculturation in worship. It is not something new arising out of world Christianity; it is the very nature of worship. Several of the key papers in this colloquium illustrate the fact that this process continues. M. L. Daneel and Dana L. Robert describe the worship amongst the Apostles and Zionists in Southern Africa, giving us

---

12. See James E. Force, *Essays on the Context, Nature and Influence of Isaac Newton's Theology* (Boston: Kluwer Academic Publishers, 1990); J. P. Ferguson, *Dr. Samuel Clarke: An Eighteenth Century Heretic* (Kineton: The Roundwood Press, 1976); James E. Force, *William Whiston: Honest Newtonian* (Cambridge: Cambridge University Press, 1986).

an insight into how certain independent churches have amalgamated and adapted forms of worship inherited from missionaries with a more independent African religious spirit. What is interesting in this account is the place given to the Holy Spirit, and this might invite comparison and contrast with manifestation of the Spirit in some African American congregations. It is perhaps no accident that the African American slaves tended to prefer camp revivalist meetings to more liturgical services, perhaps a kindred spirit with being moved by the Spirit. The marking out of sacred space in the open again has echoes of brush arbor services as well as the camp meeting and so the authors rightly draw attention to the origins of the camp meetings in American adaptation of the Scottish communion seasons, combined with Methodist open-air revivalist preaching. But particular cultural elements that characterize African religions are also prominent, such as the concern for purity, the use of distinctive dress to show purity, and the adaptation of traditional music to Christian worship.

Miguel Palomino and Samuel Escobar give an insight into models of worship that have emerged in Latin American Protestant/Pentecostal groups. Once again, music style is an important ingredient, but also there is a move from the personal testimony style of the received tradition towards a more eschatological concern with the Kingdom of God. However, we also see the impact of modern technology, shared in common with North American Pentecostalism, put at the disposal of worship. Thus we have an interesting mix of Latin American culture, North American Pentecostal spirituality and worship patterns, overlaid with late modern and postmodern technology.

Yet another perspective is presented by Charles Farhadian. In his paper on the Glory Hut Farhadian presents yet another picture of inculturation, where Papuan melodies old and new meet in a synthesis, and where the worship space becomes both a symbol of openness to the world and a defiant proclamation in the face of attempts to Indonesianize the community. But again we find in the urban areas the adaptation of late modern and postmodern cultural forms, the electronic instruments.

Questions

What happens when worship comes to one culture from an alien culture, and for one reason or another is made resistant to the process? What happens when this is recognized, and some liturgical genetic engineering takes place? And at what point does the culture intrude to a point where the gospel is compromised?

In the early modern period it was certain Roman Catholic missionaries who first realized that the older Western and then subsequent Tridentine rites embodied not only things divine, but also things heavily Italian and European. The missionaries in the New World and China sought to introduce cultural elements to de-Westernize the liturgy, most of which was subsequently condemned by Rome. Ancestor worship in China, for example, was deemed as being different in theology from the cult of the Christian saints. That same problem was lost on most Protestant churches until a later date, when they re-thought the doctrines of predestination and divine providence and also became serious missionaries. The result of course was that in Africa, for example, in the case of Anglicanism, it depended whether the home mission was Anglo-Catholic or evangelical as to the style of worship; but regardless of that, converts were treated to the seventeenth-century English liturgy, together with Victorian hymnals. In Korea, nineteenth-century American Presbyterian worship, already itself adapted to the American situation, was introduced as the norm. In most instances, Tridentine Catholic forms, the Anglican *Book of Common Prayer*, and American Presbyterian forms of worship were introduced as *the correct and authentic form of worship*. As Peter Phan comments of the Roman Catholic Church, the Roman rite, however it is understood, *is itself a cultural form*, embodying a particular and local way of seeing the world, performing divine worship, and living the Christian faith, especially through its linguistic medium and the theology enshrined in its texts and rituals.[13] As Seung Joong Joo notes in his case study, in order to become Christians, Koreans had to cut off their culture and their own traditions from their lives, resulting in a great disjuncture between their lives as Christians and their lives as Koreans, and being taught that American culture was a genuine Christian culture! In the 1920s, J. C. Winslow, J. E. G. Festing, D. R. Athavale, and E. C. Ratcliff wrote a book with a plea for a distinctive liturgy for the Anglican Church in India.[14] They argued that the late Stuart 1662 book was not appropriate to Asian culture, and suggested

---

13. Peter Phan, "Liturgical Inculturation," p. 70.

14. J. C. Winslow et al., *The Eucharist in India: A Plea for a Distinctive Liturgy for the Indian Church* (London: Longmans, 1920).

that the liturgy of St. James, used by the Thomas Christians in India, being Middle Eastern in origin, was more akin to the spirit of India than the English book. In other words, it has often been recognized by those responsible for worship on what might be termed the mission front that worship needs to be adapted, and the Eurocentric human elements must give way to the native culture and custom. However, human nature is often perverse. On the one hand, such worship was recognized to be a foreign import; on the other, precisely because it was foreign it became a mark of being a Christian, in a largely non-Christian culture. The classic example of that in the twentieth century was the mass for India, pioneered in the early 1970s by the Bangalore Institute. The mass adopted ritual gestures consonant with Hindu religious gestures — arti lamps, flowers, squatting — rather than Western ecclesiastical ceremony. New texts were authored, attempting to reflect the religious and cultural idea of India. The Eucharistic prayer gave thanks for distinctive elements found in the teachings of the other religions of India; for example, it gave thanks for God's inscrutable decrees, suggested by Islam. While many Western scholars were enthralled by this venture, many Indian Catholics were highly offended. First, the language was of the Brahmin caste, and thus offensive to Catholic Indians whose ancestry was from lower castes. In addition, many Catholics protested that they had left Hinduism to become Christian, and did not want to be dragged back into Hindu worship gestures.

Another example is the rite of Zaire. In 1972 the Episcopal Conference of the Democratic Republic of Congo (then called Zaire) asked the evangelization commission to undertake a methodic study of the appropriate modes of expression for the celebration of the Eucharist in Zaire. It took as its base the Roman rite, but found inspiration in the Ambrosian, Ethiopic, and Oriental rites on the one hand, and on the other hand from the socio-cultural context of local traditional congregations. The Zaire rite was approved on 30 April 1988, and is performed in four stages: The Opening Rite, the Liturgy of the Word, the Liturgy of the Eucharist, and Concluding Rite. Some of the characteristics are as follows:

1. The invocation of saints, including the ancestors. Leon Ngoy Kalumba explains, "The presence of God materializes itself through the invocation of the saints, which means entering into communion with the celestial family of God, where our own ancestors preceded us, the saints of our terrestrial families, men with good hearts, allied of

God, mediators of his kindness. Ancestors are, for Africans, those from whom came life, wisdom and the kindness of which only God is the source and the plenitude; those whose good example guides our communal march towards the Father."[15]

2. The Kyrie eleison comes after the proclamation and the explication of the Word and the Creed, and is then followed by the exchange of peace. Kalumba suggests that this reflects the African palaver, where speech implies total frankness, dialogue, and communion.

3. Liberated from artificial inhibitions and constraints, the believer expresses belief through bodily movements, especially dance and swaying of the body.

A great deal of preparatory work, consultation, and reflection went into the making of this rite. The Roman Catholic liturgical scholar Anscar Chupungco distinguishes between *accomodatio,* or *adaptation, acculturation,* and *inculturation.*[16] Following Aylward Shorter, he explains *acculturation* as an encounter between two cultures in which they stand side by side. Put in a formula, $A + B = AB$. *Inculturation,* on the other hand, entails interaction, assimilation, and *transculturation,* $A + B = C$. Both the Mass for India and the Zaire rite must fall into the category of *inculturation.* However, both raise questions of whether this liturgical genetic engineering really does produce a genuine incultured liturgy. At the Societas Liturgica Conference held at York in 1989, after a number of core papers exploring culture and theology, the final paper was given by Aidan Kavanagh of Yale Divinity School. In a withering paper Kavanagh ridiculed the whole idea of being able to engineer an incultured liturgy.[17] Inculturation, argued Kavanagh, happens without anyone having to agonize over it. It issues forth most commonly in the visual forms of architecture and art, and then music, and perhaps particular observances peculiar to a particular place, and in customs particularly associated with rites of passage. On the one hand, of course,

15. Leon Ngoy Kalumba, SJ, "The Zairean Rite: The Roman Missal for the Diocese of Zaire (Congo)," pp. 92-98; p. 98.

16. Chupungco is the author of several books on this subject. See for example *Liturgical Inculturation: Sacramentals, Religiosity, and Catechesis* (Collegeville, Minn.: Liturgical Press, 1992).

17. Aidan Kavanagh, "Liturgical Inculturation: Looking to the Future," *Studia Liturgica* 20 (1990): 95-106.

Kavanagh in his usual devastating way was calling in question such enter-prises as the Indian Mass. Many who heard the paper thought that was his point. Some missed the other side of his coin: if it happens, then there is no such thing as a neutral or a-cultural liturgy, and perhaps certain popular practices and customs in the Western rites, Catholic and Protestant, were more cultural and less Christian than was perceived. One only need look at the liturgical calendar in *Chalice Worship,* the denomination book of the Disciples of Christ. There a bare traditional calendar of the church seasons is overwhelmed by days marking the American secular calendar. We might like to think this was reclaiming the secular for the gospel, but actually it probably illustrates the synthesis of American civic religion.

Assessing the Balance

One of the problems is that often it is only someone from another culture who can spot the cultural elements in another's liturgy, and who may per-haps alone be the best judge of the balance between the human and divine. Here I would like to suggest three examples.

The first is the Vodun related services found in some Caribbean churches. In his book, *Old Ship of Zion,* Walter Pitts noted that the Orisha in Trinidad combines elements of Roman Catholic, Anglican, and Spiri-tual Baptist ritual with Yoruba religion.[18] Followers still recognize gods such as Ogun, Shango, and Oya. The use of incense, incantations, candles, and crucifixes witnesses to the influence of Roman Catholic worship. The frenzy of dancing, the secret knowledge, and the trance all have echoes and parallels in African worship and religious customs.

My second example is perhaps less obvious. It is a description from the *New Haven Register,* dated 8 June 2003, under the title "High-Tech Worship."

> With the click of a mouse, Ben Therien of Hamden outputs inspira-tion from a modem during Sunday worship. Therien, a professional-yet-volunteer computer consultant at the Calvary Life Christian Cen-ter, a non-denominational congregation, runs a slide show on a huge digital screen that portrays pristine images of a sun emerging from the clouds, biblical verses and song lyrics.

18. Walter F. Pitts, *Old Ship of Zion* (Oxford: Oxford University Press, 1993), pp. 106ff.

. . . Two cameras film the Sunday worship services, and fragments are beamed onto the screen the next week. The computer-generated graphics operate like a sports highlight clip, in which snapshots of individual spiritual rapture are shown amid applause and cheers by worshipers. . . . The atmosphere is a cross between a concert and a choreographed theater production: stage lights, a sound engineer leveling microphones, ushers with walkie-talkies, a band and a six-member dance team. . . .

. . . The Rev. John Muratori of Wallingford, a senior pastor, said he decided to blend technology, artistic expression and worship to make the church more appealing to the ordinary person. . . . "We are trying to bring a 21st-century outlook to church."

While Muratori acknowledges his worship format is a sharp departure from the prototypical service, he hopes this will reach people in search of "new experience."

The third example is the Liturgy of St. Gregory of Nyssa Church, San Francisco. This Episcopal church was purposely built in order to celebrate a stational liturgy, which is a traditional Western Eucharistic rite overlaid with eclectic Eastern elements. The vestments, made from material with African tie-dye coloring, are suggestive of the Ethiopic Orthodox Church, which the umbrellas and hats worn by the clergy also suggest. The liturgy of the Word is celebrated on a raised platform, with a bema at one end, with the congregation seated in collegiate style. For the liturgy of the Eucharist, clergy and congregation dance in line down to the square table in the rotunda, and stand in circles around the table. The rite ends with a circular dance. Much of the music is composed especially for the service, and is sung a capella.

At first consideration, these three accounts have little in common. But in fact they might be viewed as three examples of where cultural considerations have intruded to obscure — albeit in different proportions — the gospel. The Vodun rites, despite being an amalgamation, do not give a balanced synthesis. The concern with spirits and power, in a sinister sense, as well as the syncretism, all make it extremely difficult to place this within Christianity. What has happened is that the Christian element has been subsumed under quite alien and contrary elements to a point where such worship is deemed outside the parameters of orthodox Christian practice and belief. But perhaps a similar criticism may be made of the other two examples. The New Haven high-tech worship is exactly that. The culture has set the tone and agenda. Here the world of MTV and Microsoft has become the medium for a message, but at what price? It is almost as though the message is unable to stand without the complexity of the virtual image and cyberspace. At what point is the worship mainly about using modern/postmodern entertainment rather than the presentation of the gospel? And St. Gregory of Nyssa? It can be seen as a brave attempt at postmodern worship without abandoning the traditional format, and that is certainly one valid assessment.[19] Another is that this is an eclectic liturgy for a small eclectic congregation, and could only be a product of California. It does not appear to attract people from the nearby African American neighborhoods; its use of a Shinto shrine for the reserved sacrament, its use of Eastern gongs, its parody of Ethiopic Orthodoxy, its liberal West Coast inclusivity, all might suggest that a particular pastiche or bricolage culture, pick and mix, the religious mall Eastern style, has invaded the rite.

This brings us to the central question. Given that inculturation happens, what safeguards might there be to make sure that the divine elements are not distorted or even replaced by the human elements?

Stretching Niebuhr's Categories

Some categories or guides that have proved useful are those which have been borrowed by Richard Niebuhr's classic book *Christ and Culture*.[20] In that book he outlined five categories — Christ against Culture, Christ of Culture, Christ above Culture, Christ and Culture in paradox, and Christ the transformer of Culture. In his recent book *Worship Seeking Understanding,* John Witvliet has suggested that liturgists have tended to divorce the categories from Niebuhr's original stated purpose or the genius of the original analysis, and use them in a way that Niebuhr did not intend.[21] This may be the case, but the categories or headings are useful and suggestive, and in any case Niebuhr did not touch on the topic of worship directly. Let us explore three which I think are the most helpful and useful in

19. See "Back to the Future," *Christian Century,* Nov. 20–Dec. 3, 2002, pp. 18-22.

20. H. Richard Niebuhr, *Christ and Culture* (New York: Harper & Row, 1951).

21. John D. Witvliet, *Worship Seeking Understanding: Windows into Christian Practice* (Grand Rapids: Baker Book House, 2003), pp. 91-123.

assisting a decision as to whether the things of earth have intruded too far into the things of heaven.

Christ of Culture

Since the world is created by God, and has been redeemed, not everything is *a priori* bad. It is self-evident that liturgy assumes certain things as being an acceptable medium for adoration towards the Godhead. Human gestures, human words, human music, human artifacts are obvious examples. What might this mean? First, it is difficult to distinguish categorically between sacred and secular music. It may be that some music styles and traditions are able to evoke transcendence and things eternal better than others. But certainly there is no sacred Western music over against music of other cultures. Michael Hawn's recent book on global singing is a welcomed witness to the riches that different cultures bring.[22]

Second, because of the unstable nature of the evolving North European vernaculars, the Western church retained Latin for its rites, but this eventually was given a quasi-theological justification, as though Latin was superior. Luther made the point that the Holy Spirit did not wait for everyone to come to Jerusalem to learn Hebrew, but gave gifts of speech. Indeed, insofar as Pentecost is the theological reversal of the Tower of Babel, every human language is a medium for worship of the triune God. Again, it may be that within a particular language, certain colloquial styles are less appropriate than more formal styles, but nothing is *a priori* barbarous.

Styles of architecture are another example. The Syrian Indians very quickly adapted the style used in Hindu sacred architecture for their churches in Kerala. Anglo-Saxon wooden churches were built in the style of the central tribal hall. The evolution of Gothic architecture may well have been a statement in stone about the grandeur of God in the medieval West, but the later nineteenth-century concept that there was only one style of Christian architecture, Gothic, led to what can only be described as a nineteenth- and twentieth-century dark ages of church design. Wherever Christians adopt and then adapt the local for the glory of God, there Christ of culture is affirmed. Here we may note that the Syrian church in

22. C. Michael Hawn, *Gather into One: Praying and Singing Globally* (Grand Rapids: Eerdmans, 2003).

India did not simply copy Hindu temples; it adapted the architectural style and features to produce Indian church buildings. In some ways this paradigm is expressed by the incarnation: perfect divinity and perfect humanity in one person. Yet the incarnation expressed perfect humanity, not flawed humanity. We use the things of culture that are intrinsically good, or at least neutral.

Christ against Culture

God is creator, but also judge; the beginning, and the end; the alpha, and the omega. The incarnation, which affirms the world and human life, is inseparable from the atonement, resurrection, and the hope of the world to come. The world is passing away, says the book of Revelation, and there will be a new heaven and a new earth. There are certain things in the creation itself, and which manifest themselves in human activity, which are contrary to the goals and standards of the Kingdom. These sinister elements of the world are what Karl Barth termed Nothingness. Nothingness is certainly not nothing, but the dark side of creation, perhaps seen in the utter waste in interstellar space, with stars dying, with space debris causing destruction, and captured in anti-myth in the Genesis story where it is the serpent, and not simply humans, who unleash the negative in this world. There are certain activities that contradict the gospel, and should be challenged by worship: racism, greed, indifference, persecution, fear, and misuse of power. How far do the examples I cited — Vodun, the New Haven high-tech service, and St. Gregory Nyssa, San Francisco — challenge their surrounding cultures, or how far do they simply reflect them?

Here perhaps I may be permitted to cite two high profile, but certainly not equal, memorial services. The first is the memorial service/funeral of Princess Diana. There was a huge outpouring of popular cultural emotion, with flowers, candles, teddy bears, pictures, and public weeping, which some also interpreted as an outpouring of guilt and remorse by a nation that had forgotten how to express itself ritually. The service itself took place in Westminster Abbey, a Royal Peculiar, where the Dean and Chapter have considerable leeway in their use of rites and ceremonies for such occasions. There was of course much pomp and circumstance, as befits an English royal funeral, but the service itself was a careful weaving of Latin choral texts, readings, and prayers. The cultural element was of course Elton John's

Candle in the Wind, where a song written for Marilyn Monroe was rewritten for Diana. And there was the angry address by Earl Spencer. But these cultural elements, which for some earthed the rite, were held in check by the formal, careful use of music and carefully crafted prayer, and the focus on fragile humanity *coram deo.* The liturgy kept the earth in check.

Contrast this with the memorial service for Laci Peterson in California. Here there was a large Baptist choir, and it took a bizarre form of a cross between a charity concert, a pre-trial of her husband, and American sentimentality at its worst. The culture and emotion simply took over, and nothing held them in check. This was a "cultural incantation," and commemorated not just two lives cut short, but also that, whatever the hereafter might hold, it could never compensate for loss of this life in California.

Another example concerns the oft-asked question of whether bread and wine at the Eucharist are simply cultural. Can they be substituted in cultures where they are expensive commodities? Of course, on the one hand it can be argued that these are part of the culture of particularity that comes from the Semitic setting of the incarnation, and are reminders that to be incarnated is to be alien and intruder. The Lord's body and blood always intrude, and are never simply a nice meal. In other words, it can be argued that these are part of the givenness of the gospel. On the other hand, it is argued that they represent both the staple diet and the festal celebration of Semitic culture, and rice bread and some local alcohol could substitute for this. Far less convincing is the fear of microbes and alcohol that led to Welch's huge fortune from grape juice for the timid. Even more inappropriate is the use of Coca Cola, which students have sometimes used in a bid to be modern. In that context Australian liturgist Robert Gribben made this important point:

> The clearest theological comment came from our Cuban brother, Juan, who muttered about "the black waters of capitalism" — but his political point was also theological. He was really asking if Coca Cola can bear the theological weight of the Blood of Christ — and the answer is (I think) absolutely not. It is indeed one of the most famous products of international capitalism, and even if it is now available everywhere, it is a classic part of the westernization of culture, and that is its chief symbolic value. It carries messages about how young people should see themselves; it preaches certain ways of understanding "life." It is not ethically neutral. Compared with locally produced drinks, it is

relatively expensive, it is reputedly addictive, and it is bad for you! How can it preach Christ?[23]

Indeed, one might add that its chief symbolic value is global capitalization, and not global Christianity.

Christ against culture might obviously mean a severe cleaning up, or simply abandoning, of Vodun rites. It may require John Muratori to ask who profits from his huge investment of high-tech equipment for worship, and what this says about the expensive equipment needed, apparently, for the gospel to be proclaimed and the crucified God to be worshiped. Or rather is this just the postmodern high-tech shops of the mall come to church? And St. Gregory of Nyssa? Surely the question must be asked: why has not this style, if it is postmodern, caught on elsewhere? Why does it not attract the African American population from nearby?

Christ the Transformer of Culture

Central to the call to the Kingdom is the word *metanoia,* translated as *repent,* but its more usual meaning is *to turn around.* The present world and its ways are held up against the eschaton — against what they are intended to become. Worship, therefore, should convey a call or challenge to metanoia, for transformation. I have suggested elsewhere that, for example, in a Hindu culture this may mean a challenge to the cyclical view of the world — time is linear, or at least can be best envisioned as linear, and thus things can and do change. The gospel and worship should hold out the truth that Christians are called to work for change, and that by God's grace, things can be changed. But what of Western culture? Here it is more difficult — after all, nearly all liturgical scholars and "experts" are either Westerners or Western trained, and we are frequently blinkered to the faults of our own culture. In certain Third World contexts, the liturgy must articulate and hold up gospel justice. (I deliberately avoid the term *social justice,* which is often simply what liberal Westerners view as politically correct, regardless of whether it stems from the gospel or not.) It may mean in Western cultures challenging the idea that wealth and power are

---

23. Given at the International Anglican Consultation in Berkeley, California, 2001. I am grateful to Robert Gribben for providing me with the script.

gifts of God, which come without a terrible burden of responsibility. It may mean using properly made bread and proper wine, as a protest against fast-food corporations whose food is often not particularly healthy. It may mean deliberately eschewing anything in architecture, design, and furnishing that endorses without question global capitalism and the corporate office. St. Aldate's Church in Oxford has been recently re-ordered as a brave attempt to adapt a medieval parish church for modern English evangelical worship. But the south nave stage for the band and worship leaders, the vast audio centre and the hanging monitors convey little sense of transcendence or the other, but only intermittent entertainment at a small-town airport. Christ as transformer of culture may mean using technology in worship only insofar as it helps articulate worship as a counter-culture. To use John Howard Yoder's typologies, the liturgy must articulate the activist church, the conversionist church, and the confessing church — particularly the latter.[24] It will envision an alternative polis. It should inspire renewed effort in the world, to transform the world and announce that the kingdoms of this world will become the kingdoms of Christ.

In a recent paper given at Calvin College, I invoked the term from 1 Peter made popular by Stanley Hauerwas and William H. Willimon: *resident aliens*.[25] Whatever culture of the globe Christians come from, since the good news comes from outside, all are resident aliens. As a resident alien in the United States I have a Green Card, which allows me to come and go. But my birth certificate and passport say that my citizenship is elsewhere. As much as I enjoy the United States, it is not home, and there are things that I miss, and things which I find strange, and some things that I do not like. That is the lot of the Christian, wherever he or she is. By the new birth of baptism, the old birth is seriously qualified and changed. Whatever may be encountered in worship that is of our temporary domicile, be it high-tech screen or Tania bowl, worship itself should be a reminder of our true home, and reveal things of heaven. The things of the earth will pass away; the things of heaven are of eternity.

---

24. John Howard Yoder, "A People in the World: Theological Interpretation," in James Leo Garrett, ed., *The Concept of the Believer's Church* (Scottdale: Herald Press, 1969), pp. 252-83.

25. Stanley Hauerwas and William H. Willimon, *Resident Aliens* (Nashville: Abingdon Press, 1989).

Interfaith Comparisons and Assessment — Muslim Worship: Interfaith Assets and Ecumenical Shortcomings

LAMIN SANNEH

Editor's Introduction

"A Christian who is accustomed to pray cannot help recognizing that the Moslem who he sees praying is doing something similar. And seeing a Hindu bowing down before his god stirs the Christian, because he himself has learned to bow his head before the God who appeared to us in Jesus Christ." So wrote J. H. Bavinck in *The Church Between Temple and Mosque*. "It is not sufficient to merely witness, because [the church] will somehow have to say what it thinks of these other religions," Bavinck wrote. "[W]hatever the church may meet, it is clear that it has the duty to speak honestly and with dignity with the other religions. . . . The great encounter must take place."

The fruits of this encounter are many. We may find points of common ground and cordial fellowship between different faith traditions. We may find it necessary to clarify our own concepts and assumptions we had not examined carefully enough. We may view our own practice in a new light.

In this intriguing interfaith study of worship in Islam, Lamin Sanneh traces points of commonality between Muslim and Christian piety and worship. In Islam, Sanneh shows, "worship implies holy, undivided devotion to God." Through an extensive look at the texts of Muslim prayers, Sanneh brings out some central themes: awe of the Creator, holiness, plea for mercy, and gratitude as the opposite of rebellion. Prayer is a fundamental way of positioning the believer in relation to God. Ultimately, Sanneh establishes worship as "not just an occasion of divine encounter, the occasion of separation from the world and self and attachment to God, but also the space for training and formation in the spiritual life."

253

These themes will resonate deeply with the Christian reader. Indeed, Sanneh points out the striking parallels between Muslim piety in prayer and the piety of Christian psalms and hymns (as well as Augustine's image of the beggar before God). Although Sanneh says the theme of the holy and mysterious name of God has been neglected in Western Christianity, he lays out a beautiful expression of this from Russian Orthodoxy and notes its parallels to Muslim prayers.

By placing the prayer of these two religions side by side and drawing these parallels, Sanneh shows for us the fundamental sacredness of the act of prayer that transcends cultures and traditions, and gives us much fertile ground for mutual understanding between these two religions. He leads us to reflect on some central questions: What do Muslim and Christian prayers tell us about the similarities and differences between the worship practices of these two significant monotheistic religious traditions? How might this discussion remind Christians of riches within their own tradition? What implications does this discussion have for Christian witness? These are questions that demand a close examination of Muslim practices, based not only on anecdotal experiences, but also on foundational source documents.

•   •

Verum, a quocumque dicatur, a Spiritu santo est.

THOMAS AQUINAS

Tucked away at the back of the Catholic Catechism is a section on Christian prayer that opens with the declaration of the great mystery of God and with prayer as the basis of the believer's relationship with God. The Catechism emphasizes that the foundation of that relationship of prayer is humility. The Catechism declares that only when we humbly acknowledge that "we do not know how to pray as we ought" (citing Romans 8:26) are we ready freely to receive the gift of prayer. It recalls the words of Augustine to the effect that "man is a beggar before God."[1]

---

1. *Catechism of the Catholic Church* (Vatican: Libreria Editrice Vaticana, 1994), pp. 613-14. For a detailed study of interfaith issues in the prayer and worship life of Islam and Christianity, see Kenneth Cragg, *Alive to God* (London: Oxford University Press, 1970). See also these titles by the same writer: *The Dome and the Rock* (London: S.P.C.K., 1964), *The*

That note of the believer in prayer and worship as a beggar before God happens to be a prominent theme in Muslim devotion and piety, and it seems appropriate to turn to it for an interfaith perspective on what it means to acknowledge the Creator in faith and gratitude. I will deal almost exclusively with prayer and worship as supererogatory, supplicatory rites *(adi'yah,* sing. *du'á')* rather than with the canonical obligation of *salát,* with its prescribed formulas and its set order. It is important to stress, however, that it is *salát,* as we shall see presently, that frames and controls prayer and devotion in the Muslim religious life. *Salát* is not dispensable for the Muslim. Furthermore, *salát* is exclusive to Muslims and is forbidden territory to non-Muslims. Not so, though, are the invocations and the supplicatory rites.

In his acclaimed apologetic work on Islam, *The Spirit of Islam,* Sir Syed Ameer Ali of India describes the central role of prayer and worship in the Muslim life, saying prayer is what distinguishes Islam from other religions, with the Prophet of Islam himself setting a personal example of discipline in devotion. The Prophet's teachings and examples "leave to the individual worshipper the amplest scope for the most heartfelt outpouring of devotion and humility before the Almighty Presence."[2] The Qur'án enjoins the believer to "perform the prayer; prayer forbids indecency and dishonour. God's remembrance [*dhikr*] is greater" (29:44). Muhammad himself is quoted as praying in the following words:

> O Lord! I supplicate Thee for firmness in faith and direction towards rectitude, and to assist me in being grateful to Thee, and in adoring Thee in every good way: and I supplicate Thee for an innocent heart, which shall not incline to wickedness; and I supplicate Thee for a true tongue, and for that virtue which Thou knowest; and I pray Thee to defend me from that vice which Thou knowest, and for forgiveness of those faults which Thou knowest. O my Defender! Assist me in remembering Thee and being grateful to Thee, and in worshipping Thee with the excess of my strength. O Lord! I have injured my own soul, and no one can pardon the faults of Thy servants but Thou; forgive me

---

Call of the Minaret, 2nd edition (Maryknoll: Orbis Books, 1985), and *Sandals at the Mosque* (London: SCM Press, 1958 and New York: Oxford University Press, 1959).

2. Syed Ameer Ali, *The Spirit of Islam: A History of the Evolution and Ideals of Islam* (London: Chatto & Windus, 1964), p. 162.

of Thy loving-kindness, and have mercy on me; for verily Thou art the forgiver of offences and the bestower of blessings on Thy servants.[3]

The caliphs as the successors of the Prophet continued this tradition of prayer and worship. Accordingly, the caliph and the Prophet's son-in-law, 'Alí, is credited with the following prayer:

Thanks be to my Lord; He the Adorable, and only to be adored. My Lord, the Eternal, the Ever-existing, the Cherisher, the True Sovereign whose mercy and might overshadow the universe; the Regulator of the world, and Light of the creation. His is our worship; to Him belongs all worship; He existed before all things, and will exist after all that is living has ceased. Thou art the adored, my Lord; Thou art the Master, the Loving and Forgiving; Thou bestowest power and might on whom Thou pleasest; him whom Thou hast exalted none can lower; and him whom Thou hast lowered none can exalt. Thou, my Lord, art the Eternal, the Creator of all, All-wise Sovereign Mighty; Thy knowledge knows everything; Thy beneficence is all-pervading; Thy forgiveness and mercy are all-embracing. O my Lord, Thou art the Helper of the afflicted, the Reliever of all distress, the Consoler of the broken-hearted; Thou art present everywhere to help Thy servants. Thou knowest all secrets, all thoughts, art present in every assembly, Fulfiller of all our needs, Bestower of all blessings. Thou art the Friend of the poor and bereaved; my Lord, Thou art my Fortress; a Castle for all who seek Thy help. Thou art the Refuge of the weak; the Helper of the pure and true. O my Lord, Thou art my Supporter, my Helper, the Helper of all who seek Thy help. . . . O my Lord, Thou art the Creator, I am only created; Thou art my Sovereign, I am only Thy servant; Thou art the Helper, I am the beseecher; Thou, my Lord, art my Refuge; Thou art the Forgiver, I am the sinner; Thou, my Lord, art the Merciful, All-knowing and love. Bestow, my Lord, all Thy knowledge and love and mercy; forgive my sins, O my Lord, and let me approach Thee, my Lord.

O my Lord, Thou the Ever-praised, the Eternal, Thou art the Ever-present, Ever-existing, the Ever-near, the All-knowing. Thou livest in every heart, in every soul, all-pervading; Thy knowledge is ingrained in every mind. . . . He bears no similitude, has no equal, One, Eternal;

3. Cited in Ameer Ali, *The Spirit of Islam*, p. 162.

thanks be to the Lord whose mercy extends to every sinner, who provides for even those who deny Him. To Him belong the beginning and the end, all knowledge and the most hidden secret of the heart. He never slumbers, the Ever-just, the Ever-wakeful. He forgiveth in His mercy our greatest sins, — loveth all creation. I testify to the goodness of my Lord, to the truth of His Messenger's message, blessings on him and [on] his descendants and companions.[4]

Muslim prayer and canonical devotion begin with the declaration of God's incomparable greatness, the *takbír, alláh-u akbar,* "God, than whom is nothing greater." The *takbír* of the divine mystery exalts the Creator while humbling the believer at the same time.

No name more sums up what the believer should be than that of servitude. For God, ever to be praised and exalted, said in the description of the Prophet on the night of the Mi'ráj [the ascension into heaven], at this moment of greatest honour in this life, "Most high praise to Him who carried His servant (*'abd*) by night from the Mosque of Mecca to the Mosque of al-Aqsá [in Jerusalem]; and that other world: And He revealed to His servant what He revealed" (Qur. 53:10). Had there been a nobler title than that of servitude, He would have given it to the Prophet.[5]

In worship believers surrender their wills and seek the will of God, indicating thereby that believers may worship God only by denying themselves. In Muslim worship this idea of worship as exclusively God's is represented by the act of *sujúd,* of prostration. Muslims worship because God has commanded them; Christians worship because they are motivated. In Islam, worship is something God does to you; in Christianity worship is something you do to yourself. Expressing the sense of worship as divine command and as human obedience, a Muslim worshiper declares:

My worn mortal face is prostrate before Thine everlasting, ever abiding Face. My face is prostrate, dust-soiled, before its Creator, and meet and right is this prostration. My face is prostrate before Him who created and formed it and pierced for it [the openings of] hearing and

4. Ameer Ali, *The Spirit of Islam,* pp. 163-64.
5. Constance Padwick, editor and translator, *Muslim Devotions: A Study of Prayer Manuals in Common Use* (London: S.P.C.K., 1961), p. 4.

sight. Blessed be God, the Best of Creators. My miserable and lowly face is prostrate before the Mighty, the Glorious.[6]

The *takbír* daily summons the Muslim to worship. A Muslim master of the devotional life begins by reminding the faithful that "God created His servants for the purpose of worshipping Him." Worship of God is the favor God grants believers in order to enjoy communion with Him. Says one devotee, "My God, how sweet are the inner impulses inspiring our hearts to remembrance of Thee!" Another declares, "O Transcendent in Praise and in Holiness, make me to taste the bliss of the converse of 'Approach and fear not, thou art of those who are secure,'" referring to the encounter of Moses and his Lord in the Burning Bush (Qur'án 28:31). Worship implies holy, undivided devotion to God. "O God! O God! O God! And (we ask) that Thou wilt turn away our faces from any other goal than Thyself and grant us to gaze towards Thy noble countenance till we see Thee in everything."[7] This is the Beatific Vision *(tawajjud)* that gives rise to the ecstatic outpourings of the mystics.[8]

In all true devotion the merit of the act lies in the intention, for it is by the sincere intention *(ikhlás al-níyah)* that actions acquire moral worth. Counsels one authority:

> Rightness of intention as between you and God is the direction of your heart to the giving of due weight and glory to God and to God's commands and to that which God has commanded to be done. As between you and fellow-servants of God, rightness of intention is the direction of heart with sincerity towards them, performing your dues towards them, not seeking for special favours, and meeting opposition with patience towards God and submissive trust in Him.

One rule for the prayer life says that sincerity in the outward performance must be combined with heart-presence so that there may be symmetry of the inner and outward man (cf. Rom. 2:29, 7:22). Intention carries a sacramental meaning, as the following passage intimates:

> Now the place of the "intention" is the heart; its time is at the beginning of the actions of the prayer-rite, its method is a binding control of the

6. Padwick, *Muslim Devotions*, p. 11.
7. Padwick, *Muslim Devotions*, p. 62.
8. The idea is based on a trenchant verse of Scripture, Qur'án 2:109.

heart and of the members. It is built up of four elements[:] purpose, determination, desire, and act of will, all of these united in one idea. And the "intention" has two aspects, first the direction of the heart in the rite with full awareness, and secondly[,] single-heartedness towards God out of longing for the reward that He has to give and desire for His countenance.[9]

The true nature of "intention," concurs a guide for devotees, is that once you enter upon it you must cast out of your mind anything other than the one thing intended. Worship is an act of self-renunciation, and that means the worshiper must abandon all secret ideas of recourse save that of exalting God. The perfection of worship is the sense of unstinting companionship with God.

Thus surrendered and sanctified, the heart becomes the sanctuary of the divine presence, the inner sanctuary about which mystics speak. "Make us," pleads a devotee, "those in whose hearts is written the record of the awe of Thee, till the secret tongues of those hearts whisper to Thee with the long-drawn-out *miserere* of their solitude in the *mihrábs* of the holy fear of the lowly-hearted."[10] For the devout, the *qibla,* the facing towards Mecca, becomes an act of personal consecration and identification.

> I have turned my face towards Him who created the heavens and the earth, a sincere monotheist and no polytheist, verily my prayer and my devotion and my lifetime and my death time belong to God the Lord of the worlds, to Him who has no fellow. And thus I am commanded, I being of the Muslimín.[11]

Strains of the Christian *sanctus* are echoed in the Islamic *taqdís,* also *tasbíh,* the praise and glorification of God. The worshiper must not presume upon his or her right to approach God but instead must plead for that privilege.

> My God, were it not incumbent upon me to obey Thy commands, I should have considered Thy transcendence too great for me to direct my invocation to Thee. My invocation is only according to my power,

---

9. Padwick, *Muslim Devotions,* p. 54.
10. Padwick, *Muslim Devotions,* p. 59.
11. Padwick, *Muslim Devotions,* p. 60.

not according to Thy power. Perhaps my power may even attain to finding a place for the declaration of Thy transcendent holiness *(taqdís)*, since one of Thy greatest blessings to us is that Thou hast set our tongues to the invocation of Thyself, and that Thou dost permit us to call on Thee and to declare Thy transcendence *(tanzíh)* and [Thy] glory *(tasbíh)*.[12]

Oliver Chase Quick describes a similar attitude of praise in Christian worship:

In Christian thought holiness always contains within itself a double movement, a movement first of separation away from everything that is "common" or "profane," and a movement secondly of inclusion, whereby the separate holy goes forth again to draw into itself everything from which its separation has removed it. This duplicity of movement is exactly represented in the difference between the holiness of Jehovah in the Old Testament and the holiness of the Father of Jesus Christ in the New.[13]

In the Qur'án and in religious thought in general worship in its entirety is a form of thankful praise *(tahmíd)* to God. Gratitude to God, thanksgiving for the divine benevolence, is the mark of true faith. The one who does not thank God is an unbeliever; indeed, the ungrateful person is a rebel against God.[14] One Lenten prayer in Ramadán expresses the devotional aspects of *tahmíd* thus:

Praise be to Him who when I call on Him answers me,
    slow though I am when He calls me.
Praise be to Him who gives to me when I ask Him,
    miserly though I am when He asks a loan of me.
Praise be to Him to whom I confide my needs
    whensoever I will and He satisfies them.
My Lord I praise, for He is of my praise most worthy.[15]

12. Padwick, *Muslim Devotions*, pp. 69-70.

13. O. C. Quick, *The Christian Sacraments* (New York and London: Harper & Brothers, 1927), p. 107.

14. See L. Sanneh, "Gratitude and Ingratitude," *Encyclopedia of the Qur'an*, vol. ii, E–I (Leiden and Boston: Brill, 2002), pp. 370-73.

15. Padwick, *Muslim Devotions*, p. 81.

The theme is magnified up in the pithy, metrical lines of Hafsa of Granada, Spain:

Vouchsafe to me
A scroll, I pray
My shield to be
In fate's affray.
Let your right hand
Inscribe thereon:
"Praise God Most High,
Praise Him alone."

The efficacy of worship and prayer lends itself to invocations of refuge-seeking *(ta'awwudh)* with God and against the evil one. "I take refuge with God from Satan the accursed one" *(a'udhibi-lláhi mina-sh-shaytáni ar-rajím)* is a familiar cry in Muslim Scripture and in popular piety. The *ta'awwudh* is considered protection against a multitude of hazards, known and unknown, present and future.

I take refuge with Thee from the tyranny of every tyrant and the cunning of every deceiver and the oppression of every oppressor and the magic of every magician and the envy of every envier and the defection of every traitor and the snare of every ensnarer and the hostility of every enemy and the calumny of every calumniator and the backbiting of every backbiter and the ruse of every trickster and the malice of every malicious one and the secret rancour of every grudge-bearer.[16]

The worshiper finds recourse to God in the *ta'awwudh* for earthly security and heavenly blessing as well as against sins of the flesh.

O God I take refuge with Thee from miserliness and I take refuge with Thee from cowardliness and I take refuge with Thee from the seductions of the Anti-Christ and I take refuge with Thee from the pains of the tomb.[17]

I take refuge with Thee from the evil of my hearing and the evil of my seeing; from the evil of my tongue and the evil of my heart and from the evil of my sexual life.

16. Padwick, *Muslim Devotions*, p. 88.
17. Padwick, *Muslim Devotions*, p. 90.

I take refuge with Thee O God from unprofitable knowledge, and from a heart without reverence, and from an ever-demanding self, and from unheard petition. From these four I take refuge with Thee.

I take refuge with Thee from hunger, the worst of bedfellows, and from treachery that ruins friendship, and I take refuge with Thee from the evil suggestions of the breast and from frustration of affairs and the temptation of the grave.

O God with Thee do I take refuge from Thy torments on the day when Thou shalt raise Thy servants, from a speedy torment and a harsh judgment, for Thou art swift in punishment.[18]

According to the religious masters the fullest praise to God is the praise God gives Himself. Said Fakrud-Dín ar-Rází: "Thou art as Thou hast praised Thyself," implying that our praise of God must necessarily be inadequate, and only by God's mercy is our inadequate praise not imputed to us as a fault. Good pleasure and wrath are divine attributes equally; we deserve wrath and have no right to God's good pleasure. In worship we are, accordingly, doubly obligated to God. The ta'awwudh acknowledges the double duty that polarities of the divine attributes impose on us. 'Abd al-Qádir al-Jílání (d. 1166) declared: "O God we take refuge with Thy friendship from Thy aversion, with Thy nearness from Thy distance, and we take refuge with Thee from Thee." That way worship is not prevented by "the insistent paradoxes of experience" from concentrating on God, and that the reconciliation in God of polarized attributes allows us divine access in spite of persistent conceptual obstacles. St. Paul challenges us to be mindful of "the goodness and severity of God" (Rom. 11:22). St. Augustine also gives voice to a similar idea when he declares, reflecting on Psalm 33: "What way have I but to fly from Thee to Thee?"

Worship becomes not just an occasion of divine encounter, the occasion of separation from the world and self and attachment to God, but also the space for training and formation in the spiritual life. Who God is and what God desires are the foundations of the prayer life that demands our humility, as the Catechism points out. Trembling hearts, proclaims a Muslim prayer, are quieted by the recollection of God's name. As the Prophet of Islam declared, "It is not a sixth nor a tenth of a man's devotion which is acceptable to God, but only such portion thereof as he offers with understanding and true devotional spirit."[19] The psalmist testifies in the same

18. Loc. cit.
19. Cited in Ameer Ali, *The Spirit of Islam*, p. 166.

spirit, that a broken and a contrite heart God will not despise (Ps. 51:17).[20] What we need for life and spirit God will provide generously in worship and prayer. "My God," pleads a worshiper, "in Thee depressed hearts find rest, and in the knowledge of Thee divided hearts are made whole. Nor are hearts [at peace] save by the invocation of Thyself, nor souls quieted till they meet with Thee."[21]

Even when our needs and desires are the object of prayer, they must not be allowed to take the place of God. The worshiper, tempered in the spiritual discipline, knows to be mindful of the humility required for true enjoyment of God as the divine prerogative. Three prayers speak directly to this issue:

A. My God, if I ask Thee for succour, I have asked something beside Thee. If I ask for what Thou hast guaranteed to me I show suspicion of Thee. If my heart rests in aught else but Thee I have been guilty of the sin of association *(shirk)*. Thine attributes in their majesty are above contingency, how then can I be with Thee? They are transcendent of causes, how then can I be near to Thee? They are exalted above the dust of the earth,[22] how then can my stay be other than Thee?

B. O God, Thy riches are absolute and ours are limited.[23] We ask Thee then by Thy limitless riches to enrich us with riches that leave no room for poverty save our continued need of Thee.

C. My God, Thou hast created me, a body, and with it hast given to me instruments of obedience or disobedience, and hast appointed for

---

20. The Qur'án confirms that godliness is a matter of the sincere heart. "We have appointed for every nation a holy rite, that they mention God's Name over such beasts of the flocks as He has provided them. . . . The flesh of them shall not reach God, neither their blood, but godliness from you shall reach Him" (22:35, 38). See also 2:173.

21. Padwick, *Muslim Devotions*, p. 123.

22. In the Bible dust and ashes are a symbol of humility. Abraham repents of presuming to speak to God, seeing he is but dust and ashes (Genesis 19:27). Job recants his loud complaining against God by repenting in dust and ashes (Job 42:6). Tamar shows her extreme penance by putting ashes on her head and tearing the ornamented robe she was wearing (2 Samuel 13:19). The Psalmist testifies to God's sustenance without which people perish and return to dust (Psalm 104:29). Daniel turned to God pleading in earnest prayer with fasting, sackcloth, and ashes (Daniel 9:3).

23. This is an allusion to Qur'án 16:97: "What is with you comes to an end, but what is with God abides" *(má 'indakum yanfadu wa má 'inda 'lláhi báqin).*

me in my own nature a soul claimant for selfish ends, and after this Thou hast said to me, "Abstain, my servant!" Through Thee (only) can I guard my innocence. Keep me from evil. Through Thee (only) can I be shielded from sin. Then do Thou keep me.[24]

The heart dwelling on God as its true and only refuge awakes from its slumber into consciousness as a beggar before God, pleading its unworthiness against what it sorely needs and to avert what it patently deserves.

O God, Thy pardon of my sin, Thy passing over my errors, Thy covering of the ugliness of my doings, Thy long patience with my many wickednesses whether I did them in error or of set purpose, have made me ask in hope that to which I have no right.[25]

I have lost my purpose, I am stripped of will, lacking in strength and power. O God my soul is a ship wandering in the seas of (her own) will where there is no refuge and no shelter from Thee but in Thee. Appoint for her, O God, in the name of God, her course and its harbour.

Once quickened, the heart of the faithful stirs with a lively realization of its sin and disobedience, and is driven for timely remedy to God.

My God, my Lord and Master, this is the position of him who now makes confession of many a fault, many a disobedience, many a misdeed, of lack of moral control. I sinned as I did from inability to deny my own sinful desires. Thy case against me is a clear one, Thy judgment on me must take effect, and there is none that can help my weakness against Thee, save Thee Thyself.

O God I confess before Thee that I do not know a single believer on the face of the earth with more of disobedience and transgression than I, nor in a worse spiritual condition, nor with less of holy fear than I, O Thou Guide of the erring. O God my sins outweigh the sins of them all, the first and the last.[26]

---

24. Padwick, *Muslim Devotions*, pp. 135, 174.

25. Padwick, *Muslim Devotions*, p. 203. Compare Rom. 7:15ff.

26. Padwick, *Muslim Devotions*, p. 182. Compare with the parable of Jesus about humility in prayer, Luke 18:9-14.

In the setting of worship and prayer, words uttered before God must be spoken with a sincere heart and a guileless tongue, and that means no evading the truth of our miserable plight before God. In that respect the worshiper is a sinner throwing herself on God's sovereign mercy, pleading to "confront" God, to see God's face, as the answer to her blind willfulness. Only the sinner who acknowledges her sin can accept God's forgiveness, and with that comes the unblocking of the channels of faith, praise, and devotion. That condition is essential and necessary to being acceptable in the sight of God.

Sin assumes many forms in confessions in Islamic devotion, one of which is that sin is a blemish, something unsightly carrying the stigma of shame (compare Daniel 1:4). It occurs as such in prayers that ask God to cover our defects and our shame and to cleanse our hearts. Another form is one in which sin has the notion of profligacy, self-squandering, and self-ruin. It finds a parallel in the parable of the Prodigal Son (Luke 15:11-32). Then there are sins of omission: falling short, forgetting, doing too little, and leaving undone.

We spoke earlier of how worship need not be handicapped by "the insistent paradoxes of experience," and how polarized attributes ascribed to God may allow us divine access in spite of intractable conceptual problems. That assurance may explain why in the devotional life confession of sin may proceed with the help of polarized couplets: sin as overdoing it and falling short, of sinning secretly and openly, outwardly and inwardly, by lack of seriousness and by over-seriousness, by premeditation and by carelessness, by omission and by commission, willingly and unwillingly.[27]

The polarized couplets of sin belong with the insistent paradoxes of experience and help to put the worshiper in a state of haunting humility, what Augustine describes as the beggar in God's presence. In one Muslim prayer the seeker is described as one who "haunted the thresholds and stood at the door like a doorkeeper," adding, "For all who travel arrive, and he who haunts the threshold enters."[28]

Worship as threshold experience is an apt way to describe what is a pivotal act in the religious life. Shaykh Shiháb al-Dín al-Suhrawardí (d. 1234), a famous Qádirí spiritual master and missionary pioneer *(murshid, muqaddam)*, adopted a radical regime of prayer by transposing

---

27. Padwick, *Muslim Devotions*, p. 197.
28. Padwick, *Muslim Devotions*, p. 214.

it into the language of effort, of striving, and of personal uprooting. In a guide for his disciples, al-Suhrawardí instructs them to tear themselves from native land, from friends and familiar things, to exercise patience in calamity, and to expunge from their hearts all that causes obstinacy, intolerance, and blindness. Dead skins, he says, like old habits, coarsen and turn inflexible with time, and can be restored to their potential of softness and of supple delicacy of texture only by the unrelenting rotation of fasting, prayer, devotion, and moral rectitude, and just so can hardened hearts, and their corrosive traits of natural corruption and innate coarseness, be smoothened by the "tanning of travel."[29] That metaphor of "tanning" describes with laconic clarity the pivotal, transformative power of worship, and, indeed, of work itself as a spiritual vocation. There can be no slipping back into the void, no retreat into self-selected boundaries.

The liminal image of travel as spiritual "tanning" might stand for the "threshold" mission of mosque and church, of communities of faith as haunted frontiers of encounter with the transcendent, rather than of mosque and church as neighborhood social gathering places where people come to celebrate one another and no one else. Seeking God is in the quest, in the journey, not in leisure, display, or social agreeability.

The worshiper on the threshold, on the boundary of faith and earnest expectancy, is a common theme in the prayers, and with it comes a significant shift of mood and emphasis. Self-conscious motives are now introduced into the prayers, with bargain, exchange, gain, benefits, and advantages defining the relationship and focusing on what God offers, in contrast to the spirit of the earlier prayers with their stress on the divine attributes, and particularly on God's sovereign majesty. True enjoyment of God as the divine prerogative remains a virtue known now more in the breach than in the observance, so that something real and tangible from pre-Islamic popular piety survives into the conversion to Islam and now, given an extended life, surfaces with the undiminished vigor and directness of appeal of the ancient tribal code.

The prayers, accordingly, speak of God as the generous patron at whose door stand the beggars, with their hands outstretched, of the worshiper taking up her station at God's door, of the slave at the door begging

29. Shiháb al-Dín al-Suhrawardí, *Al-'Awárif al-Ma'árif* — "The Bounties of Divine Knowledge," ed. and trans. Wilberforce Clarke (Calcutta, 1891); reprinted as *A Dervish Textbook* (London, 1980), p. 26.

for forgiveness and mercy, of the destitute one in God's courtyard, of poor servants standing at the threshold of the courtyards of God's majesty, in great need but not daring to intrude or presume on God's largesse. In all these prayers a running theme is the idea of God as the generous host who is bound by the rules of oriental hospitality to entertain the guest and the client. The prayers, accordingly, plead with God as the "best of those besought," stressing the fact that "Thy servants the Arabs, when a fugitive seeks shelter at the ropes of their tents, will shelter him. And Thou, Creator of the Arabs and the non-Arabs, at Thy door I seek shelter, in Thy courtyard I alight."[30]

God is besieged as one who is generous to the person whose travel provision is small and who is penniless in the bargain, but whose sin is great. Far be it from God to send off with reproaches the beggar at His door, given the fact that God is of potentates the most generous, insists one prayer. It is inconceivable, says another prayer, that a well provisioned host with water to spare would refuse succor to a thirsty one who came for help in a day of burning heat, for in that case such a host would be of all misers the most miserly. God is similarly beholden to the plight of the needy worshiper.

> Thou who givest to a slave when he asks of Thee, and when he hopes for what is in Thy house sendest it to him, and when he approaches Thee dost draw him nearer. My God, who ever came seeking Thy hospitality without Thy giving it to him? Who ever halted his camel at Thy door hoping for Thy liberality, without Thy bringing him in? Is it seemly that I should return from Thy door driven away with contumely when I know no other lord than Thee whose quality is beneficence?[31]

In these prayers the needs of the worshiper hold center stage and compete for attention with the contemplative enjoyment of God simply as God. For a while, it would seem as if making complaint of one's adversities has taken the place of magnifying God, with worship an act of self-interest. What rescues this feature of the prayer life, however, from crumbling into complete neurosis as witless psychic sediment is a theological principle, namely, Islam's theistic claims.

Islam's tradition of mystical humanism expresses this tension well. The mystics have expounded three notions of the self: the ambiguous self

---

30. Padwick, *Muslim Devotions*, p. 216.
31. Padwick, *Muslim Devotions*, p. 216.

(*al-nafs al-ammarah,* Qur'án 12:53), the false self (*al-nafs al-lawwamah,* 75:2), and the self at peace (*al-nafs al-mutma'innah,* 89:27). The ambiguous self knows what is right but, regardless of that, is inclined to the wrong; the false self finds all paths to escape from itself blocked, and so suffers from the rooted sorrow of deprivation; while the self at peace is such from abiding in God. As al-Junayd of Baghdad (d. 910) expressed it, this is the state of absorption in God when God wills, works, and creates in the devotee, effacing all sense of self and existence. Still, even for the contented soul, what will prevent relapse from peace with God and descent into forlorn alienation is not clear, as these enigmatic lines concede:

> Awhile, as wont may be,
> Self I did claim:
> True self I did not see
> But heard its name.
> I, being self-confined,
> Self did not merit,
> Till, leaving self behind,
> Did self inherit.[32]

An early Muslim mystic looks to remedy this elusive problem in the following prayer:

> I have loved Thee with two loves, a selfish love
>   And a love that is worthy (of Thee),
> As for the love which is selfish, I occupy myself
>   therein with remembrance of Thee to the exclusion of all others,
> As for that which is worthy of Thee, therein Thou
>   raisest the veil that I may see Thee.
> Yet there is no praise to me in this or that,
>   But the praise is to Thee, whether in that or this.[33]

In the final analysis, the worshiper is just the creature pleading before the Creator, and that gap as a moral gap remains infinite and without parallel. As we saw earlier, the prayer of the caliph 'Ali upholds this princi-

---

32. The poem is by Jalál al-Dín Rúmí (d. 1273). Cited in K. Cragg, *The Wisdom of the Súfis* (New York: New Directions, 1976), pp. 12-13.

33. Cited in Margaret Smith, trans. and ed., *Rabi'a: The Life and Work of Rabi'a and Other Mystics in Islam* (Oxford: Oneworld Publications, 1994), p. 126.

ple: "O my Lord, Thou art the Creator, I am only created; Thou art my Sovereign, I am only Thy servant." Muslim theologians, accordingly, insist that God reveals and commands without reason or cause, *lá yuhtada bi-qiyás*. In two prayers made famous by the Rábi'a (d. 801), a woman Súfí, this theistic emphasis comes to the fore:

> O my Lord, if I worship Thee from fear of Hell,
> Burn me in Hell, and if I worship Thee from hope
> Of Paradise, exclude me thence, but if I worship Thee
> For Thine own sake then withhold not from me Thine
> Eternal Beauty.
>
> O my God, my concern and my desire in this world,
> Is that I should remember Thee above all things of
> this world, and in the next, that out of all who are
> in the world, I should meet with Thee alone. This is
> what I would say, "Thy will be done."[34]

However meandering the path of wandering in the wilderness, the path will lead inescapably and inevitably back to God, for, in the affirmation of Scripture, to God is all our returning. In that theistic assurance the worshiper finds her sanctuary, the threshold that adorns the edifice and interior space of prayer. Scripture describes the faithful as being rewarded with admission into the halls of divine pleasure:

> Surely the pious shall be in bliss,
> Upon couches gazing;
> thou knowest in their faces the radiancy of bliss
> as they are given to drink of a wine sealed
> whose seal is musk. . . .
>
> Qur'án 83:21ff; also 76:5-23 (Arberry)

The holy desire for the divine bounty is the archway through which the believer gains fellowship with God. That is the experience the Qur'an describes as the *al-nafs al-mutma'innah:* "O soul at peace, return unto thy Lord, well-pleased, well-pleasing" (89:27). In the following prayers the believer is asleep to the things of the day and awake to the things of the night.

---

34. Smith, *Rabi'a*, p. 50.

The stranglehold of routine preoccupations is loosened by the summons of prayer, and the believer turns to God in trust and intimacy:

> My God, in my very riches I am poor, how great then my destitution when I am poor! My God, I am ignorant in my very knowledge, how shall I not be crassly ignorant in my ignorance! My God, from me comes what accords with blame, but from Thee comes what accords with generosity. My God, Thou didst show Thyself kindly and compassionate to me before my evil deeds were done. Wilt Thou then deprive me of Thy kindness and compassion after those deeds?

> Thy door is open to the beggar . . . all means have failed Thy servant and all doors are locked against him.

> My God and my Lord, eyes are at rest, stars are setting, hushed are the movements of birds in their nests, of monsters in the deep. And Thou art the Just who knowest no change, the Equity that swerveth not, the Everlasting that passeth not away. The doors of kings are locked, watched by their bodyguards; but Thy door is open to him who calls on Thee. My Lord, each lover is now alone with his beloved, and Thou art for me the Beloved.

The nineteenth-century Christian hymnodist Charlotte Elliott (1789-1871) lends her reverential, laconic pen to an attitude parallel to the one in the last prayer when she writes:

> Blest be that tranquil hour of morn,
>   And blest that hour of solemn eve,
> When, on the wings of prayer upborne,
>   The world I leave.

> Hushed is each doubt, gone every fear;
>   My spirit seems in heaven to stay;
> And e'en the penitential tear
>   Is wiped away.

> Lord, till I reach yon blissful shore,
>   No privilege so dear shall be,
> As thus my inmost soul to pour
>   In prayer to Thee.

All this makes clear that worship is a matter of the inward life, of the intention consecrated to God and to unceasing traffic in God's remembrance *(dhikr)*. Echoes of the *dhikr* abound in the strains of another Christian hymn, "Breathe on me, Breath of God," especially the lines, "Breathe on me, Breath of God, till I am wholly thine, till all this earthly part of me glows with thy fire divine." That interfaith spirit is preserved in the following Muslim prayer:

> O Light of Light who dost illumine the obscurity of non-being with the effulgence of Thy Light, make Thy Light the lamp of my subconscious being and of my mind and my soul and spirit and heart and body and all of me and each part of me, till I shall be only light flooded with the Light of Thy Unity.[35]

The practice of remembrance and meditation on the name and mystery of God is a widely observed phenomenon in Islam, and, it turns out, in Eastern Orthodoxy, but it is largely a neglected theme in the Western Christian tradition. The formal rules of worship in the Western tradition do not allow or encourage communal or personal meditation and contemplation, while the rhythm of worship as only a weekend, hour-long social routine inculcates habits alien to such spirituality. In the Western tradition, worship is enlightened self-affirmation. We may, therefore, once more turn the interfaith concerns of this paper in an ecumenical direction with an example of the rules of contemplative prayer in a Russian Orthodox setting, an example that parallels a similar experience in Islam.

> Sit down alone and in silence. Lower your head, shut your eyes, breathe out gently and imagine yourself looking into your own heart. Carry your mind (i.e., your thoughts) from your head to your heart. As you breathe out, say, "Lord Jesus Christ, have mercy upon me." Say it moving your lips gently, or simply say it in your mind. Try to pull all other thoughts aside. Be calm, be patient, and repeat the process very frequently.
>
> Here is a rosary. Take it, and to start with say the Prayer three thousand times a day. Whether you are standing or sitting, walking or lying down, continually repeat, "Lord Jesus Christ, have mercy upon me." Say it quietly and without hurry, but without fail exactly three thou-

---

35. This prayer echoes the theme of the famous Light Verse of the Qur'án 24:35-38.

sand times a day, without deliberately increasing or diminishing the number. God will help you, and by this means you will reach also the unceasing activity of the heart. (Later on the number of recitations was increased.)

In my lonely hut I said the Prayer of Jesus six thousand times a day for a whole week. I felt no anxiety. Taking no notice of any other thoughts, however much they assailed me, I had but one object — to carry out my staretz's [director's] bidding exactly.

At times I do as much as forty-three or forty-four miles a day, and do not feel that I am walking at all, I am aware only of the fact that I am saying my Prayer. When the bitter cold pierces me I begin to say my prayer more earnestly and I quickly get warm all over. When hunger begins to overcome me, I call more often on the Name of Jesus, and I forget my wish for food. When I fall ill and have rheumatism in my back and legs, I fix my thought on the Prayer and do not notice the pain. If anyone harms me, I have only to think, "How sweet is the Prayer of Jesus" and the injury and the anger alike pass away and I forget it all.

After no great lapse of time I had the feeling that the Prayer had, so to speak, by its own action passed from my lips to my heart. That is to say, it seemed as though my heart in its ordinary beating began to say the words of the Prayer within, at each beat. Thus, for example, *one* "Lord," *two* "Jesus," *three* "Christ" and so on. I simply listened carefully to what my heart was saying.[36]

Conclusion

Reflecting the challenge of religious pluralism in an increasingly secular world, Sir Syed Ameer ʿAli remarked on the significance of prayer for the worldwide Muslim community, including his own Shiʿi tradition. The appeal of Islam, he argued, rested on the place given to the outpouring of the human soul in love and gratitude to God. By making the practice of devotion regular, the Prophet of Islam impressed on the Muslim character the discipline of regular observance of prayer. Ameer ʿAli suggests that the unity of Islam is a unity of practice rather than of bureaucratic order, and

36. R. M. French, *The Way of a Pilgrim*, 22-23, cited in Padwick, *Muslim Devotions*, pp. 19-20.

for such practice the figure of the Prophet and the sacrament of the orientation *(qiblah)* toward Mecca are crucial. "With the true instinct of a prophet [Muhammad] perceived the consolidating effect of fixing a central spot round which, through all time, should gather the religious feelings of his followers; and he accordingly ordained that everywhere throughout the world the Moslem should pray looking towards the Ka'ba."[37]

Ameer 'Ali's views are confirmed by experienced non-Muslim observers, such as Stanley Lane-Poole, the authority on Arabic philology:

> Mecca is to the Moslem what Jerusalem is to the Jew. It bears with it all the influence of centuries of associations. It carries the Moslem back to the cradle of his faith, the childhood of his Prophet, it reminds him of the struggle between the old faith and the new, of the overthrow of the idols, and the establishment of the worship of the one God; and, most of all, it bids him remember that all his brother Moslems are worshipping towards the same sacred spot; that he is one of a great company of believers, united by one faith, filled with the same hopes, reverencing the same things, worshipping the same God. Mohammed showed his knowledge of the religious emotions in man when he preserved the sanctity of the temple of Islam.[38]

37. Ameer Ali, *The Spirit of Islam*, p. 167.
38. Stanley Lane-Poole, Introduction to the *Selections from the Koran*, p. lxxxv.

Afterword: Inculturation, Worship, and Dispositions for Ministry

John D. Witvliet

The project undertaken in this volume, while in some ways only barely begun, promises to change and deepen both the way we think and worship as well as the underlying dispositions and attitudes that shape our work. This brief afterword allows us to reflect on three of these themes — with the hope that future work on the hundreds of countries and denominations we have not explored in this volume will continue to challenge and deepen us along these lines.

Our Conceptual Frameworks for Contextualized Ministry

Our topic points to one certain universal experience, which is that all Christian worship is shaped by culture. It all reflects a process of contextualization, indigenization, acculturation, and inculturation, whether self-conscious or inadvertent. All worship is shaped by local languages, communication styles and habits, patterns of dress, sense of time, and body language.[1]

With respect to worship, the theme of contextualization has been especially prominent since Vatican II's 1963 Constitution on Sacred Liturgy.

---

1. Mark Francis, "Liturgy and Popular Piety in Historical Perspective," in *Directory on Popular Piety and the Liturgy: Principles and Guidelines* (Collegeville, Minn.: Liturgical Press, 2005), and John D. Witvliet, "Theological Models for Worship and Culture," in *Worship Seeking Understanding: Windows into Christian Practice* (Grand Rapids: Baker Academic, 2003).

Against the backdrop of the universal use of Latin liturgy all over the globe, the Council offered this arresting statement:

> Even in the liturgy, the Church has no wish to impose a rigid uniformity in matters which do not implicate the faith or the good of the whole community; rather does she respect and foster the genius and talents of the various races and peoples. Anything in these peoples' way of life which is not indissolubly bound up with superstition and error she studies with sympathy and, if possible, preserves intact. Sometimes in fact she admits such things into the liturgy itself, so long as they harmonize with its true and authentic spirit.[2]

It is a call that brings to mind John Calvin's admonition that "for the upbuilding of the church those things not necessary to salvation ought to be vigorously accommodated to the customs of each nation and age."[3] Indeed, as the church has repeatedly discovered, its practices unfold in unpredictable ways that are constantly responding to local cultural conditions.

But that is not to say that worship practices are all equally valid or all reducible to simple cultural explanations. Christianity is about a person, Jesus Christ, who lived as a Jewish male, but embodied and enacted a gospel of transcultural truth and significance. That is, while many discussions of culture stop with the message "be relevant," the New Testament, and Jesus' life in particular, offers a more complex message. True, Jesus became "fully contextualized" in a particular time, place, and culture. But Jesus also challenged culture, throwing the money changers out of the temple. Jesus also crossed cultural boundaries, speaking with the Samaritan woman at the well. Jesus transcends cultures, embodying a gospel that has a remarkable record of crossing vast cultural divides. And Jesus' message also transforms culture. It never lets a culture stay where it is, but rather pushes toward more compassion, more justice, and more humility than any culture would ever recommend on its own. The perennial challenge of all Christians is to discern how a transcultural faith can be practiced faithfully in a contextually appropriate way.

This challenge is explained in an especially helpful and succinct way in the Lutheran World Federation's Nairobi Statement on Worship and

---

2. Constitution on the Sacred Liturgy, paragraph 37.
3. John Calvin, *Institutes of the Christian Religion*, IV.X.30.

Culture (for the complete document, see the Appendix). This brief document challenges each congregation to worship and witness in a way that

- expresses the transcultural character of the gospel,
- is contextually embodied,
- is eager for cross-cultural learning and encounters, and
- is counter-cultural in prophetic words and actions.

The document is helpful because it calls *each* of us to give attention to *each* of these four dimensions of the gospel. To those of us who have pursued cultural relevance with just about all our attention and energy, it calls us to dwell with the transcultural dimensions of the faith and determine which parts of our culture we should resist. To those of us inclined to make universal pronouncements, the document calls us to see the contextual nature of our own formulations and to learn from formulations from other cultural contexts that may challenge, complement, or enrich our understanding. To those of us with few, if any, contacts with people unlike ourselves, it invites us to the risky and rewarding prospects of forming cross-cultural friendships. The document challenges every leader, every congregation, and every denomination not only to celebrate their strengths, but also to address and correct their weaknesses.

In sum, the conversation about contextual or inculturated worship recognizes the significance of cultural forms, but also articulates the practices, images, and themes that are transculturally significant. It dances on the Pauline teeter-totter that beckons us to be in, but not of, the world. Good work on contextualization challenges both under- and over-accommodation to culture. Studying worship worldwide should cause us to grow in appreciation both for how culturally relative some forms are and how transcultural the Christian gospel is.

It is this point that has enormous value for local ministry in any time and place — for every pastor and worship leader reading this book. It challenges us to think of our own worship (whatever that may be like) as inculturated.[4] It promises to give us wisdom to make better decisions about how to relate to culture here and now. It challenges us to think of ourselves not as a center of Christian experience, but rather as one strand

---

4. Mark R. Francis, *Shape a Circle Ever Wider: Liturgical Inculturation in the United States* (Chicago: Liturgy Training Publications, 2000).

of a rich tapestry of practice. As Michael Hawn has argued, "moving from a center-based model to a spectrum-oriented understanding of worship practice is much more challenging than naively embracing the new, exotic, and quaint."[5]

The effect that a worldwide vision could have on our local worship is difficult to predict. Encounters with forms of worship very different from our own might well lead us to be more boldly "of" culture or may cause us to resist local cultural pressures. On one hand, noted Roman Catholic sacramental theologian David Power suspects that a worldwide vision would make Western Catholics more open to innovation.[6] On the other hand, it may make those with free and less formal liturgical structures more inclined to assess carefully any proposed innovation.

Consider two examples. First, several years ago at an ecumenical Christian caucus, North American Christians expressed concern to some African leaders that their prayers were syncretistic because of the way they referred to their ancestors in worship. The African leaders responded by expressing worry that North American worship can become syncretistic because of the presence of Sony Jumbotron screens in the front of sanctuaries, symbols of North American capitulation to materialism — even as one African prayer book offers the prayer "save us from materialism in the West." However the discussion about ancestors was resolved, few North Americans would experience that encounter without gaining profound awareness of the way in which wealth has shaped our worship practices.

Second, as Neal Plantinga noted some years ago, many North American Christians have grown very reluctant to name and confess sin in public worship.[7] Meanwhile, the Zaire rite offers its prayer of confession this way: "Lord our God, as the leech sticks to the skin and sucks human blood, evil has invaded us. . . . Who will save us, if not you, our Lord?"[8] North American readers who encounter such bracing language have a profound opportunity to ponder the relative strengths and weaknesses of our own practice.

5. C. Michael Hawn, *Gather into One: Praying and Singing Globally* (Grand Rapids: Eerdmans, 2003), p. 9.

6. David Power, foreword to Lumbala, *Celebrating Jesus Christ in Africa*, p. xiv.

7. Cornelius Plantinga, *Not the Way It's Supposed to Be: A Breviary on Sin* (Grand Rapids: Eerdmans, 1995).

8. Elochukwu E. Uzukwu, *Worship as Body Language: Introduction to Christian Worship: An African Orientation* (Collegeville, Minn.: Liturgical Press, 1997), p. 304.

Could North American culture, which hates talk about sin, also be depriving us of a vivid awareness of the radical nature of divine intervention that saves us?

In the past year, I have heard passionate arguments for the "universal" validity of both pipe organs and PowerPoint in North American worship. I have heard Jesus presented as a proponent of cutting-edge ministry, as the ultimate time-manager, as the model of both heroic and adaptive leadership. In fact, church life is fueled by all kinds of overly simplistic claims about universal strategies. Careful work on contextualization grows in us appreciation both for how culturally relative some forms are and how transcultural the Christian gospel is.

Recognizing the transcultural elements of worship helps us sort out what is truly essential in Christian worship from what is less so. Although my own perceptions are themselves culturally conditioned, what emerges for me in this work is renewed appreciation for what is truly transcultural in worship: baptism in the name of the triune God, the Lord's Supper as a celebration of both memory and hope, the thoughtful, vernacular reading and preaching of scripture, communal prayers of thanksgiving, confession, praise and lament, all offered in the name of Jesus, and expressions of genuine Christian hospitality.

In other words, we learn to major in majors and minor in minors. Our sense that the Lord's Supper is an eschatological feast grows; our worries about how to distribute the elements weakens. Our sense of the importance of congregational singing grows; our holding on to particular musical instruments weakens.

In this way, studying worship worldwide gives us a sense of pastoral equilibrium. We are less likely to embrace trendy strategies that do not promise long-term maturity. We are less likely to fear change or adaptation of non-essential elements of the Christian life. And we learn to celebrate the way that these non-essential elements can reflect the unique insights and creative impulses of local congregations.

Depth and Texture in Worship

But all of this is about more than conceptual or pastoral equilibrium — it also affects our weekly practice of worship. For one, awareness of worldwide practice challenges us to become more intentional, comprehensive, and concrete in our intercessory prayers. Several observers of worship have anecdotally observed that North American worshipers can be notoriously self-centered in our prayer life. We are much better at praying for ourselves than praying for others. Yet the vocation of the church is to intercede on behalf of the world, to pray in such a way that prayers for others are as significant to us as prayers for ourselves. As one pastor with whom our office recently worked noted, "From time to time we mention the church throughout the world in our prayers, but, quite frankly, not as often or as creatively as we could."[9] For another, thinking about worship worldwide also deepens our worship by giving us new perspectives on our own worship. We may learn again that vitality and formality can go together, or that reverence and exuberance are not mutually exclusive. Cross-cultural encounters challenge the false dichotomies and assumptions that any culture may fall into. Reflecting on one particular example, Michael Hawn perceptively notes that often when North American Christians talk about "traditional vs. contemporary worship" as *the* defining spectrum of liturgical practice, they "perpetuate a colonial mentality that denies the multicultural reality of society in the United States."[10] Thinking about worship from a worldwide perspective frees us from the imprisoning effects of the traditional-contemporary worship dichotomy that still stymies so many North American congregations.

Studying worship worldwide also invites the cross-cultural sharing of practices, as Michael Hawn examines in Chapter Ten. We may discover that Christian communities have come up with better ways of doing something. For example, in recent years many North American congregations have been enriched by learning new ways of passing the peace that come from other cultures. A few North American congregations, as a result of reflecting on worldwide practice, have thrown away the 60-minute timer that governs their worship planning. Similarly, the musical diets of many congregations have been enriched by singing music from a worldwide chorus of voices.

When we sing music and pray prayers from other parts of Christ's body, we anticipate the coming kingdom of God. Although the topic of worship worldwide is about much more than singing songs from other parts of the world, this practice should not be dismissed lightly. At its best,

9. www.calvin.edu/worship/stories/egypt.php
10. Hawn, *Gather into One*, p. 4.

this practice of cross-cultural singing and praying is an eschatological discipline that points us to our ultimate destination. There is always a danger in this borrowing that we will co-opt something. However, this need not prevent us from borrowing. One of the greatest compliments one person can give another, or one church can give another, is to say that the ideas or practices of the other have become invaluable for deepening its own prayer life. As Hawn suggests, the challenge is to receive these borrowed practices humbly, to express gratitude, and to resist any kind of economically and culturally exploitive misuse of a given resource.

Holy Restlessness and Eschatological Doxology

Finally, consider the effect of this subject on the attitudes or dispositions we bring to both scholarship and ministry.

To be honest, the subject of contextualized ministry often evokes anxiety. It suggests that nothing is sure and certain. Many of us who work in congregations do so because we were inspired by or are adept at a particular form of ministry. When that form is challenged, it is natural to feel a little queasy. One congregation twenty years ago let go of its organists in favor of a culturally contextual praise band. Now its praise band leaders are being pushed out by a new generation that wants more mystery and silence in worship. In both cases, what was believed to be universal turned out to be transient. In both cases, leaders who were passionate about their craft were disenfranchised and became bitterly disappointed.

Whenever this queasiness sets in, it is instructive to remember that the contextualization or inculturation of the gospel has been going on for 2000 years, and that this history has much to teach us. In the New Testament period, the Corinthian church arguably struggled the most with how to engage culture properly. One way of thinking of Paul's writings to the Corinthians is as advice about how to manage the tension between local cultural practices and the gospel.

Inculturation continued throughout the early church. When Christians started praying in Latin, their written prayers became shorter and more orderly. When the Greeks started using oil in their baths, so did Christians at baptism. In the medieval period, the feudal political system led theologians like Anselm to explain the Christian faith using terms and images from that political world. In fact, church historian Richard Muller calls Anselm's writings on the atonement a "perfect example of successful contextualization."[11]

The history of Christian missions gives us even more poignant examples. In seventeenth-century China, the Catholic Church was polarized because of the desire of Jesuit missionaries to worship in Chinese. In nineteenth-century Bali, Dutch Reformed pastors traded in their dark, black robes for white ones because of the associations of the black color. Twentieth-century missionaries in many places faced especially complex worship wars when they suggested that indigenous song should replace traditional (North American) hymns that had been taught by previous generations of missionaries.

Indeed, the entire history of Christianity features the push and pull of both reflecting and contesting cultural influence. Sometimes the church erred by refusing to engage culture; in other periods, it was nearly swallowed up by it. With all of this complexity, no wonder that Andrew Walls notes that "the global transformation of Christianity requires nothing less than the complete rethinking of the church history syllabus."[12] That statement is as true for syllabi in theology, worship, and ministry as it is for history.

The history of Christianity challenges us to be alert to subtle (and often not so subtle) ways that culture is changing — and changing us. All of this reminds us that the balancing act of engaging while resisting culture never comes to a stop this side of heaven. We are left in a state of restlessness.

Of course this feeling of restlessness is nothing new to missionaries. Lesslie Newbigin, the noted Protestant missionary to South India, summed up one period of his ministry in this way: "I have found it harder here than anywhere else to discern the right path. Yet I have no doubt that we are moving forward, and that in this realm as in many others we are being led through tension and difficulty to deeper obedience."[13] Likewise, in an appreciation of Vincent Donovan (a noted Catholic missionary to Tanzania), Lamin Sanneh describes the missionary life as "one of unexpected

11. Richard Muller, *The Study of Theology* (Grand Rapids: Zondervan Publishing House, 1991), p. 209.

12. Andrew Walls, *The Missionary Movement in Christian History* (Maryknoll, N.Y.: Orbis Books, 1996).

13. Geoffrey Wainwright, *Lesslie Newbigin: A Theological Life* (New York: Oxford University Press, 2000), p. 273.

challenge, of fundamental stocktaking, and of an uncompromising reappraisal of settled practice, received wisdom, and accepted custom."[14]

Indeed, missional Christianity lives in a constant, question-asking, liminal, restless state — a kind of holy restlessness that comes from loving people and loving the gospel at the same time. Restlessness about culture is a sign of health this side of the coming kingdom. For now, it is the way things are supposed to be. Whenever this restlessness fades, whenever the question-asking stops, whenever practices are perpetuated just because "we've always done it that way" on the one hand or just because "it's on the cutting edge of ministry" on the other — then it is time to worry.

But if the topic of contextual ministry leaves us in a state of restlessness, it also provides a window into some of the most beautiful dimensions of the gospel. Anyone who reads almost any newspaper or listens attentively to the television news with a heart plugged in is on a road that can lead to despair. The news always seems so very bad — even though commercials desperately attempt to inoculate our souls to the tragedies of life on this little planet. Awareness of Christianity worldwide at times heightens our despair as we learn of persecution, churchly corruption, or plight. But it also cultivates genuine hope. Even an hour of surfing the Internet can put us in touch with Christians worldwide and reveal remarkable stories of hope and courage. The church is so very big, and God is so very good, which we can perceive more clearly if only we have the patience to look deeply into the big picture.

Keeping the momentum of this volume going by further reading, study, and reflection can give all of us a kind of expanded awareness of the life of Christ's church and a deeper empathy for other Christians. It can instill in us a deep awareness and hopefulness about the work of God in the world, the ways that God has been and is at work beyond what we would otherwise hope or think.

There is an underlying tone of pessimism in much writing about the church in North America. And much of it is well justified. We need jeremiads as much as the ancient people of Israel. Yet this must not ever erode our conviction that the church belongs to God and not to us.

There are several dimensions to this gospel-shaped optimism. For one, we discover again that in Christ, we have an identity that is even

14. Lamin Sanneh, foreword to the twenty-fifth anniversary edition of Vincent J. Donovan, *Christianity Rediscovered* (Maryknoll: Orbis Books, 2003), p. 156.

deeper than culture. As N. T. Wright asserts, "The gospel itself stands against all attempts to define ourselves as Catholic or Protestant, Orthodox or Methodist, Anglican or Baptist, still less by national, cultural or geographical subdivisions of those labels. Our definition must be that we are in Christ; the praxis that goes with that is love for one another and the loving announcement of Jesus Christ to the whole world." Praise God that "there is no longer Jew or Greek, there is no longer slave or free, there is no longer male and female; for all of you are one in Christ Jesus" (Gal. 3:28).

For another, we discover how many practices transcend culture. Honest, common prayer in Jesus' name, faithful preaching of particular scriptural texts and Christ-centered celebrations of the Lord's Supper and Baptism are worthy goals for worship in any congregation in any culture. There is perhaps nothing quite as moving as participating in a Lord's Supper service in which you do not understand a word, but also do not have to, because of common faith in the gospel of Christ. This helps us see that questions about culture challenge not only false universal claims, but also unchallenged relativism. They point us in the direction of articulating transcultural values and looking for creative, adaptive ways of embodying those values in particular times and places.

Andrew Walls extends this thesis even further by observing, "It is a delightful paradox that the more Christ is translated into the various thought forms and life systems which form our various national identities, the richer all of us will be in our common Christian identity."[15] In fact, Walls argues, "the crowning excitement which our own era of Church history has over all others, is the possibility that we may be able to read them together. Never before has the Church looked so much like the great multitude whom no one can number out of every nation and tribe and people and tongue. Never before, therefore, has there been so much potentiality for mutual enrichment and self-criticism, as God causes yet more light and truth to break forth from his word."[16] Profound worldwide awareness grows in us all not only a sense of abiding hope, but also new learning and spiritual growth. It is an exercise in Christian maturity. It is a part of sanctification, of growing in the knowledge and faith of Jesus Christ.

Finally, the topic of culture points us to our future in Christ. As Richard Mouw explains in his memorable exposition of Isaiah 60: "When the

---

15. Walls, *The Missionary Movement in Christian History*, p. 54.
16. Walls, *The Missionary Movement in Christian History*, p. 15.

end of history arrives, there is something to be gathered in. Diverse cultural riches will be brought into the Heavenly City. That which has been parceled out in human history must now be collected for the glory of the Creator." It is this glorious vision that motivates our ministry today. As Mouw concludes, "The Christian community [now] ought to function as a model of, a pointer to, what life will be like in the Eternal City of God. The church must be, here and now, a place into which the peoples of the earth are being gathered for new life."[17]

Ultimately, the topic of culture and contextualized ministry leads not to despair, but to hope. It leads us to consider things far greater than we would ever imagine on our own. And it reminds us that the source of our confidence in ministry does not rely on any culture-bound form, but rather on the sturdy fact that the church belongs to Jesus Christ our Lord.

Above all, thinking about worship worldwide also deepens our worship by opening our eyes to breadth of the church. Studying worship in history cultivates a living awareness of the breadth of God's activities over time. Studying worship in Christianity worldwide cultivates a living awareness of the breadth of God's activities over space. Each is essential for opening up the power and mystery of Christian prayer.

One of the most luminous convictions of so many historic Christian liturgies is the notion that we sing "in union with all the saints and angels and all those who sing God's praise." Whether we gather in vast cathedrals with their professionally trained choirs or in a homeless shelter or prison, we are joining a chorus of voices that spans the world. Cultivating appreciation for this awareness is a counter-cultural struggle in our privatized musical world so often bounded by headphones. Yet this awareness is one of the beautiful gifts that come with the Christian faith.

Thinking this way transforms our prayer and worship. It invites us to worship that is less prosaic and more poetic, more of something that is filled already now with "wonder, love, and praise."

---

17. Richard J. Mouw, *When the Kings Come Marching In: Isaiah and the New Jerusalem,* rev. ed. (Grand Rapids: Eerdmans, 2002), p. 93. As John De Gruchy similarly notes: "Christians of European background and African Christians are more likely to discover one another at the aesthetic level than through doctrine or ethics . . . if churches are seriously engaged in seeking to express their unity, then the role of art could be a powerful means to that end." *Christianity, Art, and Transformation* (Cambridge University Press, 2001), pp. 251, 233.

The Nairobi Statement

This statement is from the third international consultation of the Lutheran World Federation's Study Team on Worship and Culture, held in Nairobi, Kenya, in January 1996. The members of the Study Team represent five continents of the world and have worked together with enthusiasm for three years thus far. The initial consultation, in October 1993 in Cartigny, Switzerland, focused on the biblical and historical foundations of the relationship between Christian worship and culture, and resulted in the "Cartigny Statement on Worship and Culture: Biblical and Historical Foundations." (This Nairobi Statement builds upon the Cartigny Statement; in no sense does it replace it.) The second consultation, in March 1994 in Hong Kong, explored contemporary issues and questions of the relationships between the world's cultures and Christian liturgy, church music, and church architecture and art. The papers of the first two consultations were published as *Worship and Culture in Dialogue*. The papers and statement from the Nairobi consultation were published as *Christian Worship: Unity in Cultural Diversity*. In 1994-1995, the Study Team conducted regional research, and prepared reports on that research. Phase IV of the study commenced in Nairobi and will continue with seminars and other means to implement the learnings of the study, as LWF member churches decide is helpful. The Study Team considers this project to be essential to the renewal and mission of the Church around the world.

This text is available online at http://www.worship.ca/docs/lwf_ns.html.

Nairobi Statement on Worship and Culture

Contemporary Challenges and Opportunities

1. Introduction

1.1. Worship is the heart and pulse of the Christian Church. In worship we celebrate together God's gracious gifts of creation and salvation, and are strengthened to live in response to God's grace. Worship always involves actions, not merely words. To consider worship is to consider music, art, and architecture, as well as liturgy and preaching.

1.2. The reality that Christian worship is always celebrated in a given local cultural setting draws our attention to the dynamics between worship and the world's many local cultures.

1.3. Christian worship relates dynamically to culture in at least four ways. First, it is transcultural, the same substance for everyone everywhere, beyond culture. Second, it is contextual, varying according to the local situation (both nature and culture). Third, it is counter-cultural, challenging what is contrary to the Gospel in a given culture. Fourth, it is cross-cultural, making possible sharing between different local cultures. In all four dynamics, there are helpful principles which can be identified.

2. Worship as Transcultural

2.1. The resurrected Christ whom we worship, and through whom by the power of the Holy Spirit we know the grace of the Triune God, transcends and indeed is beyond all cultures. In the mystery of his resurrection is the source of the transcultural nature of Christian worship. Baptism and Eucharist, the sacraments of Christ's death and resurrection, were given by God for all the world. There is one Bible, translated into many tongues, and biblical preaching of Christ's death and resurrection has been sent into all the world. The fundamental shape of the principal Sunday act of Christian worship, the Eucharist or Holy Communion, is shared across cultures: the people gather, the Word of God is proclaimed, the people intercede for the needs of the Church and the world, the eucharistic meal is shared, and the people are sent out into the world for mission. The great narratives of Christ's birth, death, resurrection, and sending of the

286

Spirit, and our Baptism into him, provide the central meanings of the transcultural times of the church's year: especially Lent/Easter/Pentecost, and, to a lesser extent, Advent/Christmas/Epiphany. The ways in which the shapes of the Sunday Eucharist and the church year are expressed vary by culture, but their meanings and fundamental structure are shared around the globe. There is one Lord, one faith, one Baptism, one Eucharist.

2.2. Several specific elements of Christian liturgy are also transcultural, e.g., readings from the Bible (although of course the translations vary), the ecumenical creeds and the Our Father, and Baptism in water in the Triune Name.

2.3. The use of this shared core liturgical structure and these shared liturgical elements in local congregational worship — as well as the shared act of people assembling together, and the shared provision of diverse leadership in that assembly (although the space for the assembly and the manner of the leadership vary) — are expressions of Christian unity across time, space, culture, and confession. The recovery in each congregation of the clear centrality of these transcultural and ecumenical elements renews the sense of this Christian unity and gives all churches a solid basis for authentic contextualization.

3. Worship as Contextual

3.1. Jesus whom we worship was born into a specific culture of the world. In the mystery of his incarnation are the model and the mandate for the contextualization of Christian worship. God can be and is encountered in the local cultures of our world. A given culture's values and patterns, insofar as they are consonant with the values of the Gospel, can be used to express the meaning and purpose of Christian worship. Contextualization is a necessary task for the Church's mission in the world, so that the Gospel can be ever more deeply rooted in diverse local cultures.

3.2. Among the various methods of contextualization, that of dynamic equivalence is particularly useful. It involves re-expressing components of Christian worship with something from a local culture that has an equal meaning, value, and function. Dynamic equivalence goes far beyond mere translation; it involves understanding the fundamental meanings both of elements of worship and of the local culture, and enabling the meanings and actions of worship to be "encoded" and re-expressed in the language of local culture.

3.3. In applying the method of dynamic equivalence, the following procedure may be followed. First, the liturgical ordo (basic shape) should be examined with regard to its theology, history, basic elements, and cultural backgrounds. Second, those elements of the ordo that can be subjected to dynamic equivalence without prejudice to their meaning should be determined. Third, those components of culture that are able to re-express the Gospel and the liturgical ordo in an adequate manner should be studied. Fourth, the spiritual and pastoral benefits our people will derive from the changes should be considered.

3.4. Local churches might also consider the method of creative assimilation. This consists of adding pertinent components of local culture to the liturgical ordo in order to enrich its original core. The baptismal ordo of "washing with water and the Word," for example, was gradually elaborated by the assimilation of such cultural practices as the giving of white vestments and lighted candles to the neophytes of ancient mystery religions. Unlike dynamic equivalence, creative assimilation enriches the liturgical ordo — not by culturally re-expressing its elements, but by adding to it new elements from local culture.

3.5. In contextualization the fundamental values and meanings of both Christianity and of local cultures must be respected.

3.6. An important criterion for dynamic equivalence and creative assimilation is that sound or accepted liturgical traditions are preserved in order to keep unity with the universal Church's tradition of worship, while progress inspired by pastoral needs is encouraged. On the side of culture, it is understood that not everything can be integrated with Christian worship, but only those elements that are connatural to (that is, of the same nature as) the liturgical ordo. Elements borrowed from local culture should always undergo critique and purification, which can be achieved through the use of biblical typology.

4. Worship as Counter-cultural

4.1. Jesus Christ came to transform all people and all cultures, and calls us not to conform to the world, but to be transformed with it (Romans 12:2). In the mystery of his passage from death to eternal

288

life is the model for transformation, and thus for the counter-cultural nature of Christian worship. Some components of every culture in the world are sinful, dehumanizing, and contradictory to the values of the Gospel. From the perspective of the Gospel, they need critique and transformation. Contextualization of Christian faith and worship necessarily involves challenging of all types of oppression and social injustice wherever they exist in earthly cultures.

4.2. It also involves the transformation of cultural patterns which idolize the self or the local group at the expense of a wider humanity, or which give central place to the acquisition of wealth at the expense of the care of the earth and its poor. The tools of the counter-cultural in Christian worship may also include the deliberate maintenance or recovery of patterns of action which differ intentionally from prevailing cultural models. These patterns may arise from a recovered sense of Christian history, or from the wisdom of other cultures.

5. Worship as Cross-cultural

5.1. Jesus came to be the Savior of all people. He welcomes the treasures of earthly cultures into the city of God. By virtue of Baptism, there is one Church; and one means of living in faithful response to Baptism is to manifest ever more deeply the unity of the Church. The sharing of hymns and art and other elements of worship across cultural barriers helps enrich the whole Church and strengthen the sense of the communio of the Church. This sharing can be ecumenical as well as cross-cultural, as a witness to the unity of the Church and the oneness of Baptism. Cross-cultural sharing is possible for every church, but is especially needed in multicultural congregations and member churches.

5.2. Care should be taken that the music, art, architecture, gestures and postures, and other elements of different cultures are understood and respected when they are used by churches elsewhere in the world. The criteria for contextualization (above, sections 3.5 and 3.6) should be observed.

6. Challenge to the Churches

6.1. We call on all member churches of the Lutheran World Federation to undertake more efforts related to the transcultural, contextual, counter-cultural, and cross-cultural nature of Christian worship. We call on all member churches to recover the centrality of Baptism, Scripture with preaching, and the every-Sunday celebration of the Lord's Supper — the principal transcultural elements of Christian worship and the signs of Christian unity — as the strong center of all congregational life and mission, and as the authentic basis for contextualization. We call on all churches to give serious attention to exploring the local or contextual elements of liturgy, language, posture and gesture, hymnody and other music and musical instruments, and art and architecture for Christian worship — so that their worship may be more truly rooted in the local culture. We call those churches now carrying out missionary efforts to encourage such contextual awareness among themselves and also among the partners and recipients of their ministries. We call on all member churches to give serious attention to the transcultural nature of worship and the possibilities for cross-cultural sharing. And we call on all churches to consider the training and ordination of ministers of Word and Sacrament, because each local community has the right to receive weekly the means of grace.

6.2. We call on the Lutheran World Federation to make an intentional and substantial effort to provide scholarships for persons from the developing world to study worship, church music, and church architecture, toward the eventual goal that enhanced theological training in their churches can be led by local teachers.

6.3. Further, we call on the Lutheran World Federation to continue its efforts related to worship and culture into the next millennium. The tasks are not quickly accomplished; the work calls for ongoing depth-level research and pastoral encouragement. The Worship and Culture Study, begun in 1992 and continuing in and past the 1997 LWF Assembly, is a significant and important beginning, but the task calls for unending efforts. Giving priority to this task is essential for evangelization of the world.

Contributors

M. L. "Inus" Daneel served for sixteen years as senior professor in missiology at the University of South Africa, Pretoria. Daneel has written extensively on African Traditional Religions and indigenous African Christianity. He has held research fellowships at the University of Zimbabwe, Harare; the Center for the Study of World Religions, Harvard University; and the African Studies Center at Boston University. Daneel's publications include, among others, *God of the Matopo Hills* (Mouton, 1970), *Zionism and Faith-healing* (Mouton, 1970), *Old and New in Southern Shona Independent Churches*, vols. 1-3 (Mouton, 1971, 1976, 1988), *Quest for Belonging* (Mambo, 1987), *Fambidzano: Ecumenical Movement of Zimbabwean Independent Churches* (Mambo, 1989), and *African Earthkeepers: Interfaith Mission in Earth Care* (Orbis, 2001). Presently, Daneel spends six months a year in Masvingo, Zimbabwe, and six months in Boston, where he is co-director, with Dana L. Robert, of Boston University's Center for Global Christianity and Mission.

Samuel Escobar was born in Peru, graduated in Arts and Education from San Marcos University in Lima, and obtained a Ph.D. (Cum Laude) at the Complutense University, Madrid, Spain. From 1959 to 1985 he worked as a traveling secretary, evangelist, and editor for the International Fellowship of Evangelical Students in Peru, Argentina, Brazil, Canada, and Spain. He is one of the founders of the Latin American Theological Fraternity and was its president between 1970 and 1984. He was a visiting scholar at Calvin College (1983-1984) and since 1985 he is the Thornley B. Wood Professor of Missiology at the Eastern Baptist Theological Seminary in Wynnewood,

Pennsylvania. As a missionary from American Baptist Churches he teaches at the Baptist Seminary of Madrid, Spain, during the Spring semester. He is president of the United Bible Societies, and received an honorary Doctor of Divinity degree from McMaster University in Hamilton, Canada. Among his most recent books are *Changing Tides: Mission in Latin America* (Orbis, 2002) and *A Time for Mission* (IVP, 2003).

Charles E. Farhadian is Associate Professor of World Religions and Christian Mission at Westmont College, Santa Barbara, California. He is the author of several articles on mission, conversion, and non-Western Christianity. Farhadian is particularly interested in the intersection of religions and cultures, having made numerous visits to Southeast Asia and South America. He was a recipient of a grant from The Pew Charitable Trusts for studies of Christian Mission and World Christianity, administered by the Overseas Ministries Studies Center, New Haven, Connecticut, for his research on culture, religion, and society in eastern Indonesia. His area interests include Southeast Asia and the Pacific. Farhadian holds a B.A. from Seattle Pacific University, an M.Div. from Yale University, and a Ph.D. from Boston University. He is the author of *Christianity, Islam, and Nationalism in Indonesia* (Routledge, 2005) and is currently engaged in recording and editing non-Western faith narratives compiled in a series called *The Testimony Project.*

C. Michael Hawn assumed the position of Associate Professor of Church Music at Perkins School of Theology, Southern Methodist University, in the fall of 1992. Hawn holds D.M.A. and M.C.M. degrees from Southern Baptist Theological Seminary, Louisville, Kentucky, and a B.M.E. degree from Wheaton College. A frequent contributor to many journals, Dr. Hawn has published over seventy articles. Hawn is also a student of global music, having received several fellowships for study of music around the world, including Africa, Asia, and Latin America. This research led to the publication of a global collection, *Halle Halle: We Sing the World Round* (Choristers Guild, 1999), and, more recently, two books on multicultural music and worship: *Gather Into One: Praying and Singing Globally* (Wm. B. Eerdmans, 2003) and *One Bread, One Body: Exploring Cultural Diversity in Worship* (The Alban Institute, 2003).

Seung Joong Joo graduated from Presbyterian College and Theological Seminary (M.Div., Th.M.). He received his Th.M. degree at Columbia

Theological Seminary in 1991 and his Th.D. degree at Boston University School of Theology in 1997. Dr. Joo has been teaching worship and preaching at Presbyterian College and Theological Seminary (PCTS) since 1997. He is currently Associate Professor of Preaching and Worship and Dean of the Graduate School of Ministry.

Thomas A. Kane, a Paulist priest, is an internationally known ritual maker and videographer. His research interests include the area of arts, communication, liturgy, and culture. Dr. Kane studies contemporary worship and celebration and has written and lectured on liturgy, dance, and creativity in the United States and abroad. In his research, he has documented liturgical inculturation in three videos — *The Dancing Church of Africa, The Dancing Church of the South Pacific,* and *FIESTA! Celebrations at San Fernando Cathedral,* published by Paulist Press. Kane teaches preaching, liturgy, and the arts at the Weston Jesuit School of Theology in Cambridge, Massachusetts, and has authored three faculty handbooks on methods in teaching preaching as well as articles on liturgical dance and creativity.

Ogbu U. Kalu is Henry Winter Luce Professor of World Christianity and Mission at McCormick Theological Seminary, Chicago, after serving as Professor of Church History at the University of Nigeria, Nsukka, for twenty-three years. A native of Nigeria and an elder in the Presbyterian Church of Nigeria, Professor Kalu was educated in Canada and the United States and has taught in the United States, Korea, Nigeria, Edinburgh, Canada, and South Africa. Professor Kalu has published and edited sixteen books, including *Power, Poverty, and Prayer: The Challenges of Poverty and Pluralism in African Christianity 1960-1996,* and more than 150 academic articles. Most of his research focuses on African Christianity, African church history, African traditional religions, English history, historiography, and theology. Most recently he has been teaching courses that unearth the history of worldwide Pentecostalism.

Miguel A. Palomino is a Peruvian ordained minister of the Christian & Missionary Alliance (CMA). From his early years in ministry, he actively worked with his church in Lima, Peru, as part of the program "Lima al Encuentro con Dios," which was an urban mission strategy that led the CMA to a rapid growth in the city. From 1981 to 1984 he was elected president of the National Evangelical Council of Peru (CONEP), a period in which the Peace & Hope Commission was founded to help the victims of the Shining Path terrorist group. After these years, he and his family moved to Philadelphia to pursue studies at Eastern Baptist Theological Seminary while pastoring an ethnic church in one of the most deprived areas of that city. In 1996 he was appointed as the Director of the newly formed Facultad Teológica Latinóamericana Alianza (FATELA), which is a graduate school of theology and mission working now in Argentina, Brazil, Chile, Colombia, Ecuador, and Peru. During this time he has extensively traveled throughout the region, training pastors and leaders, and ministering in different churches. He earned his Ph.D. from the University of Edinburgh, and currently resides in São Paulo, Brazil.

Robert J. Priest is Professor of Mission and Intercultural Studies and Director of the Doctor of Philosophy in Intercultural Studies at Trinity Evangelical Divinity School, where he has served since 1999. Dr. Priest earned the Master of Divinity from Trinity Evangelical Divinity School, the Master of Arts in social science from the University of Chicago, and the Doctor of Philosophy in anthropology from the University of California, Berkeley. Prior to coming to Trinity, Dr. Priest served nine years as a professor at Columbia Biblical Seminary and Graduate School of Missions. He has served in a variety of ministries, including the roles of youth director and assistant pastor. Born to career missionaries, he was raised in Bolivia and eventually returned to South America, conducting nearly two years of anthropological field research among the Aguaruna of Peru, focusing both on traditional religion and on conversion to Christianity.

Dana L. Robert is Truman Collins Professor of World Mission and Co-Director of the Center for Global Christianity and Mission at Boston University. Her most recent books are *Occupy Until I Come: A. T. Pierson and the Evangelization of the World* (Eerdmans, 2003); *African Christian Outreach, Vol. 2: Mission Churches* (South African Missiological Society, 2003); and *Gospel Bearers, Gender Barriers: Missionary Women in the Twentieth Century* (Orbis, 2002). With her husband, M. L. Daneel, she edits the book series "African Initiatives in Christian Mission" and works with a Theological Education by Extension program in rural Zimbabwe.

Lamin Sanneh, a naturalized U.S. citizen, is descended from the *nyanchos,* an ancient African royal house, and was educated on four continents. He went to school with chiefs' sons in the Gambia, West Africa. He subsequently came to the United States on a U.S. government scholarship to read history. After graduating he spent several years studying classical Arabic and Islam, including a stint in the Middle East, and working with the churches in Africa and with international organizations concerned with inter-religious issues. He received his Ph.D. in Islamic history at the University of London. He was a professor at Harvard University for eight years before moving to Yale University in 1989 as the D. Willis James Professor of Missions and World Christianity, with a concurrent courtesy appointment as Professor of History at Yale College. He is an Honorary Research Professor at the School of Oriental and African Studies in the University of London, and is a life member of Clare Hall, Cambridge University. He serves on the board of Ethics and Public Policy at Harvard University, and the Birmingham Civil Rights Institute in Birmingham, Alabama. He has been appointed to the Council of 100 Leaders of the World Economic Forum. He is the author of over a hundred articles on religious and historical subjects, and of several books. He was awarded an honorary doctorate at the University of Edinburgh, Scotland. For his academic work he was made Commandeur de l'Ordre National du Lion, Senegal's highest national honor. He is listed in *Who's Who in America* (1995-).

Bryan D. Spinks is Professor of Liturgical Studies at Yale Divinity School and Yale Institute of Sacred Music. He teaches courses on marriage liturgy, English Reformation worship traditions, the eucharistic prayer and theology, Christology, and liturgy of the Eastern churches. Research interests include East Syrian rites, Reformed rites, and issues in theology and liturgy. He is the author of many books and articles on liturgy, worship, and theology. Professor Spinks is also co-editor of the *Scottish Journal of Theology,* a consultant to the Church of England Liturgical Commission, president emeritus of the Church Service Society of the Church of Scotland, and fellow of the Royal Historical Society.

Andrew F. Walls is a graduate of the Universities of Oxford and Aberdeen. He began service in West Africa in 1957, working at Fourah Bay College, the University College of Sierra Leone, and at the University of Nigeria, Nsukka, where he was Head of the Department of Religion. For many years he was Professor of Religious Studies and Riddoch Lecturer in Comparative Religion at the University of Aberdeen, Scotland, before becoming founding Director of the Centre for the Study of Christianity in the Non-Western World at the University of Edinburgh, Scotland. He has lectured in all six continents, and been Visiting Professor of World Christianity at Yale and Harvard Universities. From 1997 to 2001 he was Guest Professor of Ecumenics and Mission at Princeton Theological Seminary. He is an Officer of the Order of the British Empire, a past President of the British Association for the Study of Religions, a past General Secretary of the International Association of Mission Studies, and a Fellow of the Society of Antiquaries of Scotland. Recent publications include *The Missionary Movement in Christian History* (Orbis, 1996), *African Christianity in the 1990s* (with Christopher Fyfe, Edinburgh, 1996), and *The Cross-Cultural Process in Christian History* (Orbis, 2002). Currently he serves as Honorary Professor in the University of Edinburgh, Director of the Scottish Institute of Missionary Studies at the University of Aberdeen, and Professor at the Akrofi-Christaller Memorial Centre in Ghana, where he teaches every year.

The Reverend Dr. Philip L. Wickeri, Flora Lamson Hewlett Professor of Evangelism and Mission at San Francisco Theological Seminary, holds dual standing in the Presbyterian Church (U.S.A.) and the Episcopal Church (U.S.A.), and worked for more than twenty years in Asia, with the Amity Foundation (China) and the China Christian Council, before joining the seminary faculty in 1998. He holds an A.B. from Colgate University, and both an M.Div. and Ph.D. from Princeton Theological Seminary. He teaches missiology, with a particular interest in Christianity in relation to issues of globalization and religious and cultural pluralism. He also teaches in the area of the history of Christianity in Asia, with a special focus on modern and contemporary China. Wickeri has lectured in a number of North American and Asian theological seminaries, and he continues to be involved in the work of the church and the ecumenical movement at the local, national, and international levels. He has published widely and has edited a number of conference volumes focusing on missiological themes. Wickeri is currently at work on a biography of Bishop K. H. Ting, China's foremost Christian leader in the late twentieth century, and has recently co-edited a volume of Ting's writings published by the World Council of Churches (2003).

John D. Witvliet is Director of the Calvin Institute of Christian Worship and Associate Professor of Worship, Theology, and Music at Calvin College. His responsibilities include oversight of the Institute's practical and scholarly programs, teaching courses in worship, theology, and music, and supervision of campus worship. He holds graduate degrees in theology from Calvin Theological Seminary, in music from the University of Illinois, and a Ph.D. in liturgical studies and theology from the University of Notre Dame. He is the editor of *A Child Shall Lead: Children in Worship* (Choristers Guild, 1999), author of *Worship Seeking Understanding* (Baker Academic, 2003) and *The Biblical Psalms in Christian Worship* (Eerdmans, 2007), and co-editor of *Worship in Medieval and Early Modern Europe* (University of Notre Dame Press, 2004) and *Proclaiming the Christmas Gospel: Ancient Sermons and Hymns for Contemporary Inspiration* (Baker Books, 2003).

Index

United States, 36

vaPostori, 66

Walls, Andrew, 3, 281, 283
Willimon, William H., 252
Wilson, Bp. Daniel, 80
Winkler, Gabriele, 233-34
Witt, Marcos, 109, 115
Witvliet, John, 247
Worship: and evangelism, 180; and culture, 151-53; and nature, 225-26; as
contextual, 22, 45, 92, 106, 128, 150,
154, 160-63, 240, 275; as counter-
cultural, 22-23, 152-53; as cross-
cultural, 23, 33, 218; as mission, 148-
49; cell groups, 188-89; individual
and, 16-18; liminality of, 4, 265-66;
means and ends of, 3-4; personal and
corporate transformation in, 2, 20-21,
153, 187-88; physicality of, 180-82, 227-
28; political aspect, 4, 175-77; space
(sacred), 179-80, 226-27; symbols, 11-
16, 53, 55; technology, 114-15, 174; temporal and spatial features, 21-23;
transcultural, 21-22; wars, 8
Wright, N. T., 283
Wuthnow, Robert, 15
Wynans, Roger, 132, 140, 143-44

Yoder, John Howard, 252

Zionist Apostolic Church (Zimbabwe),
48-50
Zion Christian churches (ZCC, Zimbabwe), 58
Zobi, Yohanan bar, 235-37